BE YOUR OWN

Architect

GENE B. WILLIAMS

TAB Books
Division of McGraw-Hill

New York San Francisco Washington, D.C. Auckland Bogotá
Caracas Lisbon London Madrid Mexico City Milan
Montreal New Delhi San Juan Singapore
Sydney Tokyo Toronto

The author wishes to thank Jerold L. Axelrod for the use of several floor plan designs from **Dream Homes: 66 Plans to Make Your Dreams Come True** *(TAB book number 2829).*

Thanks also to Ernie Bryant, whose book **The Building Plan Book: Complete Plans for 21 Affordable Homes** *(TAB book number 2714) inspired many of the designs in this book.*

© 1990 by **TAB BOOKS.**
TAB BOOKS is a division of McGraw-Hill, Inc.

pbk   8 9 10 11 12 13 14 15 FGR/FGR 9 9 8 7
hc   1 2 3   4   5   6   7   8   9 FGR/FGR 9 9 8 7 6 5 4 3 2 1 0

Library of Congress Cataloging-in-Publication Data

Williams, Gene B.
    Be your own architect / by Gene B. Williams.
        p.   cm.
    ISBN 0-8306-8336-4   ISBN 0-8306-3336-7 (pbk.)
    1. Architecture, Domestic—Amateur's manuals.   2. Architecture,
Domestic—Designs and plans.   I. Title.
    NA7115.W48   1990
    728′.37—dc20   89-48464
                            CIP

Acquisitions Editor: Kimberly Tabor
Book Editor: Joanne M. Slike
Director of Production: Katherine G. Brown

Contents

PART TWO

PART THREE

Introduction

A few years ago, my wife and I lived in a two-bedroom, two-bath home. My office was the spare bedroom, and the second bathroom was used as a darkroom. As my career began to take an upswing, I found myself getting crowded out—and I was about to be *shoved* out. With a baby on the way, my office would be needed as a nursery.

We were left with three choices: 1). I could rent office space; 2). we could build an addition; 3). we could move to a new home. Renting office space was expensive, and besides I *like* working at home. Building an addition was fine, but we'd been thinking about how crowded the area was becoming.

So it was decided. We'd find a new place to live.

Now we went from just two choices to an almost overwhelming number of choices. We could try to find a good used home, or we could buy new. With either comes a long string of choices and decisions. It can be confusing, especially if you haven't thought out your needs.

You can get a used home. The cost is generally, but not always, lower than a new home, and often the savings are offset by needed repairs. More, you still end up with a home that may not suit your specific needs.

With a new home you can be more selective as to floor plan. There are plenty available—as you'll find out. Among these are so-called "custom homes." Despite the name, these houses are still someone else's idea of how things should be. You're allowed to make minor changes to the existing floor plans, but only minor ones. The

basic design might still be wrong—and that's no longer a minor change.

If the available models or floor plans don't suit you, your third option is to begin paging through the books of floor plans that are available. (Many publishers, including TAB, produce books of this type.) This particular method will also serve well even if you *do* design your own home. I *highly* recommend *The Building Plan Book: Complete Plans for 21 Affordable Homes* by Ernie Bryant and published by TAB. I don't say that just because TAB happens to be my publisher as well, but because this book, in my opinion, is one of the best you can find to both give you some ideas of available plans, and to show you the complexity of making your own designs. (In fact, I'd recommend this book to anyone who lives in any home. It provides a wonderful education of just how a home goes together.) Another excellent source book for floor plans is *Dream Homes: 66 Plans to Make Your Dreams Come True* (TAB book number 2829) by Jerold L. Axelrod. This book contains many unique and beautiful designs, covering a wide range of architectural styles.

Your next choice is to hire someone to design the home for you, which generally means finding an architect. If you go by one of his existing plans, or a modification to one, or even if you give this person creative control, you're basically back at that second choice mentioned above.

When you begin to take creative control for yourself, you enter the realm and purpose of this book. This way you can design exactly the home you want. Even if you use the services of a professional to come up with the final drawings, the home will still be uniquely yours.

In my family's case, we wanted two main bedrooms (one for ourselves and one for our child, Daniel, who was born a month after we moved in, and a third bedroom for a possible future addition to our family and, meanwhile, as a guestroom. Most of the time we spend in the bedrooms is while unconscious, so large bedrooms were not a priority. (The same is true with most families.)

We wanted to give extra room to the kitchen/dining area and wanted that to be a single large room rather than two separate rooms. (We would use a formal dining room maybe once every five years, if that often.) Another spot of importance for us was the family room, which was to contain a very special fireplace—a handmade unit that was in the home where my wife was raised.

Since I work at home, I needed a large work area, a fair-sized research library, darkroom facilities, and a big room that can be used for project coordination and as a photographic studio. With all of this, we also had to keep in mind that the day might come when we'd sell and move. That meant that everything had to be easily modifiable to meet the needs of someone else. (Not everyone needs a built-in darkroom.)

We started to look at homes, both used and new. We went through at least a hundred model homes. We borrowed from the library and bought books full of floor plans—thousands of floor plans. In all of that, we found a handful that would work if we made some modifications, but not one that was just right.

I wasn't surprised. You shouldn't be, either.

Most families have certain things in common. Homes are designed to suit the so-called "average family." Still, you'd be hard-pressed to find two families that are exactly alike. One might need just one bedroom, while the next might want six. I know one couple who haven't eaten anything at home but midnight snacks for three years. They don't need a large kitchen. For others, the kitchen and dining room are where the family gathers most often.

You might like to build things and want a roomy shop for this purpose. Maybe you have a boat for fishing and waterskiing and want it kept locked safely in a garage. Someone else might need only a basic roof to keep the sun off the car.

We kept looking for *the* perfect home. After several months and a confusing number of floor plans, I became convinced that the only solution was to design our own home.

With this book to help you, you can do the same thing. It doesn't matter if you have drafting skills or not. You certainly don't need a degree in architecture to come up with a design that exactly suits you.

Yes, it's possible. It's not as difficult—or as expensive—as you might imagine. By careful planning, intelligent design, and shopping for a contractor, we actually saved money over a comparable home built to someone else's specifications. Of course, it was expensive, but all homes are. It still remains that if we'd bought a house of the same size, with the same features (such as extra insulation), we'd have paid more and still would have ended up with someone else's idea.

We drew up the plans and hired an architectural draftsman to do the final drawings. If I'd been less skilled, the cost would have been a little higher. The draftsman could have worked from crude sketches. By providing him with complete drawings, done to scale, his job was easier, less expensive, and the end results were exactly what we wanted.

What is important is that designing a home—*your* home—is almost certainly within your own talents and capabilities, whatever those might be. The more you can do, the better it will go and the less it will cost.

If you can't draw a straight line, use a straightedge. If the symbols give you problems, use a template. Professionals do both.

This book will help to show you how to use the right drafting tools, how to get your ideas down on paper, and how to make that dream house a reality.

How to Use This Book

This book is divided into three parts. The first part will give you the overall considerations you'll need to keep in mind before you begin.

You can get by with just a few basic tools. The better they are (to a degree), the better your drawing will be, but you can quite easily get everything you need for under $10. All of this, and how to use the tools, is in Chapter 1.

The key to getting your first idea down on paper is to know basic outside sizes. How big is the lot? You can't put a 200-foot-wide house on a 150-foot-wide lot. Chapter 2 takes care of this and shows you have to design your home to best fit the land.

You'll need to know how the home will be constructed. Will it be a traditional frame home? Or do you prefer block? What are the advantages and disadvantages of each? Although this isn't necessarily critical to the overall internal design, it's an important factor in the overall appearance. Chapter 3 will show you how to consider these factors and weigh the costs of various types of materials and construction. It will also let you know something about stresses and loads so that your design makes sense. (For example, it's easy to span 15 or 20 feet, but difficult and expensive to span 50 feet.)

Like it or not, for comfortable living you'll need heating, air conditioning, or both. These cost money to operate. You can reduce the cost of construction, and the ongoing cost of utilities, by properly designing the system and installing the right amount of insulation needed to reduce the bills. (The correct time for this is during construction, *not* after the home is up.) This is the subject of Chapter 4.

Surprisingly, few people think about the electrical system and plumbing of a house. Where are the lights? Are there enough outlets? Can you expand in the future? Are the pipes in the right places? This becomes especially important in a multilevel structure, where "stacking" the plumbing can both reduce costs and future plumbing problems. Chapter 5 will tell you about these considerations.

Chapter 6 is about common sense. People *do* move around inside a home—and outside it. It's called traffic flow. You wouldn't put the refrigerator in the bedroom, the stove on the back patio, and the sink in the front yard. Neither should you place them improperly even in the same room. You wouldn't care to have someone tromping through your bedroom to get to the only toilet. This chapter will show you how to figure traffic patterns for maximum efficiency and convenience.

Chapter 7 completes the basics with another item so many people forget until after they've moved in: storage. There's an old saying that however much storage room you have, you'll need and want more.

With the basics of Part One aside, you're ready to get down to work. The purpose of Chapter 8 on overall design is to set in your mind that all things in the home must work together.

The kitchen and dining areas, discussed in Chapter 9, are where most families spend much of their time together. You might be the exception, but most people who leave these areas for last in the design find themselves having to start all over again. These areas represent the first primary function of a home—a place to eat.

Chapter 10 is about the personal areas of your home: the bedrooms and bathrooms. The bedroom area represents the second primary function of a home— a place to sleep.

Once you've decided on the two primary functions, you can approach the living room areas. Big? Small? Do you do a lot of entertaining? Does your family watch television together? Would a pool table be nice to have? Chapter 11 will show you the options available, and how to make use of them.

Chapter 12 covers other kinds of rooms. I work at home, so I needed both an office and a library. You may not want either, but perhaps you'll want a sewing room, or just a room to get away from the distractions. There are a variety of uses for a spare room, some of which require special planning.

In Chapter 13 you'll learn about building down instead of up. Basements are at least partially, and often completely, underground. This might be the perfect solution for more room at lower construction costs: basements also require very little in the way of heating or cooling.

Chapter 14 is concerned with those basically outside areas with roofs: garages, carports, and patios. You might want them attached to the house or separate. Either way, you still have to determine what you want and how it will affect the structure.

The word "elevation" sounds like it refers to how tall something is. In architecture it means how the structure will look once completed. Will it be stucco or have a brick veneer? Even if you're not artistic enough to draw exactly what you want, Chapter 15 can help you visualize what the final effect will be.

By the time you get to Chapter 16 you'll have (hopefully) some rough sketches of the basic house. How does it all go together? How do you create the sketches you'll need so that the final drawings can be made? This chapter will guide you along.

Before construction can begin, you'll need final drawings and copies of those drawings (*blueprints*, from the days when the photo process for copying large sheets involved white lines on blue paper). You'll probably hire someone to make these drawings for you. Just what goes into this is split between Chapters 17 and 18.

Part Three involves the final steps. You have your basic design, and now it's time to do something with it.

There are hundreds of little details to consider: paint color, carpet and tile, plumbing fixtures, cabinets and woodwork, lighting fixtures, and doors. Sooner or later you'll have to make all those decisions. Chapter 18, on specifications, will help you.

In Chapter 19 we return to the question of hiring a draftsman or an architect. The focus this time is on finding and working with this person to get the job done properly.

Someone has to build the house, and that means a contractor, or contractors. This can be a trying experience—especially if you do some of the subcontracting yourself. Chapter 20 can help you to get things done efficiently, while avoiding some headaches.

Chapter 21 continues from the previous chapter. The home is now under construction. The problems are no longer theoretical but very real. The promises made to get the contracts signed might have slipped a bit.

The remainder of the book is made up of charts, tables, and other assorted goodies you might need for reference (just how *do* you show an electrical outlet?).

In short, everything you need is here, from coming up with the general plan to figuring the individual rooms to putting your concept out on bid to watching your new home being constructed.

You won't become an architect from just this book. That's not the purpose nor even a possibility. It's also not necessary. When designing your home, you don't need to know exactly how a particular part of the house will be built—although a general idea of how a footing and foundation are made is good to know, especially if your home is unusual or is on an unusual lot.

Your goal is to understand enough about construction and design to be able to come up with a sensible floor plan—and then to get your ideas onto paper so you can communicate them accurately to those who will be handling the actual construction.

That is the purpose of this book—to show you how to come up with an effective and intelligent design and to communicate your idea to professionals so that you can move into a home that began as a dream and became a reality.

Part
ONE

1

Drafting tools & techniques

You don't have to be a trained draftsman to design your own home. Nor do you need to spend thousands of dollars for special tools and equipment. You can do a passable job with little more than a decent table, a pencil, and an accurate straightedged ruler—not a great job, but adequate. And, depending on how deeply you wish to be involved, this may be all you need.

Many people find that after they've tried a few drawings with such elementary tools, they're only making the job more difficult. Walls come out crooked. Parallel lines aren't quite parallel. Worse, those imperfections end up taking more time.

One of the ideas behind designing your own home is to come up with something that is perfect for you, and to then communicate your ideas to others. If your sketches are inaccurate or misleading, this could become impossible. Even if you intend to hire a professional draftsman to make the final drawings (an excellent idea!) you'll have to present this person with drawings that can be followed. The better your own drawings are, the closer your house will be to your dream.

The basics begin with a clean, smooth surface for drawing, and sufficient light from more than one direction to prevent unwanted shadows. You'll need at least one pencil with a medium lead, and at least one good-quality eraser. A brush for wiping away the erasure crumbs isn't abso-lutely necessary but should be included if you want to avoid smears. Standard typing paper will be sufficient at the start, but later you will need larger sheets and perhaps quadruled paper, also. An accurate ruler with a smooth edge is a must. And you'll need at least one triangle. (See FIG. 1-1.)

Drawing Surface

The drawing surface must be smooth and clean. There's nothing quite so frustrating as trying to make a clean drawing only to have a nick in the table cause a big mark or tear—or for a rough pattern on the table surface to come through. A kitchen table is okay, but only if it's smooth and clean.

There is a distinct advantage in having a drawing board—especially if the only table you can use is rough or has a texture. The drawing board, or drawing table, will have a perfectly flat, smooth surface and squared edges—features that most kitchen tables don't have. Another advantage is that you can tape or tack the paper to the board without worrying about damaging it (FIG. 1-2).

You can buy or make a drawing board or drawing table. The cost of buying one can be any-thing from a few dollars to several hundred. The cost of making one will generally be less, but of course, it will require your time, some effort, and at least minimal skill.

Fig. 1-1. *The basic drawing kit: paper, pencils, eraser, ruler, and triangle.*

Fig. 1-2. *A drawing table.*

If at all possible, the size should be at least 2 inches larger than the largest paper to be used. For a 24-by-36-inch sheet of paper, the smallest board would be 28 by 40 inches. This gives you enough room for the paper, and a slight margin all around.

Many professionals prefer a surface with a little "give" to it. Others like a hard surface. You can determine your own preference very simply by drawing a few lines on a piece of paper placed on a hard surface (such as a Formica counter) and then on something softer (a piece of smooth wood or a few sheets of paper beneath).

You might prefer to work with the surface and paper flat. Professionals usually prefer to have the surface at a slant. This is considered to be more efficient and less of a strain. Most commercial drawing tables are adjustable from flat to about 30 degrees. Commercial drawing boards often have folding legs on one side to provide a tilt.

Which way you work is up to you. Try both. The "down and dirty"—and easiest—way is to simply place some books under the far side of a board to provide the tilt. Now make a few sketches to see how you like a tilt as compared to flat.

Pencils and Erasers

The common wooden pencils are simply rated No. 2. This is a fairly soft lead and will leave a dark line. Unfortunately, it also has a tendency to smear. (The softer the lead, the more is left behind, which means a darker line but more smear.)

The standard lead used by professionals is 2H. This is hard enough for good use and less smear, but not so hard that making a line is difficult, or that the line comes out too dim. The "H" means "hard." The higher the number, the harder the lead and the dimmer the line. A 4H, for example, is harder than the 2H; it will leave a lighter line.

Although the standard wood pencil will probably suit your needs just fine, you might prefer to use a different lead than the No. 2. Other hardnesses are available, both in wooden pencils and in leads to be used in a mechanical pencil. Commonly available leads range from 3B (very soft) to 9H (very hard).

The wooden pencils will fit into a standard pencil sharpener (if you have one—and you *must* have a good one). Of course, each time you sharpen the pencil, it will get shorter. The advantage of a mechanical pencil is that it's always the same length. When you need more lead, you simply push the button on the back of the pencil. The investment isn't necessary, but it's not one of high cost.

There are actually two types of mechanical pencils. One holds very thin leads. These tend to break easily and are generally not considered suitable for drafting work. Each break isn't just irritating, it can leave marks on the paper, and increases the chance that the line will be crooked or doubled. For drafting, a holder and thicker leads are used. These leads are roughly the same thickness as the leads in wooden pencils; therefore, they are stronger and less likely to break.

There are special sharpeners for these leads, but there is a less expensive method. The lead sharpener need be nothing more than some fine sandpaper. For a small cost, special sharpening "sticks" are available, with narrow sheets of sandpaper on a cardboard holder. These are relatively inexpensive, and you can peel off and throw away the sheets as they become dirty.

Consider also getting some colored pencils. These can help you map out certain things quickly and easily. Professionals use lines of different densities and different patterns to indicate various things. For your needs, color might be easier to use and to see. (When I designed and installed my sprinkler system, I color-keyed both the design and the pipes. It was easy to do and if repairs are ever needed, I know just where the pipes are located. Once I dig down I know which pipe is which when more than one is in a trench.)

Paper

You're going to need at least two kinds of paper. Smaller sheets can be used for rough sketches and for detailed drawings of small sections of the whole. Standard $8^1/_2$ by 11 typing paper will do fine. Better yet, get quadruled paper—paper with squares printed on the surface. It's a little more expensive, but the cost is worth it. Not only do you have lines and right angles to follow, you have a built-in method of measuring and scaling.

The most common type of quadruled paper had $1/_4$-inch squares, which means that a standard $8^1/_2$ by 11 sheet is 34 squares wide and 44 squares long. If you use a scale of 1 square equals 1 foot, the maximum drawing would represent 34 feet by 44 feet (actually a bit smaller, since you'll want to leave a margin). This is usually just fine for doing a detail, such as for the cabinets.

By using another scale—$1/_4$ inch equals 5 feet, for example—the sheet can be used to represent 170 feet by 220 feet, which is more than ample to handle most plot plans—at least in the crude-sketch stage. You'll also need larger paper—24 inch by 36 inch should be sufficient unless the home you're designing is extremely large.

Quadruled paper comes in the smaller sheets and also in these larger sheets. If ruled in $1/_4$-inch squares, that 24-by-36-inch sheet is 96 by 144 squares. Even if your chosen scale is $1/_4$ inch to 1 foot, that represents a sizeable structure (96 feet by 144 feet).

This paper isn't sufficient for the true final drawings, but might be handier for your own finals (the ones you'll be turning over to the draftsman or architect). Once again, there are printed lines to follow, which makes your job easier and more accurate.

The final drawings will be done on a high-quality, semitransparent paper somewhat similar to high-quality tracing paper. Most often vellum will be used. If you hire a draftsman or architect to make the final drawings (see Chapter 19), you need not use the vellum paper.

You can also buy specially printed "job" paper, with ruled sections for name, date, description, etc. If you care to spend the money, fine, but it's not necessary.

Ruler and Straightedge

That 39-cent ruler might seem to be accurate enough, but if you really care about accuracy, give that one to the kids and get a quality one for yourself. One 18 inches in length is best, but a shorter one will do, especially if you have a T-square (see p. 7).

You don't need high accuracy for making crude sketches, but without accuracy, your final drawings—and the final home—may not be what you had in mind. A line you draw might translate into more than 6 inches of real space. Two of those make a foot. It adds up in a hurry if you're not careful. (Two 10-inch-thick exterior walls and four 5-inch interior walls means that your sketch is going to be off by more than three feet. More, it's very easy to find a wall or doorway a foot or more in the wrong place.)

You'll be drawing to scale, which means that you'll pick a real measurement on paper to represent a real measurement in the building. This should be as accurate as you can possibly make it, even in your rough sketches.

Scale

Which scale you use depends largely on the size of the structure, and the size of the paper. For example, you might choose to have 1 inch on the paper to be the equivalent of 10 feet in reality. Each $1/4$ inch then represents $2^{1}/_{2}$ feet.

Perhaps you can see a problem already in such a scale. While this scale might be fine for overall landscape and plot layout drawings, it's hardly sufficient when you're also trying to figure in walls that are 4 inches in thickness.

The architect's scale mentioned above has on it a variety of different scales (usually 10), with especially handy markings. The markings are in the number of units. On the $1/4$-inch scale, for example, marking "18" means eighteen $1/4$-inch units. If you're using a scale of $1/4$ inch = 1 foot, that "18" represents 18 feet. This means you can measure off distances easily and quickly, without the need to make calculations. (See FIG 1-3.)

The most common scale for the house itself is

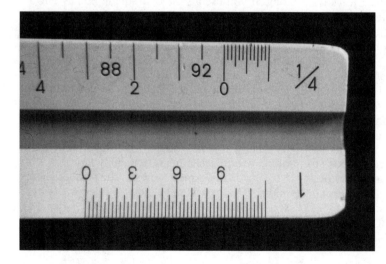

Fig. 1-3. Architect's scale.

$^1/_4$ inch equals 1 foot. This is how most quadruled paper is provided (although some of it comes with $^1/_8$-inch squares). As mentioned above, a standard 24-by-36-inch sheet then represents an area of 96 feet by 144 feet—usually more than enough for the house and immediate surroundings.

For your own use, half of the square equals 6 inches, or just slightly more than the average interior wall (just shy of 5 inches, depending on the thickness of the sheetrock). This is generally accurate enough for determining room size in your rough sketches.

T-Square

An expensive, but extremely handy tool is the T-square (FIG. 1-4). This tool forms a perfect right angle between the edge of the board and across the paper. Absolutely parallel lines can be drawn. Further, the use of the T-square and a triangle will create precise vertical lines. The job *can* be done without a T-square, but not nearly as accurately or as easily.

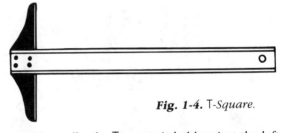

Fig. 1-4. *T-Square.*

Normally, the T-square is held against the left side of the drawing board and moved up and down, as needed, to draw horizontal lines. It also serves as a square base so that vertical lines (and others) can be drawn with a triangle.

Some drawing boards come with a built-in "square." This is actually a straightedge, attached to rails on each side of the board. Often, there are knurled screws on each side to lock the edge in place. In a sense, the board itself, and the rails, become the "T" part of the square.

Either way, the edge can be used to line up the paper so that the lines—horizontal and vertical—will be consistently square (FIGS. 1-5 and 1-6).

Fig. 1-5. *Lining up the paper.*

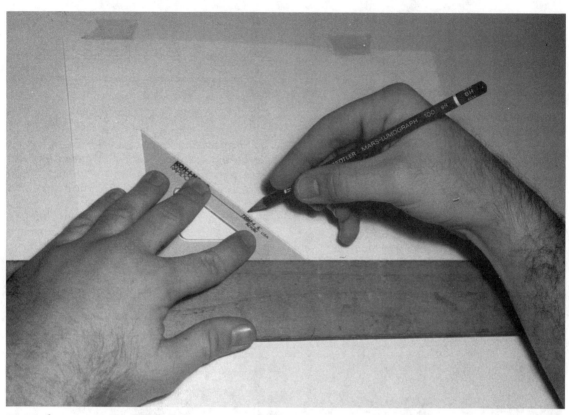

Fig. 1-6. *Using the* T-*square with a triangle.*

Triangles

The two most common drawing triangles are 45 – 45 – 90 and 30 – 60 – 90. These are not just to draw angles, but also to draw perfectly perpendicular lines.

To draw perpendicular lines you hold the triangle against the T-square. The angle between the two is a perfect 90 degrees. All the lines are then perpendicular to the base line and perfectly parallel to each other.

It's wise to invest in good triangles. They should be thick enough for easy handling, with clean corners and edges. They should also be either clear or lightly tinted. Being able to see through the triangle is a big help.

One of the triangles you get should be as long as the longest vertical line you'll be drawing. This is usually the 30 – 60 – 90 triangle, since it has the longest side. Generally, though, a triangle larger than 12 inches becomes cumbersome to handle, especially when it's also being used mostly for shorter lines. One shorter than 10 inches begins to be too small for effective use. (Using the 1/4 inch equals 1 foot scale, a 10-inch triangle can draw a line to represent 40 feet.)

Templates

There are a variety of templates available in several scales, most at very low cost. Their function is to make it possible to draw various symbols. At very least, you should get a template to aid you in drawing small circles, squares, and triangles. These are used so often in the drawings that the $1 (or less) you spend for that little piece of plastic is a very good investment. (See FIGS. 1-7 and 1-8.)

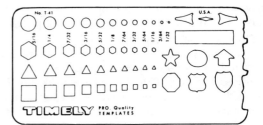

Fig. 1-7. *Template.*

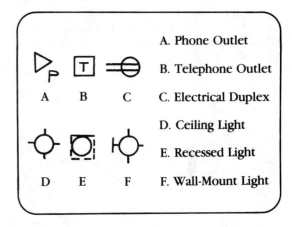

Fig. 1-8. *Some of the common symbols used in architectural drafting for which a template is useful: a) phone outlet; b) television outlet; c) electrical duplex outlet; d) ceiling light; e) recessed light; f) wall-mounted light.*

A. Phone Outlet

B. Telephone Outlet

C. Electrical Duplex

D. Ceiling Light

E. Recessed Light

F. Wall-Mount Light

Other Tools

You can spend hundreds, even thousands, of dollars for specialized drafting equipment. Only *you* can determine if they are needed or not. The basic rule of thumb is that if you'll be using the tool only once or twice, and it costs more than a few dollars, be sure that you actually need it and can't do the job any other way. (Keep in mind that since you'll probably be hiring a draftsman or architect, freehand sketching on your part is perfectly allowable.)

There are relief sheets that can be placed under a piece of paper to make the rendering of bricks, for example, as easy as rubbing a pencil over the top. You can even find relief templates for the drawing of trees, bushes, and other landscape ideas. If you're not artistic, it might be tempting to spend money on these things, but generally they are not needed by the average person.

A protractor can be used to measure and determine angles. With most homes, exact and unusual angles are rare. You might have something that is at a 45-degree angle, and your triangle can be used to create this. It's unlikely that you'll need to draw a 21-degree angle.

At the same time, protractors are inexpensive. If you have a need to figure angles, such as on the plot plan, it's a viable investment.

A good compass is the best way to draw larger circles and arcs. (A template is best for small circles.) If you intend to have a circular fountain or perhaps some arches of a specific size, a compass is the way to go about it.

In using a compass keep in mind the difference between a diameter and a radius. If an arch is to be 10 feet across at the widest point, that's its diameter. Its radius is half of that, or 5 feet. If your scale is 1 inch equals 10 feet, you'd set the compass at 1/2 inch (the radius), put the steel point at the exact center of what would be a circle, and swing the arc.

A compass can also be used to bisect (cut in half) a line. If you are using the proper scale and have an accurate ruler, bisecting a line with a compass isn't usually needed, but it's still a handy technique to know (See FIG. 1-9).

Set the compass so that the steel point and pencil tip are a little longer than half the distance to the other side of the line. Place the point on one side and swing a partial arc. Move the point to the other side of the line and do the same. Place a straightedge between the two spots where the arcs cross. That will be exactly the center of that line. If you now set the pencil of the compass to be exactly at one edge of the line and swing an arc, it will end up exactly at the other end of the same line (FIG. 1-10).

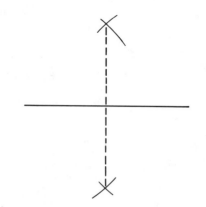
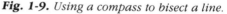

Fig. 1-9. Using a compass to bisect a line.

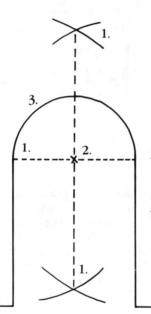

Fig. 1-10. Drawing the arc after bisecting the line. The dashed line (1) represents the line to be bisected. Using a compass, find the exact center. (2) Then, using this center for the point of the compass, measure to the edge and swing the arc (3).

2

Plot layout

There are many things to consider when it comes to planning how the home will sit on the lot. The most obvious is size. If the lot you'll be using measures 100 feet in width, and you want (or are required to have) 20 feet on each side of the house, the maximum dimension of the house in that direction will be 60 feet.

Unless you happen to live in a flat desert of hard soil—and even if you don't—there are many things to keep in mind, including the future. How is the drainage, and in which directions? This becomes particularly important if you intend to have a basement. What natural obstacles are going to interfere with your plans? If you want to build a flat, ranch-style house on the side of a hill, you're in for some trouble, or at least some preplanning. Where are the various utilities and sewer lines? What kind(s) of deed restrictions do you have on the property? What kind of landscaping do you plan to have? For that matter, how many trees, bushes, and rocks will have to be moved or removed if your plan is to be possible? Where is the road, and where will you place the driveway?

Your choice is to design a home and then try to find a lot to suit it, or find the lot and then design a home to suit. The latter is much easier to accomplish (but do keep an eye out for unreasonable deed restrictions).

The Land

It should be obvious that you should never buy any land without first seeing it. Better yet, spend some time on it. Walk the perimeter. Go across it. Make note of any possible problems you might encounter.

Many lots have already been mapped. It's possible that you can get hold of a copy of this from the seller, from the county or other government agency, or from the title search company. Don't expect anyone to just give it to you. Ask. Each step of the way, make your request known. If need be, make one for yourself.

Eventually you'll need a very accurate map of the boundaries and property lines. If you hire a surveyor (see the next section), you'll have just that. While this map defines the legal edges of the property, to design the home you need more. It isn't *just* the boundaries that matter, it's the features of the land.

If you don't already have a map of the boundaries, make one to the proper scale. This can be done by using a long tape measure or measuring wheel. For the moment, though, it might be sufficient to get just an approximation of dimensions by simply "stepping off" the property, both as to size and to location of various features. (Keep in mind that this *is* an approximation only and not sufficient for the final plot map.)

Practice at home until you can fairly accurately step off a particular dimension—usually 3 feet. Then count your steps as you walk all the way around the property. Forty steps across the front would indicate approximately 120 feet; eighty steps to reach the back means 240 feet. By making a complete circuit; you're double-checking your estimate. (That is, if you've taken 40 steps from east to west, then 80 steps from north to south, walking from west to east gives you a way to double-check the first and walking south to north checks the second.) This obviously will get a little tricky if the lot is a shape other than a perfect square or rectangle. (See FIG. 2-1.)

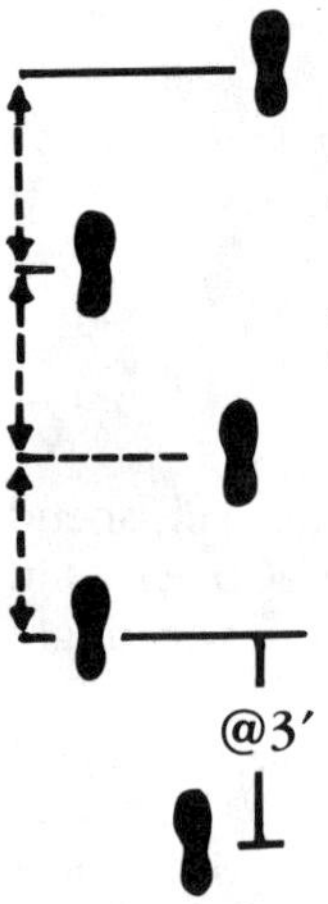

Fig. 2-1. *For most adults, one step is roughly 3 feet. To find out what your own stride is, mark several steps and measure between them.*

@3'

Once you have a scale drawing—either the official plot map or the one you've made yourself—on the overall size and shape of the property, you can mark the features of the land, including slope and drainage. Locate each as accurately as possible on your map. (Don't forget to take winds, weather, direction of sun, and easement into account.) These can also be "stepped off," but, again, you'll eventually need something more accurate. Your primary concern at this point is to note those things that will interfere with construction, and to envision what you intend for the future (FIG. 2-2).

Make copies and file away the original and one of the copies. The other copies are for scribbling notes and helping you plan the overall layout of the house on the land, the locations of underground pipes, and even plans for landscaping.

Surveys

Even if the property has been surveyed, consider having it done again—especially if the last survey is quite old. At very least, you should have an accurate survey report. And, if you can't find the corner markers while walking around on the land

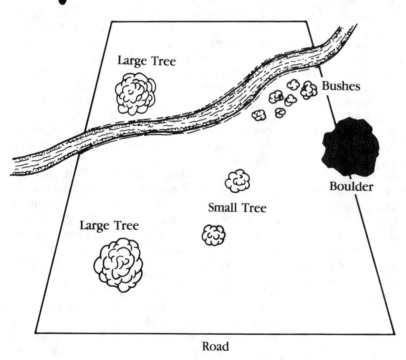

Large Tree

Bushes

Boulder

Small Tree

Large Tree

Fig. 2-2. *Make a map of the property to show features and obstacles.*

N

Road

(as above), a survey is essential! It becomes particularly important if you intend to build within 5 feet of the property line, and even more so if there will be a fence along that line.

Land that has been surveyed will generally have markers (assuming that they haven't been moved, vandalized, or somehow destroyed). Learn where the corner marks are. Best, mark them so they can be found easily in the future. The surveyor will use the land description (which will read something like, N$^1/_4$ NW$^1/_2$ Sec. 15, Township 3 South Range 9 East) and other information to locate and verify the markers, or to place them if they have been lost.

A survey of as-yet-unsurveyed land is almost unknown today. Virtually every square inch of our country has been surveyed at one time or another in one way or another. New surveys merely verify the figures and otherwise break up a larger piece of land.

The cost of a survey depends on the job. It can be as low as $100 to simply find existing corner markers, or can run into thousands of dollars for more complicated work. On the average, a survey team will cost anywhere from about $55 per hour to well over $100 per hour.

Title Search

A title search isn't always a requirement, but it is almost always a wise investment. A title search simply tracks the title backwards to be sure that there are no encumbrances on it. It lets you know that yes, this is that particular piece of land, yes, that person can sell it, and yes, if you buy it you become the real owner without obligation to someone else with a claim to the land.

Imagine the alternative. You could pay $20,000 for a piece of property only to find out that the seller had no right to sell it. Perhaps it had already been sold. Or there might be a claim against it (a *lien*). For example, the seller may have already borrowed money, using the land as collateral—or the land itself may still be unpaid, and you could find yourself paying not just the $20,000 purchase price but the $10,000 already owed on it. Land fraud is a crime, but that won't get your $20,000 back.

It's almost unheard of for a bank to lend money on land that has not had a title search and

title insurance as well. The simplest is a Condition of Title Report, which will generally cost somewhere between $150 and $200. This report verifies that the title is clear as of the date of the report. Title insurance is more expensive for the simple reason that the title company is not only verifying that the deed to the land is clear, they're insuring the investment.

You *can* do a title search on your own. The County Recorder's Office is open, and the records are not sealed. You can go in on your own. Most of these offices will even help you. One drawback is that the process is tedious, especially for someone who has never done it before. More important than this, if you make a mistake or miss something, the fault and responsibilities are your own.

Deed and Other Restrictions

Be sure to very carefully review any restrictions that will affect your home and lifestyle. No matter where or how you decide to build, you're going to be facing some restrictions. State, county, city, and townships all might have certain local requirements.

Most of these will make good sense, and most will be fairly standard regardless of where you live. The foundation and footings must be secure and able to support the structure. There will also be certain restrictions concerning placement and depths of pipes and wires.

It might seem that a local restriction on window size has little to do with plot layout, but if you're wise enough to be considering energy efficiency, this can be a concern in the overall layout. (If the code requires 12 square feet of window for a particular bedroom, should that window face north, south, east, or west?)

To keep a neighborhood (or future neighborhood) consistent, there are often restrictions concerning setback and room on the sides between the properties. This can be important even if you choose a lot in the country, and can become more so if your lot is within a development.

This can make a difference in the overall costs, general appearance, and the design you use. For example, if the lot is very large, and the deed restriction requires that the home be placed a minimum of 125 feet from the road, the savings on the land can be offset by the cost of building such a long driveway. Also, simply due to perspective, a small home set well off the road is going to look even smaller, and perhaps a little odd.

Setback restrictions will probably also apply from side to side. If the lot is 125 feet wide, but carries with it a deed restriction of setting the home no closer than 30 feet from either adjoining property, the maximum length of the house will be 65 feet. Keep in mind that this means from outer wall to outer wall. If your design doesn't take wall thicknesses into account, you could find yourself with a house plan that violates the deed restrictions.

Deed restrictions might also apply to the design itself. For example, those restrictions might limit your choice of materials, and especially those that "skin" the house. You might be required to have a two-story house, or you might be prohibited from having one. Some areas have restrictions against various kinds of antennas. Others limit, even prohibit, certain kinds of pets (or all pets).

Height, overall size, style, driveway, landscaping—all can be factors determined by local and other restrictions. All these things, and more, have to be taken into consideration. The more you know before you begin the design, the better. The less you know. . . .

If the plot is zoned for smaller homes, and your intention is for a larger one, chances are pretty good that yours is going to be the largest and most expensive in the neighborhood. That might seem fine, but later on, it's going to mean that selling your home at a decent price will be more difficult.

On the other hand, if the area is zoned for larger homes, and you can't afford to build or maintain one, the deal on the land is meaningless.

Not all of the restrictions will be listed on the deed and accompanying papers. Some will be local, or even through a neighborhood committee, but it works out to the same thing. If you have plans to install a satellite television system, the time to find out if you can is *before* you buy the property, not after.

The opposite is nearly as bad and sometimes worse. Restrictions limit what you can do, but also limit what others can do. If you buy a piece of unzoned land, only building codes will apply. And that means that one day in the future you might find yourself living next door to an industrial complex, and living in a house that can't be sold.

Keeping Costs in Mind

Unless you're so rich that money means very little, one of your first considerations in building a house will be, "How much will it cost?" As the size of a home increases, so does the cost of construction, and the cost of the lot to hold it. You should have some idea of what you can afford before beginning. It's fine, and even fun, to design your 8000-square-foot dream home, but it's not realistic to do so if you intend to keep costs below $100,000.

A rough average for construction, figuring on average-quality materials, usually comes to somewhere between $45 and $65 per square foot. Thus, a home of 1700 square feet is going to cost roughly $76,500 to $110,500 to build. You can improve on this, or worsen it, depending on how hard you try, where you live, what you've designed, and a number of other factors.

Cost of the land varies across such a wide range that even an attempt to put a range in print is useless. You might find some undeveloped land in the middle of nowhere for $1,000 per acre, or might find yourself paying $25,000 for a fraction-of-an-acre lot. No matter what, the larger the lot, the more expensive it will be, both now and in the future (property taxes). See FIGS. 2-3 and 2-4.

Another cost that many people forget to add in is that of needed improvements. Land out in the boonies might be less expensive, but could bring in the cost of bringing in water, electricity, and a telephone line.

A friend of mine had the chance to pick up a .86-acre piece of property for $10,000. This seemed like a good deal, since other property in the area was selling for $17,000 an acre. He especially liked the idea that the land was isolated, which would give him privacy, while being within just a few miles from the main road, shopping areas, and other businesses.

He almost plunked down the initial payment, but then found out that it would cost more than $12,000 to bring power and water to the property, and another $3,000 to build a passable road so he could get in and out. There was an existing structure on the land, but it was far too small and in

Fig. 2-3. *This land will probably be fairly easy to develop. Electricity, water, and phones are at the front of the property, where there is also a major paved road.*

Fig. 2-4. *Although the land might be less expensive to buy, the costs of building on it make it more expensive in the long run.*

such poor shape that it would have to be torn down and hauled away before the new home could be started. What seemed to be a good deal would actually have ended up costing him more than double the "going price" for land in that area.

It might not seem important, but location can make a big difference both in enjoyment and long-term costs. How far will you have to drive to work, shopping centers, and schools? The costs in fuel and time can add up quickly if you have to drive long distances every day. Is the neighborhood safe for children? Pets? You? If someone in your family might require emergency medical care, is it available where you plan to build?

Then comes the problem of preparing the land to take the house. Trees or large rocks might have to be removed. If the soil is too soft, special procedures might be needed to keep the house from sinking. Soil that is too hard or has bedrock or other hidden excavation problems beneath the surface can be considerably more expensive to solve.

Worse yet might be a problem with drainage. If you place the home in a natural valley, every time it rains you could be facing a flooding problem.

Look the lot over very carefully before buying it. Judge it objectively and honestly. What are the problems? How much will it cost to take care of them? You might be able to situate the house on the lot so as to reduce—even eliminate—some of those problems (which will once again restrict your design). A good deal on a piece of land that is useless for building or that will force heavy expenditure to make it of use isn't much of a deal.

Restrictions can also make a difference in costs. A required setback can end up meaning additional costs. The driveway might need to be longer, along with the lines and pipes that attach your home to the various utilities. (There's a difference in tying a house to an electrical supply 10 feet away and one 50 feet away.)

General Size

As already mentioned, two of the great limiters on size are how the house will fit on the lot, and the costs. Pushing it in the other direction is your own needs (FIG. 2-5).

Before anything else, determine your budget. Just how much home can you afford? Be *honest* with yourself. If you can afford only a 1400-square-foot home, there's not much sense in making designs that represent 5000 square feet. (*Note:* If your present financial condition allows only 1400 square feet of home, but you expect that you'll need, and can afford, something larger in the future, try to make your design so that expansion is relatively easy.) Your financial situation determines maximum size. This has to be balanced against minimums.

How many bedrooms do you need? Will a single bathroom be sufficient? (Most experts recommend a bath and a half, at the very least.) Do you need a large family room, and, perhaps, a formal living as well? What size should the kitchen and dining areas be? And how about outside areas and parking places for your vehicles?

There are four basic concerns in a home: general living and gathering; eating; privacy areas (bedrooms and bathrooms); and outside. Some space must be given to each. How much depends on your own priorities and needs (and financial status).

Begin by figuring minimums. How *small* can something be? Your dream might be to have a 20-by-30-foot master bedroom, and a 20-by-20-foot attached bathroom complete with a sunken swirling hot tub. But if the only way you can live that dream is to have no living room and a 5-by-10-foot kitchen, you're probably not going to be happy for long in the home—and you'll have a difficult time reselling.

So, what *are* the minimums?

In most cases, a minimum house should have two bedrooms, one and a half baths, a living room, a decent-sized kitchen, an eating area, a one-stall carport, and closets or storage in each room (FIG. 2-6). (*Don't forget storage space!*).

Each area should be large enough to hold those things appropriate to the room, while leaving sufficient space for normal movement. For example, a single ("twin") bed measures 39 by 75 inches, which means that it's a little over 3 feet wide and 6 feet long. Allow 3 feet on each side just for walking; if the bed is pushed up tight against a wall and into a corner, the bare minimum becomes 6 feet by 9 feet. Such a room is useless for anything but sleeping.

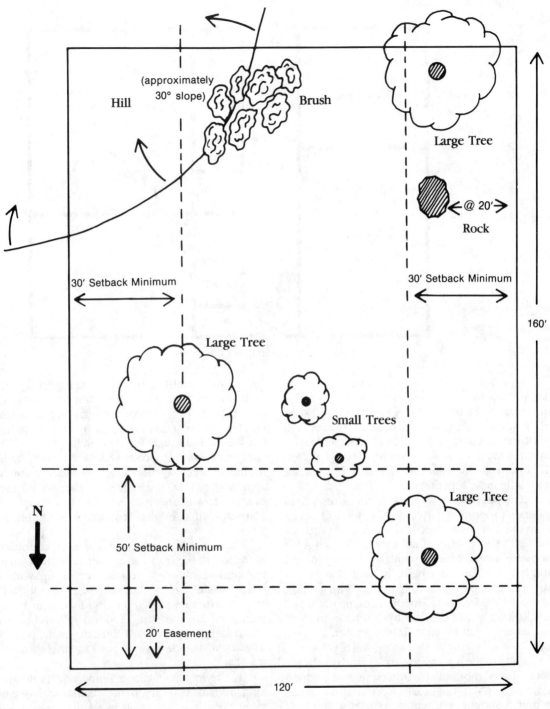

(approximately 30° slope)

Hill

Brush

Large Tree

@ 20'

Rock

30' Setback Minimum

30' Setback Minimum

160'

Large Tree

Small Trees

Large Tree

N

50' Setback Minimum

20' Easement

120'

Scale 1" = 20'

Fig. 2-5. *With the boundaries, features, setbacks, and other items of importance marked on your map, you can begin to design your home.*

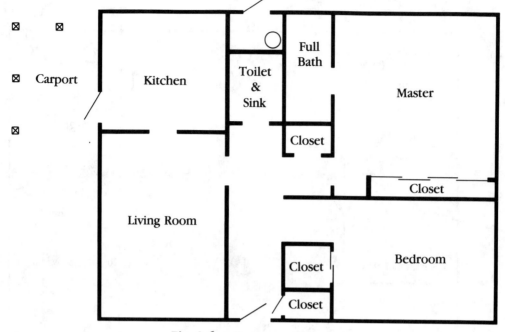

Fig. 2-6. A "minimum" house.

Now add a closet—one a mere 2 feet in depth. Now the room becomes 8 by 9 feet and is still pretty much useless except for sleeping. (Keep in mind that a door is needed, and also that wall thickness is going to "cut into" what little you have.) Adding a couple more feet (10 by 9 feet) doesn't make this bedroom spacious, but at least it's a little more functional.

If a larger bed is needed, the size has to increase proportionately. (See Chapter 10.) Going from the small twin-sized bed to a full size adds 15 inches in width—more than a foot. A queen-sized bed adds almost 2 feet in width over the twin, and another 5 inches in length. A king-size bed is about double the width of the twin. With a width of nearly 6½ feet and a length of edging towards 7 feet, a king size bed in a 9-by-10-foot room will just barely fit, and there will be no room for storage.

Many of the major items have standard sizes—beds, stoves, tubs, toilets. Others, such as refrigerators, vary in size, but usually over a narrow range. A prefab shower stall will be one of a very few sizes. If the shower is to be made of ceramic tiles, it can be pretty much whatever size you wish.

All of it might seem to be nothing more than individual factors. That's true, but it's also additive. A 10-by-10-foot bedroom may not seem like much, but two of them and a 14-by-20-foot master is a total of 480 square feet, not including the walls (which *do* take up space!). Now add two bathrooms, the hallway, the closets—suddenly you're approaching 1000 square feet. By the time the rest of the house is drawn in, you can too easily find yourself with a design that simply won't fit on the lot.

Once you know the size of the lot, condition of the lot, the setbacks and other restrictions (natural and man-made), you can come up with a rough overall size of the building. If the lot will allow a structure to be 80 by 40 feet, your maximum total size comes to 3200 square feet, but this has to include all the walls and external areas (such as garages) as well. It's *not* 3200 square feet of living space.

If the lot can't take a home that is 80 feet long, perhaps you can "bend" the house in one or more directions. (Keep in mind that each jog is going to cost, and too many can make the house look silly and ill-planned.)

General Shape

Most homes are rectangular in shape for the simple reason that this is the easiest and most practical shape for design, construction, and living.

A circular home, for example, can quickly end up being nothing but a series of triangles inside, getting smaller toward the center of the home. This makes it very difficult to design suitable rooms. It's also relatively difficult to build, which means that it will be more expensive.

Modifications on the rectangle are also common. The overall shape might be a rectangle with another rectangle jutting out in one direction or another, somewhat like an L in shape. Have the home break on both sides, and the shape is like a U. (Refer to FIG. 2-7 for house shapes.)

This is a perfectly valid technique for fitting a home onto a relatively narrow lot, but it's not free.

Each time you break away from that standard rectangle, the walls and roof also have to break. This can end up costing more than the investment in a lot that will hold a longer home with a straighter roof.

Also, if the house "breaks" in too many directions, the visual effect is one of haphazard design, as though the house was pieced together rather than properly designed.

Landscaping

Landscaping can be as simple as letting nature do its own work, or it can mean that you completely change how things look by creating hills, bumps, gulleys, and so on. Although not usually considered as a part of the landscaping, how the driveways and sidewalks are arranged has an effect on the overall plan.

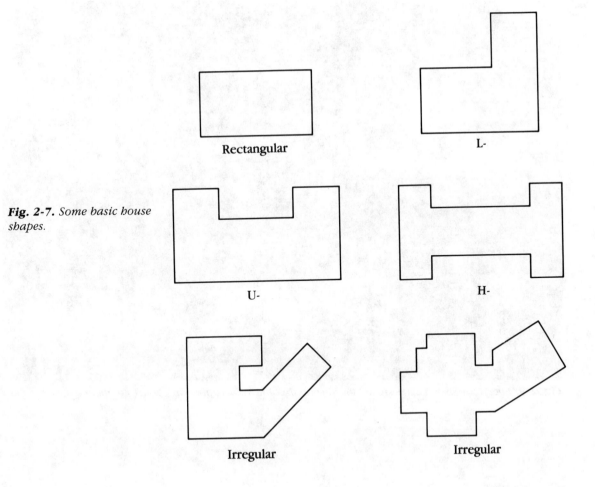

Rectangular

L-

Fig. 2-7. *Some basic house shapes.*

U-

H-

Irregular

Irregular

Fig. 2-8. *A completed elevation.*

Fig. 2-9. *Everything here was designed together so that the landscaping and house complement each other.*

When drawing concepts of finished homes (called *elevations*), a professional designer will often add a few trees and bushes to give a better idea of how the home will look after a few years and a touch of landscaping (FIG. 2-8).

It doesn't really matter if you follow that entire concept or not. It also doesn't matter if you do the landscaping now or in the future (unless deed or local restrictions require it). What does matter is that you at least have it in mind.

Some forms of landscaping are easy to plan. Other types require some thought. How you design the house, how you place it on the lot, along with other factors, determine the landscaping (see FIG. 2-9). The house and land should blend and complement each other. (This is another reason for having copies of the lot map you or someone else made earlier. You can calculate sizes and placements without any expense.)

Where will the house be placed? Do you want a larger front yard or backyard? (Will local restrictions give you the option?) Is there room for a tree on the side? How big will that tree become? If there's room now, how about ten years from now? Will the plants you have in mind grow over the sidewalk to the front door and block passage? If changes in the lay of the land are allowed, what will be the overall effects, both in appearance and in structural stability?

Structures & materials

Many people have the mistaken idea that you have to know all about construction to design a home. Not true. Much of the detail about how the house will be constructed will be left to the draftsman, architect, local regulations, and contractor. You don't really need to memorize all the specifications about which sized beam will support what weight.

At the same time, it's important to realize that limitations do exist. If your plan calls for a 50-foot-wide open space in the center of the home, that creates a long span with no support between. Doing so is possible, but fairly expensive.

Another consideration is the kind of construction you want, along with the advantages and disadvantages of each. Frame homes are made of vertical planks spaced usually 16 inches apart and covered with sheets of flat material in and out with insulation between. This is the most popular type of construction for homes. It provides a low construction cost and long-term benefit of having very good insulation qualities. It might also go up in flames since just about everything except the nails is flammable.

Slump block or cinder block structures have also been popular, largely due to the relative cheapness, sturdiness, and durability (FIG. 3-1). Since it's stone, it won't burn (although the structure might be "gutted" by fire). The trade-off is lack of insulative qualities.

Of course, a frame home can be given a veneer of stone (block, brick, or whatever you wish) or a block home can be given frame walls to allow extra insulation (which works out to about the same thing as a veneer). Or you can build a frame home and have "man-made stone" (called *stucco*) sprayed on the walls outside. (See FIGS. 3-2 through 3-4.)

Some of the considerations are structural, some just aesthetic. Giving a frame home a veneer of brick will add a little to the overall strength and durability of the home, but the true structural strength in such a case is the framing, with the brick being more for appearance.

Costs

There is another matter to consider concerning the structure and materials: costs. Many people, including contractors, try to skimp and save by using the cheapest materials. This is rarely a good idea. More often than not, the effort to save money will end up costing, both immediately and in the long run.

Lumber, for example, is graded. The best grades cost more because they are straighter and generally easier to work with. The lowest grades are the least expensive because they have the most flaws, and that, in turn, means there is likely to be more waste; therefore, you won't save much, if

Fig. 3-1. *Block construction.*

Fig. 3-2. *Frame construction.*

anything, by trying to cut costs. Costs for labor will be higher, and it's entirely possible that the waste will make the cost of materials higher than if you'd gone with quality materials in the first place.

This consideration can become even more important in the long run. A good example is the kind and quality of roofing materials. Try to save money on the roof, and the $500 you save now could quite easily cost you $3000 in five years.

And don't forget long-term maintenance costs. Some types of exterior, such as wood siding, are going to require regular and costly maintenance. It may be less expensive to install, but 10

Fig. 3-3. *Brick veneer.*

Fig. 3-4. *Stucco.*

years from now, it could be a "savings" you'll regret. (This is not to say that wood siding isn't a terrific way to finish a home—just that when calculating costs, you must also consider the future.)

There are times to save, and times to get the best available. When it comes to structural soundness, *never* skimp. Fortunately, building codes exist to help you and protect you here. At least they will in the major sense; the house won't fall down around your ears, anyway. But those codes won't protect you from having to pay thousands of dollars in maintenance over the long run.

Foundations and Footings

The foundation supports the home. It also helps to protect it from frost, water, and insects (particularly termites), and provides stability in other ways. This is one of those places to *never* skimp or try to save.

A home is a heavy thing. You can't just plop it down anywhere and expect it to stand for very long. The result of doing so will be, at very least, cracks and repair work. There is also a chance that the building will become structurally unsound. In other words, if the foundation isn't solid, the house won't be, either.

Imagine an extreme example. A house is built on a hillside. Piers are sunk into the ground to hold the weight. But then along comes an unusually heavy rain. This washes away some of the soil, thus weakening the piers. As they begin to slide, more soil washes out, causing more sliding. Eventually, the piers let go, and the house comes sliding down the hill along with the mud.

There are such cases, some of which involve homes that were built so soundly that the long slide down the hill did less damage to them than the water and mud. But the house was still a total loss.

Less extreme, but more common, are minor problems with the home. Doors and windows begin to stick. The plaster (or drywall, especially at the seams) cracks. Some nails pull loose. Shifting and settling can cause such problems; this is fairly normal.

A solid foundation is essential to minimize the little problems and eliminate the bigger ones. How it's done depends on the type of home and on the type of ground. Sometimes this means getting a soil sample to see what is under the surface to hold the house (or what problems you'll encounter in excavating a basement, septic system, and so on).

In almost every area, the building code will require that the bottom of the foundation be below the frost line. This is to prevent excessive shifting due to changes in temperature. If you happen to be in one of those rare areas where this is not required, do it anyway.

The foundation should also come up high enough so that any wood is a fair distance above the soil, which includes any backfilling that will be done.

The thickness depends on the size of the home, the materials from which it is built, the soil conditions, and other factors. Usually, the absolute minimum thickness for a slab is between 6 and 8 inches, and thicker if the home is large.

With rare exception, the foundation will sit on footings. These might be integral parts of the foundation, or might be separate (FIG. 3-5).

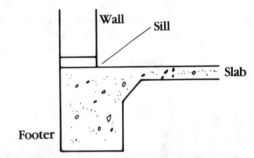

Fig. 3-5. *Footings are wider to spread the weight.*

Supporting Members

The foundation holds up the weight of the house. Various other supporting members hold up the ceilings and roof. Some span distances across a horizontal plane, while others hold up weight vertically. The strains are quite different. A single 2-by-4 upright can hold considerably more weight than a horizontal beam. (It will take a number of joists, hangers, rafters, and so forth to hold up a roof, spaced maybe 16 inches apart, while some 4-by-4 vertical posts spaced 10 feet apart will support the ends. This is an exaggeration, since there are other supports between, but it should give you a general idea.)

How far a supporting member can span depends on four main factors:

1. *The grade of lumber.* The better grades can carry more weight than the lower grades. In most cases the builder will use "No. 2 or better," which means that most of the lumber will be No. 2 in grade and some of it will be No. 1.

2. *The size of the lumber.* Obviously, the bigger the lumber, the more it can hold. A 2 by 4 will carry less weight than a 2 by 6, which will carry less weight than a 4 by 6.

3. *Spacing.* The closer the members are together, the more of them there are to spread and hold the weight. If they are spaced 2 feet apart, they'll be able to carry less weight than if they are placed 16 inches apart.

4. *Weight.* In construction there are various kinds of weight. There is the weight of the building itself, which varies depending on the materials used; the weight of the standard things the house will hold (appliances, for example); the weight of people moving around; the weight caused by things in nature such as wind, rain, and snow. In some areas other stresses, such as earthquakes, must also be taken into account.

Overbuilding

Inexperienced people often make the mistake of thinking that if the code calls for a 2 by 10 beam in a certain spot, a 2 by 12 is even better, and a 4 by 12 is better yet.

This is true to an extent, but only to an extent. Those building codes were developed after many years of study and experience. How much weight a particular length of wood will carry is well known. The size of beam needed to span a particular distance is also well known.

If you know that a section of the ceiling is going to be holding an unusual weight in the near future, plan for it accordingly. Have it drawn into the plans and properly calculated. This doesn't mean that the ceiling over the kitchen has to be strong enough to attach a mount to lift an engine from a car.

As mentioned in the previous section, there are codes and standards used to determine the size of supporting and nonsupporting members. There are many variables involved, such as the loads involved. A 2 by 6 will be sufficient as a supporting member under one circumstance, and insufficient under another. Determination of this depends on more than just distance to be spanned. However, there are books in print filled with tables to determine what is needed under just about any condition. These tables establish set minimums known to be capable of handling a given load under given circumstances. Exceeding them is fine, but is generally a needless cost.

Frame Construction

Virtually every home has some kind of wood framework, if only for the ceiling and roof. How-

Table 3-1. Some Standard Maximum Joist Spans

Size	Spacing	30# w/Ceiling	30# Open	40# w/Ceiling	40# Open
2 × 6	12"	11'6"	14'10"	10'8"	13'2"
	16"	10'6"	12'11"	9'8"	11'6"
	24"	9'3"	10'8"	8'6"	9'6"
2 × 8	12"	15'3"	19'7"	14'1"	17'5"
	16"	13'11"	17'1"	12'11"	15'3"
	24"	12'3"	14'2"	11'4"	12'6"
2 × 10	12"	19'2"	24'6"	17'9"	21'10"
	16"	17'6"	21'6"	16'3"	19'2"
	24"	15'6"	17'10"	14'3"	15'10"
2 × 12	12"	23'0"	29'4"	21'4"	26'3"
	16"	21'1"	25'10"	19'7"	23'0"
	24"	18'8"	21'5"	17'3"	19'1"

ever, when someone talks of a "frame house," they mean one that has walls built of lumber. The house might have a veneer—brick, block, or some other material—but the main structure is the wooden framework. (A block house with wood members inside to hold the drywall or allow additional insulation is not a "frame" house.)

Wood framing is one of the most common types of construction. It's relatively inexpensive, while being strong, durable, and having excellent insulation capability (FIG. 3-6).

Probably the most common size is 2 by 4. For a slightly higher cost you can go to 2 by 6 framing. This makes the house stronger, but, more important, it allows for better insulation (simply because 6 inches of insulation is better than 4 inches). The cost difference consists almost entirely of material: the lumber and the insulation. Labor—one of the major costs—stays the same.

Block Construction

There are various types of cast masonry, all of which are called "block." Various kinds of aggre-gate are mixed with the concrete to make blocks of different weights and textures (FIGS. 3-7 and 3-8).

Building with block is often the least expensive means. They can be constructed quickly, which reduces labor costs. And they are highly durable, requiring very little future maintenance. However, by its nature, block is not a good insulator, which can cause your utility bills to be higher.

One solution is to use the lightweight blocks. These are lighter because the aggregate provides more airspace. A limit is reached, however. Then other things have to be done to increase the insu-lative qualities.

A frame house can have a veneer of brick, block, or other material, with the frame providing the structural strength and space for the insulation. Similarly, a block house can be built with the block providing structural strength and with wood furring strips attached to the block for the added insulation.

It's very common for 1 by 2's to be nailed to the block as a means of holding the drywall to fin-ish the interior walls. This also allows a space for

Fig. 3-6. *A framework house being constructed.*

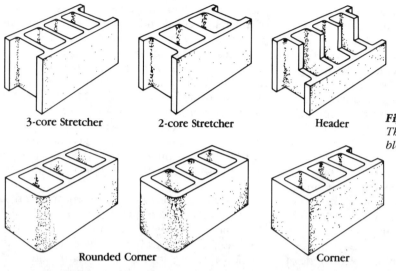

3-core Stretcher   2-core Stretcher   Header

Rounded Corner   Corner

Fig. 3-7. *Standard block shapes. The standard size for a full block is $7^5/_8$ by $7^5/_8 \times 15^5/_8$.*

Fig. 3-8. *A block home being built.*

some minimal insulation (2 inches). All too often, even this is ignored, with the furring strips being used only to hold the drywall. Unless you live in a paradise of constant moderate temperatures, *don't forget the insulation!*

Better yet, using 2 by 4's on end about doubles the space that can be filled with insulation. This allows installation of full 4-inch batts. The cost is minimal and can be "earned back" quickly in reduced heating and cooling bills.

Another solution is to fill the open channels in the block with insulative material, such as foam. One method, called Integra (by Superlite), uses lightweight block filled with foam and then put under tension to "lock down" the construction, claims to have a high R (insulative) factor.

Roofing Materials

Covering the house is the roof. The ceiling joists and roof rafters are tied together, or the roof is built of trusses. With almost every residence, a wood decking is nailed down. This is then covered with one of a variety of roofing materials.

This is one of the places in your home where you should *not* try to save money. The roof pro-tects the home from the weather. Skimping here can mean that in a few years you'll have rain coming in, which, in turn, can mean that the repair costs will be higher than just for a new roof. (See FIG. 3-9.)

Asphalt roofing products are the most common. Roll roofing is sometimes used, but more often the roof will be of shingles. These come in many different styles, colors, patterns, and thicknesses (FIG. 3-10).

A felt backing is saturated with asphalt to provide weatherproofing. Granules cover the outer surface, both to add color and to protect the backing. Some have a layer of insulation built into the shingle to protect the house both from heat and cold, and to increase fire resistance.

The warranty on asphalt shingle roof materials can be 5, 10, 15, 20, or 25 years. As a general rule, the longer the warranty, the thicker, better, and more durable the shingle. Think this over carefully in specifying the kind you will use on your home. The better and more expensive shingles cost no more to install than the cheapest (and sometimes a little less). Your added cost is for materials alone.

Wood shingles, or shakes, were once very

Fig. 3-9. *Building a roof.*

Fig. 3-10. *Asphalt shingles.*

popular, and in some parts of the country are regaining some of that popularity. They add a unique appearance to the house. Because they are a product of nature, they are not quite uniform. This and their size gives the roof a texture instead of being just a flat roof. However, unless given regular weatherproofing treatments, they tend to have a short life, will fade and discolor (which many consider to be a desirable quality), and present a fire hazard unless treated with a retardant.

To satisfy all these shortcomings, shakes made of concrete were developed (FIG. 3-11). Although expensive, they make a virtually permanent roof (assuming it isn't damaged).

A somewhat similar solution is to use roofing titles (FIG. 3-12). This is popular in the Southwest where snow isn't a problem. As with concrete shakes, the tile roof is extremely durable, as long as it isn't damaged.

It has been said twice now. Stone roofs are durable, but only if kept undamaged. Walking on a tile roof is asking for trouble. Expensive trouble.

Concrete shakes aren't quite as susceptible to damage, but you should still do everything you can to keep people off the roof.

Contrary to what a lot of people seem to think, the same applies to any kind of roof. Again, the first tip is to get the best roofing materials you can afford. You can further extend its life of the roof by doing something very simple. Keep everything and everyone off the roof as much as possible.

For example, a common practice is to put the air-conditioning unit on the roof. This came about largely because the ducting of a roof-mounted unit is easier and less expensive. However, it means that whenever the unit needs servicing, someone has to go up onto the roof. Over a period of time this can greatly reduce the life of the roof. Having the air-conditioning unit on the ground will take up some possibly precious space, but doing so will protect the roof, while also making servicing the unit easier. (It will also be easier to protect the unit from the elements.)

Fig. 3-11. *Concrete shakes.*

Fig. 3-12. *Tile roof.*

4

Heating, cooling & insulation

No matter where you live, seasonal changes in the weather will mean that you'll have to have heating and cooling if you're going to live comfortably. Which is more important to you depends on where you live. In one of the colder states, such as Minnesota, you can generally tolerate the summer without air conditioning, but you're risking your life without heat during the icy winter. If you build in the Arizona desert, lack of heat during the winter will be uncomfortable, but lack of cooling during the summer can be fatal.

Your options are many, beginning with the kind and amount of insulation to help protect the interior from the changes in temperature. This, in turn, will reduce the load on the unit(s) that keep your home warm and cool, while also helping to keep utility bills within reason.

Most of the variables involve heating. You can heat with electricity, natural gas, oil, wood, coal (in *very* limited areas), and even with the sun. Each has advantages and disadvantages.

Methods of cooling also have advantages and disadvantages, but the choice isn't as broad. Other than natural breezes and ventilation, all of the practical methods require electricity.

Duct Work

Unless you plan to heat and cool your house room-by-room, you'll need a central duct system (FIG. 4-1). An exception would be if you install a boiler and water radiators, in which case the pipes are the "ducts." You will still need ducting if you want central air conditioning.

The duct work is generally best left to the subcontractor who will be installing the heating and cooling units. It's important that the ducts match the unit(s), and that the units match the house. The subcontractor is a specialist in this.

This doesn't mean that you can forget that ducting is needed. Where the ducts run, space is needed—generally about 1 foot in height and 2 feet in width. This can become a real problem if your home has more than one floor. The ducting has to be somewhere, and if you don't allow for it in your design, you might find yourself with a 7-foot ceiling in some areas instead of the 8-foot height you wanted.

It's also important that the space planned can be well insulated, especially from the outside. Placing uninsulated metal ducting in a hot attic isn't going to provide much cooling for the house. The same applies to warm air moving through the ducts during the cold months.

During construction, take the time to see that the ducting is insulated where needed, and that every seam is thoroughly and completely sealed to prevent leaks.

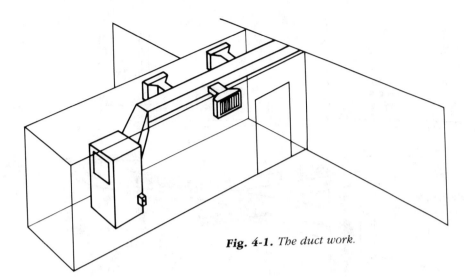

Fig. 4-1. *The duct work.*

Heating

Household heating consists of some method of generating heat and then moving it to the places where it is needed. (See FIGS. 4-2 and 4-3.) That heat can be the sun beating down on a collector, heat generated by electrical resistance, or heat from a fire (wood, coal, or gas). Movement of the heat can be from convection, from a fan blowing warmed air through ducts, or from heated water (even to the point of becoming steam) moving through pipes.

In many cases, you won't have a lot of choice. You might like the idea of using natural gas, only to find that your area has a restriction on new installations. Or you might prefer to heat your home by burning wood, but can't because there are no good local supplies and a county air pollution statute limits the use of wood as a fuel anyway.

Types of Heating

The most common types of heating are (in approximate order of most to least common, the order of which will differ from area to area): electrical, natural gas, oil, wood, and solar.

Electrical heating is a possibility just about anywhere. You'll have electrical service coming to your home anyway. Having it provide the heat is easy. And in some areas, it's the only option available. For example, some areas do not have natural gas lines. Others have the lines but do not allow new residence hookup.

The basic principle of electrical heating is that as electricity flows through a resistive wire, the wire becomes hot. The same is true of an electric dryer, coffee maker, hair-dryer, light bulb (although the last generates heat as a by-product).

Small space heaters often use reflectors to help direct the heat into the room. Sometimes fans are used to increase the effectiveness. In whole-house systems fans are almost always used.

Electrical heating is generally considered to be the cleanest and most versatile. There are no fumes, ashes, or deposits to worry about. It isn't explosive, as are gas and oil. In addition, electrical heating is usually the least expensive to install. You don't need chimneys, flues, special pipes, or storage tanks. More, electricity can be generated by a variety of fuels, including nuclear, or even by your own backyard windmill. It's a fairly secure source of energy.

It is, however, the most likely to disappear during a storm. That snow or thunderstorm won't knock out natural gas, which is underground. The same applies to snow, ice, people crashing into power poles, and so forth. (Of course, if your furnace burns natural gas but uses an electric blower, you still won't have heat if the power goes out.)

Of the direct fossil fuels, natural gas is the cleanest and most common. Although the gas is explosive, as is fuel oil, the supply is brought in through pipes instead of being stored in a tank. The risk of fire or explosion is thus reduced – but it does still exist. Care must be taken with both

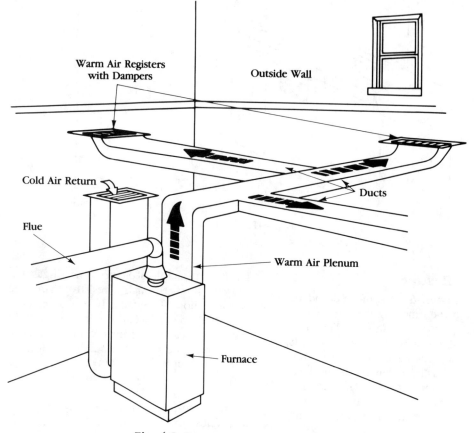

Fig. 4-2. *Furnace and forced-air system.*

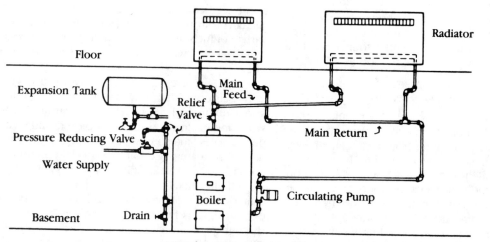

Fig. 4-3. *Boiler and heated water system.*

natural gas and oil heating systems because of the danger of fire or explosion.

Oil is stored in a tank. This brings with it a danger of having, almost literally, a bomb near the home, but it makes you independent (as long as there is oil in the tank). The same is true of using tanked propane.

Wood Heating

On the whole, fireplaces and wood-burning stoves are the least efficient means of heating a house. Much of the heat rises up the chimney and is lost. Only a relatively small portion comes into the room, and even less moves into the rest of the house. (See FIG. 4-4.)

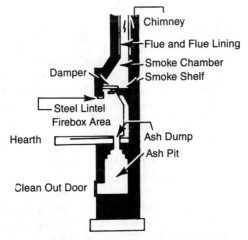

Fig. 4-4. Structure of a fireplace.

There are high-efficiency wood-burning stoves available, and modifications that can be done to a standard fireplace, such as special convection pipes to help direct the heat into the house instead of up the chimney. More sophisticated versions even tie to other rooms through special ducting. Even then, unless the house is small (and wood is abundant in your area), don't consider wood as your source of household heat.

If you can afford the room and the additional cost (at least $1000)—and if firewood is plentiful and cheap in your area—it *is* a very pleasant and romantic way to reduce the heating bills. That wood-burning unit may not heat the entire house, but it will add heat that doesn't have to be generated by other means. But spend the time to find

out about the cost and availability of firewood before you begin thinking of that wood burner as a money-saving unit. It may be, or it may not.

Don't forget to add in the cost of maintenance. Burning wood creates creosote, which is like a flammable tar. The softer woods, such as pine, are the greatest offenders, but all kinds of wood will put deposits on the inside of the chimney stack.

The end result can be a "flash fire" inside the chimney, and a disaster for your home. Regular chimney cleanings are needed to remove these deposits before they become dangerous, and regular inspections of the stack are also needed to be sure that the heat and flame can't get through any cracks.

More important than money saved – or spent—is safety. Even enclosed, a wood-burning unit is a fire in your home. It can easily get out of control. Special materials are used to build the unit to reduce the risks, but the danger isn't eliminated. Sparks can still come into the room or go up the chimney. Without proper and regular maintenance, a wood-burning unit becomes, almost literally, a bomb waiting to go off.

But, take it from a person who has one, there's nothing quite like a cozy fire!

Solar

It's no secret that most forms of energy come from fossil fuels, and that the supply of these fuels is *not* limitless. Sooner or later there will be no more natural gas, oil, or coal for home use or to power the generators that put electricity in our lines. Meanwhile, the cost of these fuels is guaranteed to go up.

The sun, however, is an effectively limitless source. (When it gives out a couple of billion years in the future, it won't matter because our planet will go with it.) And, it's free. The only thing that costs is the method of turning that energy into something directly useful.

The simplest way of using the sun is by proper placement of windows (FIG. 4-5). Allowing more sun into the home during the colder months, and keeping it out during the summer, can make a real savings on the utility bills.

Solar power doesn't have to end there. It's fairly simple to have a solar water heater installed, especially if you plan for it before the home is

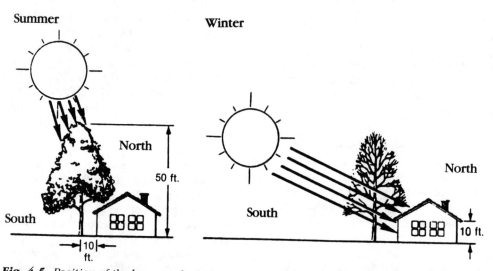

Fig. 4-5. *Position of the home and windows can make the sun work for you or against you.*

built. The complete system consists of four basic parts. Three of these will already be in the home. Exposed to the sun, and usually mounted on the roof, is the collector. As the sun beats down, water inside the collector is heated. Pipes carry it through the house (although a pump to provide pressure is often used with a solar system). If you're going to have hot water during the night, a storage tank is needed. Here, it's possible to tie the solar system into the regular water heater. That provides storage and the fourth part, a means of backup.

If the system is extended to provide heat for the home, the same basic parts hold true. They simply become more complex. The collector can provide heated water to pipes in the walls and floors, with a pump to keep the water moving. The storage tank would need to be considerably larger, and the need for backup heating is more important. (You might survive a cool shower, but not so easily an icy Midwestern winter night.)

Solar electrical (photovoltaic) power is possible, but still difficult and very expensive, made worse by the cost of the storage batteries needed. Powering a transistor radio isn't hard to do, but the power needed is just a fraction of an amp. The electrical demands of a household are considerably greater. If these solar cells are also to power electrical heating or cooling in the home, the draw becomes so large as to require a prohibitive number of solar cells and storage batteries.

The day may come when solar electrical power is economically feasible. Research continues for cheaper, and more efficient, solar cells. Meanwhile, it's more a source of experimental alternate energy (which is a subject all in itself).

Air Conditioning

The word "air conditioning" is actually a bit of a misnomer. More correctly, what most people think of as air conditioning is "refrigeration," since this is what people are actually talking about when they are saying "air conditioning."

The system works on the principle of compressing and expanding gases. When compressed, heat is created. (See "Heat Pumps" on p. 37). When allowed to expand, the gases cool. That's just what is happening in the air-conditioning unit. When the Freon gas inside the tubes expands, it becomes very cold. It then goes through a compressor and is squeezed back into its liquid state so that it can expand and cool again. During the process, some humidity is taken out of the air. (See FIG. 4-6.)

Operating a household air conditioner is expensive, but many people find it to be the most comfortable because the air coming into the home is both cool and dry. The size of the unit depends on the size and location of the house. Any local A/C contractor can tell you exactly what is needed for your house in your area. (The same people will

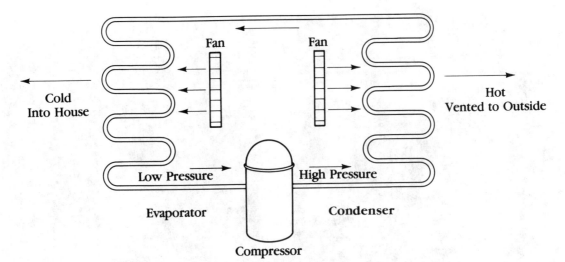

Fig. 4-6. *How an air conditioner works.*

be designing and installing the ductwork that will work most efficiently with that unit under those conditions.) You can also call the power supplier, who will also be able to advise you.

If the unit is too small, it obviously won't be able to do the job when you need it to, and it will often be strained to do a minimal job. That, in turn, is likely to shorten the life of the unit—and they are expensive to replace!

However, this is one time when bigger isn't necessarily better. If the unit is too large, your costs go up needlessly. And once again, there is a strain on the unit because it's trying to push too much air into a too-small area.

Heat Pumps

The easiest way to understand a heat pump is to think of it as an air conditioner that works in both directions. Moving around inside the tubes is a gas—usually Freon. As it expands, it becomes cold; as it is compressed, it makes heat. Such a unit can work year-round, providing cool air in the summer and warm air during the winter. Only one duct system is needed, since the same unit provides both. (See FIG. 4-7.)

Heat pumps are best in warmer climates, but don't work well in colder areas. Set outside in sub-zero weather, much of the heat generated is lost to the surroundings.

Evaporative Cooling

An option available in dry climates is the evaporative cooler. Water is pumped to run over pads. (Most commonly, the pads are made of shredded aspen wood.) A blower fan inside pulls air through the pads, causing the water to evaporate and cool the air. This cooled air is what is blown into the house. The only electricity required is to run the small water pump and the blower fan. Add to this the cost of the water and of regular pad replacements, and it's still the least expensive method of cooling a home.

The major disadvantage is that the outside air *must* be dry. The higher the humidity, the less effective the cooling unit. During humid weather evaporation is slower. The air pumped into the house won't be as cool, but will carry more moisture. On a hot, humid day, not only will the air blown inside be warmer, it will add to the humidity level, making things even more uncomfortable.

In areas where the climate is hot and humid, evaporative coolers are not an option. In drier areas they are a valid means of reducing utility bills. (In humid areas they are useless.)

Wherever used, if at all possible, also have an air-conditioning unit. In the driest areas of our country there are still hot and humid days when the evap cooler will make things inside sticky and miserable. You can survive it, but it won't be comfortable.

Fig. 4-7. *A dual heat-pump system—the larger one for the upstairs and a smaller one for the basement.*

Insulation

There is an attitude that the more insulation there is, the better. This is true to a point. Up to certain limits, adding more insulation will be of benefit. Beyond that, the cost doesn't justify the benefits.

To give yourself a guideline as to what is enough and what is too much, contact the local power company. Each area is slightly different as far as recommended insulation thicknesses. The power company will have all the charts and tables for your own area. (The heating and cooling sub-contractor might also have those specifications.)

The purpose of insulation is to reduce or control the movement of heat. Heat moves through objects (*conductivity*). Heat also rises. Your goal is to keep the heat inside the home during the winter, out of the home during the summer, and make use of the nature of heat movement. This is done in two ways. One is to slow or stop the movement of heat. Fiberglass insulation, whether in sheets or loose, has airspace between the fibers. The fiberglass itself is a fair insulator, but it's the air that does most of the work.

Another is to reflect the heat. This is why some insulation has a shiny foil side. The heat reflects off it in the same way light would. Movement of heat is then "turned around" and sent back where it came from.

How well a material resists the movement of heat is the *R-value* of that material. (See FIG. 4-8.) The higher the number, the more effective the insulation. Think of a cup of coffee. If it's in a ceramic cup, the outside of the cup will become hot because ceramic (and almost all stone materials, natural or man-made) is a poor insulator. It allows heat to move through the material easier. However, a cup made of polystyrene foam will stay fairly cool to the touch because it resists the movement of heat.

A thermos bottle resists movement of heat in two ways. One is the shiny, reflective surfaces, which "bounce heat" back into the bottle. The other is a partial vacuum between the layers of glass, which reduces the conductivity of heat.

The ceiling should always be given the highest R-value. In the hot areas of the country, this helps to prevent heat from moving into the house as the sun beats down on the roof. In the colder areas, it helps keep rising heat inside the home instead of letting it drift out through the roof.

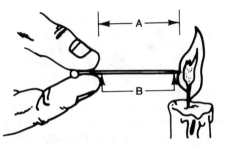

Fig. 4-8. *Movement of heat depends on the material. Air is a better insulator than metal. You'll feel more heat faster through the metal pin.*

Don't forget the insulative quality—or lack thereof—of the windows. With most homes, the windows are the greatest source of loss when it comes to heating and cooling. Glass, in and of itself, is a relatively poor insulator. Heat flows through it easily, and the sun even more so. While allowing the sun to come through for warmth during the winter is desirable, letting the heat escape through the glass is not. During a hot summer, you might want to keep the heat and the sun outside.

A dual-pane window can help in both situations. Although some heat is still transmitted

Table 4-1. Comparison of Insulation Materials

Form	Type	Approximate R-Value Per Inch of Thickness	Relative Cost 1 = least, 5 = most
Blankets &	Fiberglass	3.1	1
Batts	Rock Wool	3.7	1
Boards	Fiberglass	4.5	5
	Polystyrene	3.5 to 5.4	5
	Urethane	4.5	5
Foam	Urea-Formaldehyde	4.2	5
	Urethane	4.5	5
Loose Fill	Cellulose (blown)	3.6	2
	Rock Wool (blown)	2.9	1
	Fiberglass (blown)	2.2	1
	Vermiculite (poured)	2.1	4
	Perlite (poured)	2.7	4

Table 4-2. Thicknesses of Various Insulations and Insulating Values

R-Values:	R-11	R-19	R-22	R-30	R-38
Fiberglass blankets/batts	$3^1/2'' - 4''$	$6'' - 6^1/2''$	$7'' - 7^1/2''$	$9^1/2'' - 10''$	$12'' - 13''$
Rock wool blankets/batts	$3'' - 3^1/2''$	$5'' - 6''$	$6'' - 7''$	$8'' - 9^1/2''$	$10^1/2'' - 12''$
Fiberglass loose/blown	$5''$	$8^1/2''$	$10''$	$13^1/2''$	$17''$
Rock wool loose/blown	$4''$	$6^1/2''$	$7^1/2''$	$10''$	$13''$
Cellulose fiber loose/blown	$3''$	$5^1/2''$	$6''$	$8^1/2''$	$10^1/2''$

through the glass, the airspace between the panes serves as an insulator to reduce this.

You can also get insulated glass, which is specially made to resist the movement of heat. Another kind of glass coming into prominence in areas where the problem is in keeping the sun's rays out has a special layer inside designed to block those rays.

Both cost extra, but the time to make the decision is before the windows have been ordered for the home—actually before construction even begins. If installed during construction, your only added cost is for materials. If you wait until later, the cost of all your original windows is pretty much wasted, and the labor costs for replacing all the glass in your home is considerably higher than that of installation during the construction (which you have to pay anyway).

Other things you can do to the windows to control the sun and movement of heat include things like reflective film, screens, shades, curtains, and shutters. Most of these can be added later with little or no extra cost over doing it during construction.

Electric & plumbing

Electric and plumbing are similar in many ways. In fact, it's fairly common for those learning about electricity to be given analogies of water to help in the understanding.

Electrical wires serve as the "pipes" for the flow of electricity. If there is a break somewhere in the pipe, water won't flow—and neither will electricity if there is a break in the wire.

A light switch is like a "valve" to turn the water on or off. Just as you have one for every light, there are probably "switches" at all or most of the plumbing "outlets" (or there should be).

Most people will decide where they want lights and outlets, and leave the rest to the electricians. Generally, it's fairly easy and inexpensive to run electrical wires where you want them while a home is under construction.

You can do the same with the plumbing fixtures, but at very least you should keep design and potential problems in mind. The reason is that even though there are some similarities between electrical and plumbing systems, there are also some very important differences.

The "drain" for electricity is the return wire, which is the same size as the supply and generally runs alongside it. The drain in plumbing has to be larger, and since it works by gravity, it has to be sloped.

Since water is more "physical" than electricity, it's more affected by distance and angles. You can bend a wire almost any way you wish and the current will flow. Every bend in the plumbing reduces pressure a little.

Even if you leave the details to the subcontractors, there are some basics that must be kept in mind if your design is to meet your needs.

The Electrical System

The local power company will bring the main lines up to the house. The wires go through a meter and into the main box. Here it goes through fuses, or circuit breakers, or both, to make up the various circuits of the home (FIG. 5-1).

The minimum size of the service entrance is usually determined by building codes. Keep in mind that this *is* a minimum for the size of the home. It doesn't allow for future expansion. Because of this, it's often a good idea to specify a service entrance at least one size larger than the minimum.

The number and capacity of branch circuits will also be determined by building codes. Although these codes differ from area to area, the basic standard is to have at least one 15-amp circuit for every 375 square feet, or at least one 20-amp circuit for every 500 square feet. Again, this is a bare minimum. Both of these subjects are discussed in more detail below.

To this you must add other electrical needs.

41

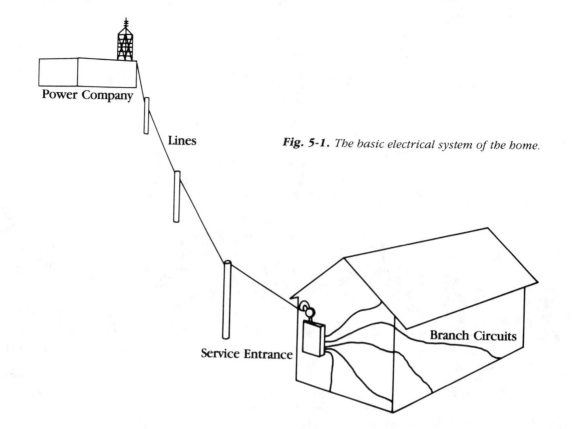

Power Company

Lines

Fig. 5-1. The basic electrical system of the home.

Service Entrance

Branch Circuits

Major electrical appliances can draw considerable power. Even something fairly small like a microwave is generally given its own, dedicated, 20-amp circuit. The electric water heater and range are usually given their own 30-amp (or larger) circuits.

Calculating Electrical Draw

You can't keep plugging more and more into the same branch circuit without having trouble. The standard household circuit will tolerate a draw of up to 15 amps.

The base formula is P = EI (or P = IE, which is the same thing and easier to remember). This means that the number of watts is equal to the current times the voltage.

By algebraic juggling, you get I = P/E (current is equal to the wattage divided by the voltage) and E = P/I (voltage is equal to the wattage divided by the current).

Since the voltage is a constant (more or less), you don't need to worry about E = P/I. Calculating wattage (P = IE) is also relatively unimportant.

Most important for the homeowner is to be able to calculate the current (draw), using I = P/E. This can be used both to calculate the size of the service entrance and what can be used on a continuing basis to determine what can and cannot be plugged into a circuit.

A perfect 100-watt device (such as a perfect light bulb) operating at the nominal household 110-volts will draw 0.9 amps. Note that the word "perfect" was used. There are losses both in the device and in the wiring. It's better to think of each 100 watts drawing 1 amp. This means that 1500 watts would be pushing that 15-amp circuit to the limit.

Many people prefer to think of some lower number, such as 1200 watts, as being the maximum loading for any individual circuit. There is a sound reason for this. Under normal conditions, the voltage supplied to your home will be within 10 percent of the nominal 110 volts. However, as the voltage decreases in value, the draw in amps increases.

Imagine that same 100-watt bulb under different conditions. At 110 volts it will draw 100/110 (P/E) or 0.91 amps. If the voltage drops to 100 volts, the same bulb will draw 100/100, or 1 amp. If voltage decreases to 60 volts, such as during a brownout, the draw becomes 100/60, or 1.67 amps.

Like it or not, the voltage *will* fluctuate at times. Usually it won't be for long periods, and it's fairly rare for it to drop dramatically. However, if the circuit is already "full," even a relatively small decrease in voltage can cause the circuit breaker or fuse to let go.

All of this is also valid for 220-volt circuits. This is one of the reasons that larger appliances use 220 volts instead of 110. When the voltage doubles, the amperage is halved for the same number of watts.

An electric range will consume as much as 8000 watts. If supplied with 110 volts, it would be drawing 73 amps (8000/110). But when supplied with 220 volts, it draws only 36.4 amps (8000/220). While this does not reduce your power bill, it means that the wires supplying the current can be smaller.

The electricians will "spread" each circuit. One might provide power to 3 outlets and 3 lights. If each of those lights draws 1 amp each, that means that the outlets can be loaded with an additional 12 amps total.

You can calculate your needs easily enough by simply thinking of which electrical devices go where and how much power they draw. As already mentioned, a 100-watt light bulb draws about 1 amp. A hot plate or toaster in the kitchen might draw as much as 10 amps.

Normally, you can figure that each major electrical appliance is going to require 30-amps and 220-volts. Some take more, some take less. It depends on what you have in mind, the size of the appliance, and other factors.

The Service Entrance

Almost without exception, electricity is supplied to your home by three wires. Two of them carry 110 volts each, and the third provides the return to complete the circuit. Using one of the "hot" legs and the neutral provides 110 volts; using both of the 110-volt wires together gives 220 volts.

Even if you don't plan to have any 220-volt appliances, be sure to get a service entrance that allows it. You might change your mind later, and having the capability will certainly make a difference in the resale value of the house.

As described above, you can calculate your electrical needs and judge the size of the entrance by that. If your home is to be 1500 square feet, you'll need a bare minimum of four branch circuits for lights and wall outlets. At 15 amps each, that's a total of 60 amps. Add an electric range using a 30-amp circuit, and the total is 90 amps. If this is all you'll have, you can just barely get by with a 100-amp service entrance (which is generally considered to be the minimum size). Better is to plan for future expansion.

A main breaker will shut off the entire box. Each branch circuit will have its own breaker of the appropriate size. On occasion, there may be an additional fuse or breaker near the electrical device.

Breaker Labels

One of the first things you should do after moving into the house is to spend the time to accurately label every circuit breaker in the service entrance. You can use a copy of the floor plan to mark which breaker controls which lights and outlets.

To make things easier on yourself, have the electricians do it for you. This is a fairly simple task if done while wiring is being installed and tested. It's a time-consuming, royal pain if done later.

Having the breakers labelled will save you problems in the future. (Be sure to indicate the room and where outlets are located.) If you don't know exactly which breaker controls a malfunctioning outlet, the only safe way to handle repairs is to shut off the entire house.

Wall Outlets

The national electrical code requires that, within a room, no spot on a continuous wall (in the door, around all the corners and back to the door again) be more than 6 feet from an outlet, which means that there has to be an outlet for every 12 feet of continuous wall (FIG. 5-2). Although there is no code concerning outlets in hallways, the general practice is to have one for every 20 running feet.

Review your needs. Come up with a balance

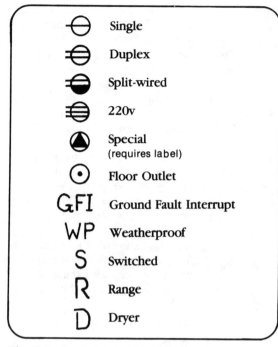

⊖	Single
⊜	Duplex
⊜	Split-wired
⊜	220v
▲	Special (requires label)
⊙	Floor Outlet
GFI	Ground Fault Interrupt
WP	Weatherproof
S	Switched
R	Range
D	Dryer

Fig. 5-2. Symbols used for various kinds of electrical outlets.

of the inconvenience of perhaps having to use an occasional extension cord to the inconvenience of having too many outlets on the walls.

Areas where you plan to have electrical equipment should be given more outlets (and from more branch circuits). For example, if a room is to have a television, two VCRs, a stereo receiver, turntable, CD player, and cassette player, you're simply not going to be able to plug it all into a single duplex outlet.

Most of the standard outlets in the home will be connected to 15-amp circuits. If you know that a certain area will have special needs, you can call for special circuits and outlets. For example, in our kitchen we have a dedicated 20-amp circuit for a microwave oven. In my office are one 15-amp and one 20-amp circuit, both dedicated. (The first is for the computer equipment; the second for ham radio gear.)

In addition to these general-purpose circuits are those assigned to specific tasks. Major appliances (stove, electric water heater, washer, dryer, air conditioners, and so on) will each have their own dedicated breakers.

Lighting and Switching

Quite often the branch circuits bringing power to the general outlets (not those assigned to a single, specific purpose) will also be connected to lights (FIGS. 5-3 and 5-4). Lights are always switched one way or another. A plug-in light will have its own switch, or the outlet itself might be switched.

Lighting is important. Installation is very simple and relatively inexpensive during construction, but just the opposite later. Plug-in lamps mean that cords might be in the way, and it's easy to run out of outlets.

It's important to consider the light that will be available in every area of the house, inside and outside, day and night. Proper design of window size and location takes care of the day, but the windows become all but useless (for lighting) at night. (See FIG. 5-5.)

You'll notice in FIG. 5-5 that every room has lights, and some of them more than one. Areas of particular importance are kitchens and bathrooms (try to prepare supper in a dimly lighted room, or to shave or apply make-up with a flashlight). Anywhere that work will be done also deserves special consideration.

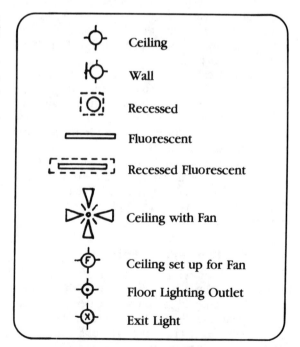

✦	Ceiling
⊩✦	Wall
⌈O⌉	Recessed
▭	Fluorescent
⌈▭⌉	Recessed Fluorescent
✳	Ceiling with Fan
(F)	Ceiling set up for Fan
✦	Floor Lighting Outlet
(X)	Exit Light

Fig. 5-3. Symbols for lighting.

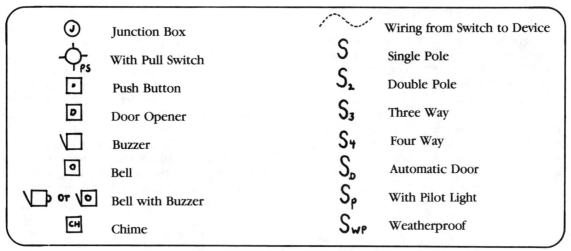

ⓙ Junction Box	∿ Wiring from Switch to Device
With Pull Switch	S Single Pole
Push Button	S₂ Double Pole
Door Opener	S₃ Three Way
Buzzer	S₄ Four Way
Bell	S_D Automatic Door
Bell with Buzzer	S_P With Pilot Light
Chime	S_WP Weatherproof

Fig. 5-4. *Other electrical symbols.*

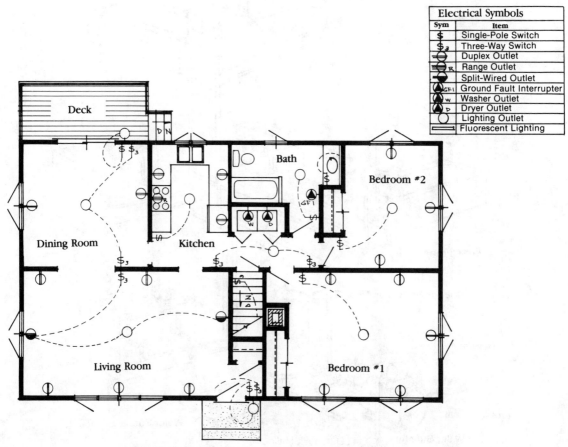

Electrical Symbols

Sym	Item
$	Single-Pole Switch
$₃	Three-Way Switch
	Duplex Outlet
R	Range Outlet
	Split-Wired Outlet
GFI	Ground Fault Interrupter
W	Washer Outlet
D	Dryer Outlet
	Lighting Outlet
	Fluorescent Lighting

Fig. 5-5. *Electrical plans for a house.*

The Basic Water System

In easiest terms, the plumbing system of a home consists of water coming in and water going out. The first is under pressure. The second works by gravity. (See FIG. 5-6.)

Unless you have your own well and pressure tank, you'll be getting the water from a local utility. Likewise, unless you have a private septic system, the household wastes will be fed into a sewer system. As mentioned elsewhere, one of your concerns in finding a lot is to determine just where these are and how much it will cost to tap into them.

The water main will be tapped and connected to a meter. The other side of the meter connects to your home. The size of pipe used depends on the needs of the house, but more on the distance between the main and the house and the pressure in the main. The water then splits into two systems—one cold and one hot. The cold continues through the house from the main. The hot comes from the water heater.

As a rule, with the exception of outside faucets and toilets, both hot and cold lines go to each room that uses water. Each is separate, and each *should* have a shut-off valve close to the plumbing fixture.

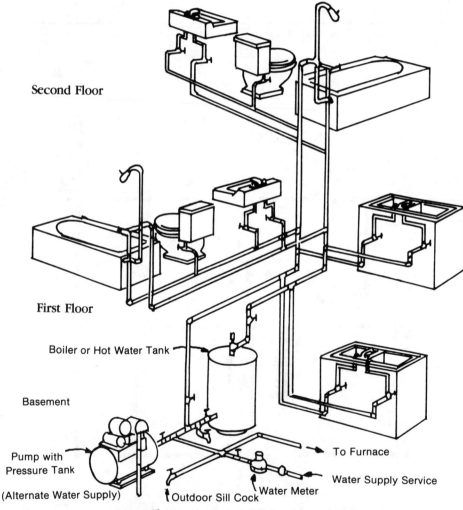

Second Floor

First Floor

Boiler or Hot Water Tank

Basement

Pump with
Pressure Tank

(Alternate Water Supply)

Outdoor Sill Cock

Water Meter

To Furnace

Water Supply Service

Fig. 5-6. *A basic household plumbing system.*

Not long after we moved into our home, I designed and installed a sprinkler system for the lawn, trees, and other plants. Fortunately, I'd thought ahead and knew where I'd tie into the household water system. A valve had been installed at this point—very inexpensive during construction. Not only did this make connecting the system easy, if anything goes wrong with the sprinkler system, I can shut it off without affecting the house. Then if it takes a few days to find and repair the problem in the yard, or to install a new faucet, no one suffers (except me).

As you design the home, include all appropriate shut-off valves. Don't rely on the builder to install them. You will note in FIG. 5-6 that there are a number of valves. Too many builders fail to install all of them.

There will be a valve at the meter. This and the meter are considered to be the property of the water company. Technically, you, as the customer, aren't supposed to touch either without permission. If work needs to be done to the line, getting permission is usually easy.

There should be a shut-off at the house, however. Things happen, and there could come a time when it's necessary to shut off the flow of water into the house in a hurry.

A water heater can last for many years, or it might "blow up" after just a few years. No matter what, the time *will* come to replace the water heater. Although you can shut off water to the house to make the change, this is going to be terribly inconvenient if the water heater goes at 2 AM on a weekend and you have to wait 12 hours or more—maybe more than a day—for a replacement. Living without hot water is bad enough, but having no water at all can be disastrous. Consequently, the inlet to the water heater should have a valve so that it can be shut off without affecting the rest of the house.

The same is true for all major fixtures. A toilet or faucet might need to be changed or repaired. Sometimes this means disassembling the fixture so that the right part can be purchased.

As a future tip, don't just have valves installed and forget them. Have a regular schedule for inspection and testing. At very least, once each year (twice a year is better) the valves should be worked closed then open to be sure that corrosion hasn't made the valve useless.

Pipe Sizes and Types

Usually you won't have to worry about pipe sizes and types. Local building codes will probably specify the right sizes for the right places. This usually means a 3/4-inch to 1-inch incoming main, 3/4 inch through the house, and appropriate reductions at the various fixtures.

Most of this will be determined by local building codes. With rare exception, following those codes will work out fine for just about any use.

More important is the question of the kind of pipe used. The local codes might preclude certain kinds and leave you no choice in the matter. The use of PVC pipe is common, especially among do-it-yourselfers, because of ease of installation and durability; however, local codes might limit its use to outside and sewage installations. It's common for copper pipes to be required inside the walls.

Some say that this code makes sense, since the copper pipes are metal and therefore stronger and more durable. Others say that the reason for the codes is a bit of under-the-table negotiation to be sure that plumbing unions (since installation of copper pipes is more difficult) and copper manufacturers are secure.

Under normal circumstances, PVC pipes can handle cold water just as well as copper, but copper is the preferred standard for handling hot water.

Hot Water

Some years ago my wife and I were taking an ill-fated trip by car. On the second day, the heater radiator in the car developed a leak. So, as we were driving into a Minnesota December, there was no heat in the car. After a freezing day of travel, we stopped at a motel.

It was going to be so nice! A nice hot shower and then a warm bed after shivering all day. But it wasn't to be.

Each room had its own water heater—tiny units with slow recovery times, apparently to save money. Not 10 minutes into her shower, the hot water disappeared. My wife had to wash off the soap in cold water, and I didn't get a shower (a *quick* one) until the next morning.

The lesson? It's important to figure your hot water needs and personal schedule. Five people taking separate baths every evening around 9 PM is going to require a very large water heater, and larger yet if you put the dirty clothes into the washer at the same time.

The minimum size of water heater needed may be determined by local regulation. As a rule of thumb, go one size larger than the minimum. Be realistic about your needs, though. If code calls for a 30-gallon tank, you are probably wasting money both immediately and long-term by installing a 100-gallon unit. A 40-gallon heater will probably be sufficient, and unless you are wasteful, a 50-gallon water heater will certainly take care of your needs in this case.

Placement of the water heater is a part of your design. There are three primary considerations. The first is that of efficiency, and not just the efficiency of the unit itself. Putting a water heater so that it is exposed to the outside temperatures will mean that it will be fighting the cold during the colder months. You wouldn't put the tank out in the middle of the yard, for obvious reasons. Likewise, putting it in a location that does little more than hide it from sight, but doesn't protect the tank, is foolish. The elements will shorten its life and increase the problems you'll have. Mean-

while, exposure to the cold is going to cause utility bills to jump. This latter problem can be reduced by placing the water heater where it is protected from the weather, and reduced even further by use of insulation around the water heater and the pipes.

Second is distance. Uninsulated pipes can lose as much as 1 degree for every foot of run. If the water heater is 50 feet away from where hot water will be needed, the pipe isn't insulated, and it is in an area where cold temperatures can affect the pipe, you could end up with little more than warm water. (And, as with all plumbing, a longer distance means lower pressure.)

Third is a combination of safety and ease of service. Imagine a ridiculous situation. The water heater is in the center of the living room. If it develops a leak, it can ruin the floor. Draining and otherwise servicing the tank is going to be messy, and changing it when that time comes will be worse yet.

If at *all* possible, locate the water heater so that you (or a service person) can get at it easily—and so if it develops a leak, the water won't run into places that can be damaged (FIGS. 5-7 and 5-8).

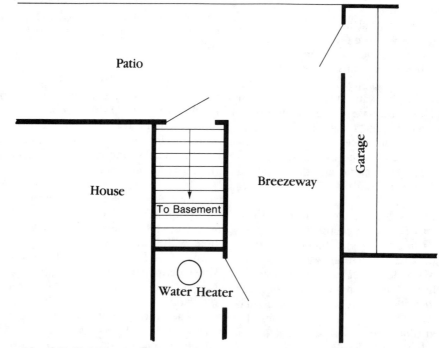

Fig. 5-7. *If this water heater explodes, it can cause water damage to the home.*

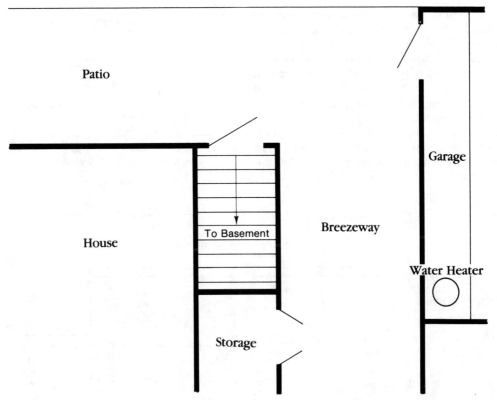

Fig. 5-8. *It's much better to locate the water heater both for ease of service and for safety.*

As an odd coincidence, even as I was writing the above paragraph, the telephone rang. It was a neighbor. Their water heater had developed a very large leak and suddenly dumped all 55 gallons, plus at least an hour's worth of filling water, right into the basement. Enough so that the drywall was saturated and coming loose. If the water had been located elsewhere, it would have still "exploded," but the house wouldn't have been damaged.

For longest life, the water heater should be drained, from the bottom, every 6 months, and no less frequently than once a year. This is to clear sediments from the bottom. Using a hose eliminates much of the mess, but the water heater still has to be close enough to an outside area where the job can be done. Much the same is true when it comes to replacing the tank.

Sewage

Most homes will connect to a sewer system. Some will connect to a private septic system. Either way,

just as water must come into the house, it, and the wastes it carries, must leave the house.

This is done by gravity. That means that the sewage carrying pipes have to be constantly sloped. Minimum is 1/4 inch for every foot of pipe. Less than that and the flow will be sluggish, and the system will have a greater tendency to clog. One-quarter inch for every foot may not seem like much of a slope, but it adds up quickly. If the sewage pipe has to go all the way across a 50-foot span, the drop will be more than a foot between one end and the other. Even that may not seem like much until you consider how much a foot is in construction.

Septic Tanks and Systems

If you're too far away from a sewer system to make a connection, installing a personal septic system is the most likely solution. The most common type consists of the lines bringing waste from the house, a holding/digestion tank, and some form of getting rid of liquids (generally either a leach field or a dry well). (See FIGS. 5-9 and 5-10.)

Local regulations and conditions will determine how a sewage system will be installed. Soil tests might be required to calculate the size and kind of leaching. Concerning tank size, once again, local regulations will give you a rough guideline—and again, as a rule of thumb it's best to go one size larger. If regulations call for a 500-gallon tank, pay the little extra to have a 750-gallon tank installed.

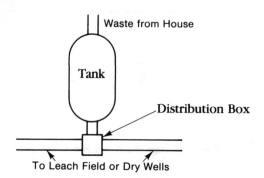
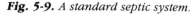

Fig. 5-9. *A standard septic system.*

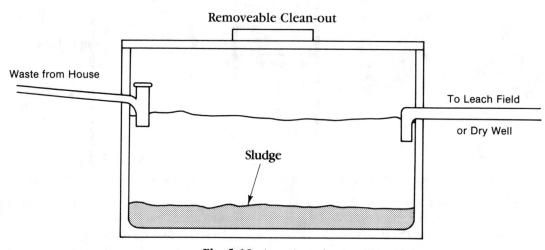

Fig. 5-10. *A septic tank.*

6

Traffic flow

There is a classic story about a very large office being designed and built at great cost. It was a beautiful structure and the inside was luxurious. The only problem was that there were no doors to the individual offices. A particular hall might have 14 offices along each side, but the only entrances were on the ends of the hall.

The idea was apparently to have unbroken walls for dramatic effect. The reality was that to get to any of the inner offices you had to go to one end of the hall and walk through all the offices between.

Normally such a design would never be built. Restrictions and building codes would prevent it. Those middle offices were not only inconvenient but were fire traps as well. Yet somehow it slipped through, and no one seemed to even notice until it was time to move in.

Still, there are other traffic-flow problems that *can* come about. If you're not thinking about it while designing the home, you can all too easily find yourself with a home that's going to drive you crazy.

You not only have to get into and out of your home, you have to move around inside. The easier you can do this, the better you'll like your home in the long run.

Just how you go about designing for traffic flow depends on your lifestyle and your basic concept of what the house should be. No matter what, your goal is to make getting movement in and around the home as smooth as possible.

General Traffic Flow

In determining placement of the doors, you also have to take the plot layout into mind. Where will the driveway be? Are there obstacles in the way? How will you get from the driveway to the house? Will your guests have an easy path to the front door?

There will be traffic flow in front, behind, between the front and the back, and into and out of the house. Keep this overall movement in mind as you design your home (see FIG. 6-1).

You or a guest will drive up to the house. Unless you park on the public street, that means some kind of driveway, with perhaps a carport or garage. For the guests, a path is needed to the front door. For yourself, the garage should have a door leading to the house, preferably into the kitchen (for unloading groceries). And if the garage is used to store lawn and garden equipment, a door should be provided for this.

There will be a main entrance, usually in the front of the house and visible. With most homes, this leads into an entry hall or directly into the living room.

A back door, usually near the kitchen, takes you into the backyard. And if the backyard is fenced, there should be a gate, at least on one side of the house. If you're thinking ahead, somewhere in the fence there should be a gate large enough to drive through, or perhaps a section of the fence that can be easily removed for this purpose.

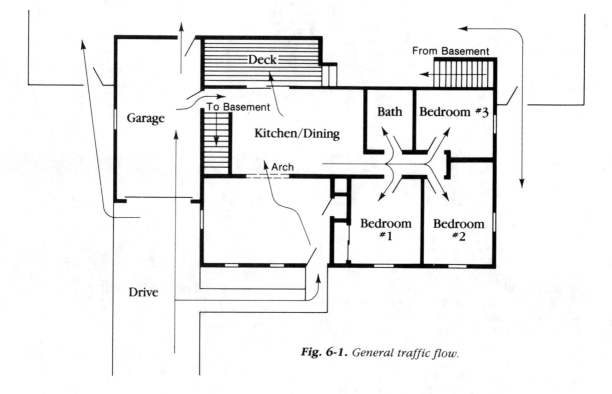

Deck

From Basement

To Basement

Garage

Kitchen/Dining

Bath

Bedroom #3

Arch

Bedroom #1

Bedroom #2

Drive

Fig. 6-1. *General traffic flow.*

The landscaping and other factors outside can affect traffic flow. If you have a swimming pool, before the first drop of water goes in, a tall and sturdy fence *all* the way around, with locking gates, should go up. This is almost certain to interfere with an easy flow of traffic, but don't skip it! Not even if you don't have children. Trees, bushes, and other plants can be attractive, but can also be a nuisance if they make it impossible to move around in the yard (FIG. 6-2).

Inside, traffic flow is set to provide easy movement and also privacy. In FIG. 6-1 visitors enter directly into the living room. This room is isolated from the private areas of the house while being close to the kitchen. You'll also notice in FIG. 6-1 that there are two stairways for the basement. This not only makes things easier, but can save your life in case of a fire. Both entrances are protected (one inside, and the other in the backyard), which reduces the chance of burglary. (*Note:* Although it's generally better to have stairways centrally located, this may not be possible in a smaller home.)

Entrances

All homes should have at least two entrances, both for convenience and for safety. The larger the home, the greater the need for more doors to the outside.

The main entrance is generally in the front. This door is the one used by strangers, casual guests, delivery people, and so on. As such, it's located in the front of the house for high visibility and ease of access. (Because of its nature, be sure that you have a secure door, complete with a peephole, and plenty of light outside for the night.)

Preferably, this door should be somewhat isolated from the rest of the house. If you're entertaining guests or having dinner, it can be disconcerting to have a nosey salesman walking into the middle of things. A classic method of handling this is to design a foyer or entrance hall (FIG. 6-3). This is like a small room from which nothing inside the home can be readily seen.

If you have a small house, an entrance may

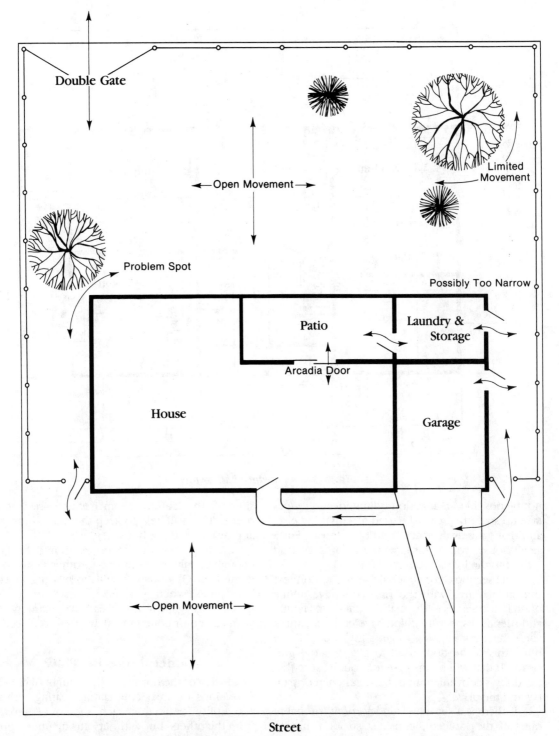

Double Gate

Limited
Movement

←Open Movement→

Problem Spot

Possibly Too Narrow

Patio

Laundry &
Storage

Arcadia Door

House

Garage

←Open Movement→

Street

Fig. 6-2. *Don't forget that there will be traffic flow in the yard.*

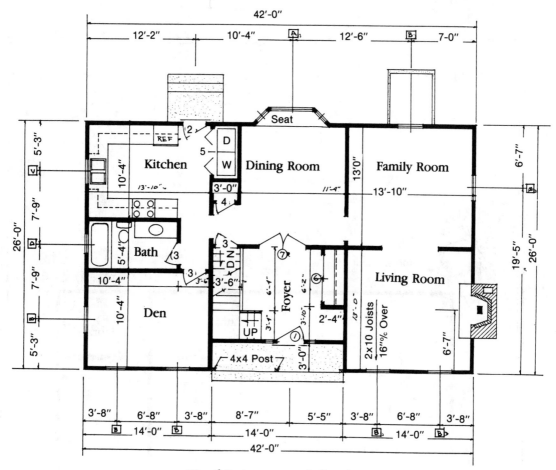

Fig. 6-3. *An entrance hall or foyer.*

not be possible. Its function is limited, and it *does* take up space that can't be used for anything else, and that takes away space from other areas. For a small house, you might have the front door lead right into the living room (FIG. 6-4).

The second door generally serves to connect the kitchen area with the yard or garage. Quite often it also serves as the main entrance for family and friends. Especially if you have children, and a yard, this door is going to get a lot of use. Quite often this is the door used to bring in the groceries. If that will be the case for you, be sure that the door is convenient to both the kitchen or pantry and the drive.

If there is a separate laundry room (probably one off the kitchen), consider strongly having doors there, too—one to the outside, and one to

shut off the laundry room from the rest of the house. This will help to keep the noise, humidity, and heat out of the house (FIG. 6-5).

At least one of the doors should be large enough to allow furniture and other items to be carried in. Obviously, you'll be moving in your belongings when you take possession of the home, and again if you ever leave. Through the years, a bed or couch may have to be replaced.

General Interior Flow

The inside of the house can be thought of as being four kinds of area: entertaining, eating, private, and utility. Preferably each should be separate from the others, but without causing undue problems with getting from one to the other.

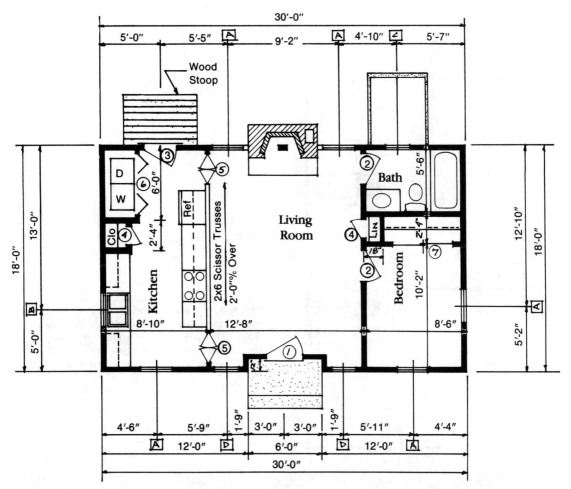

Fig. 6-4. *A smaller home might have the door lead directly into the living room.*

An "open" plan makes the house seem more spacious, but sacrifices privacy to do it (FIG. 6-6). This kind of design consists basically of a large central room with all others off of it, and few or no hallways. Traffic flow is no problem, except for how the furniture is arranged (FIG. 6-7).

Bathrooms and bedrooms are the private areas of the home. A guest bathroom located near the living or dining room can help to keep guests from having to intrude on those private areas, but this requires extra room (FIG. 6-8). If placed near an outside door, this makes an excellent place for children to get clean before coming into the house.

Depending on your circumstances, perhaps more important in separating the bathroom and

bedrooms from the rest of the house is that quiet is provided. This is especially necessary if someone in your family goes to bed early or sleeps late.

Compromises have to be made. An open plan allows for open traffic flow, but with little or no privacy. A divided home provides the quiet and privacy, but at a cost of floor space since halls are needed to get from one area to another.

Hallways

Hallways are basically a waste of space. They provide a path to get from one place to another but are pretty much useless for anything else.

The key is to eliminate hallways where possible, and to reduce them when hallways are

Traffic Flow   **55**

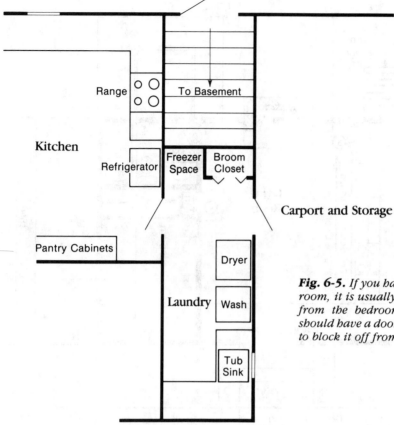

Range

To Basement

Kitchen

Refrigerator | Freezer Space | Broom Closet

Carport and Storage

Pantry Cabinets

Dryer

Laundry | Wash

Tub Sink

Fig. 6-5. *If you have the space for a laundry room, it is usually off the kitchen and away from the bedrooms. If at all possible, it should have a door to the outside and a door to block it off from the rest of the house.*

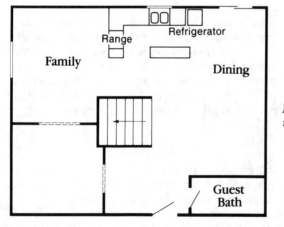

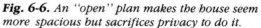

Refrigerator

Range

Family

Dining

Guest Bath

Fig. 6-6. *An "open" plan makes the house seem more spacious but sacrifices privacy to do it.*

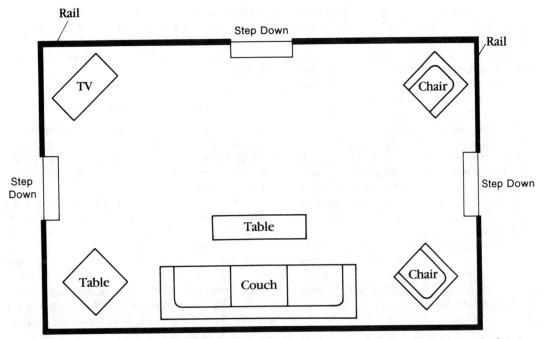

Fig. 6-7. *Furniture arrangement can become critical for traffic flow. If the design is poor, the furniture can be arranged in one way only.*

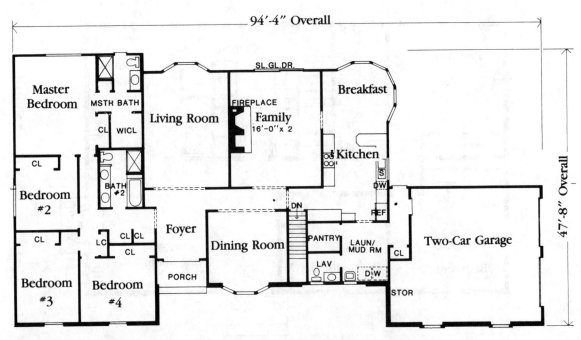

Fig. 6-8. *A more traditional floor plan separates the living areas from the private areas.*

needed. (Unless you have an "open" floor plan, chances are nearly 100 percent that you'll have at least some kind of hallway.)

A common mistake made is to design a hallway that is too narrow. Moving through the hall then becomes difficult, and trying to get a bed down the hall, around the corner, and into a bedroom might be impossible (FIG. 6-9).

Many books list 30 inches as the minimum width for a hall (and for stairs, see p. 61). That will be fine if you never have to bring a large mattress down and turn it in through a doorway or around a corner, but that's not a realistic condition. Usually the rooms down the hall are bedrooms—the very rooms that require movement of the large, bulky mattresses.

In my own opinion, 36 inches should be the minimum width. That extra 6 inches is indeed more wasted space, but it doesn't cut too badly into the rooms (if you design correctly). More important, it makes the hall at least functional. You might need those extra inches only once during move-in, and not again for another 10 years, but those times are critical. If the hall is so narrow that you can't get a bed down it and into the bedroom, that bedroom becomes useless *as* a bedroom.

The Kitchen Triangle

There are a number of standard designs for kitchens. Which you use will depend on your likes and needs. Behind them all is the so-called "work triangle." (The same idea can be used in other work areas.)

The three major sections of the kitchen are refrigerator, stove, and sink. Movement between the three should be minimal, with plenty of counter space near and between each.

A *U-shaped kitchen* is ideal for this. The sink is placed on one wall, usually beneath a window so that the person standing there, or elsewhere in the kitchen, has a clear view of what is going on outside. The refrigerator and stove are against

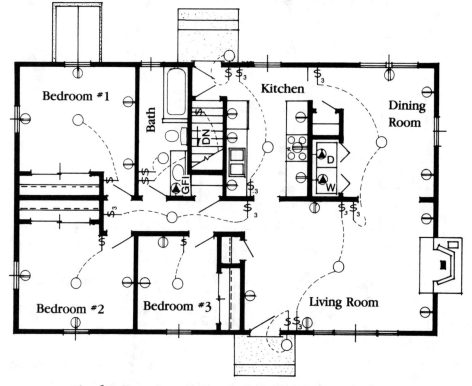

Fig. 6-9. *Try to keep the length of a hallway to a minimum.*

opposite walls at right angles to the sink. This design allows for cabinets and counter space between each of the three. (See FIG. 6-10.)

The *L-shaped kitchen* lacks one of the three walls. In this case, two of the three items are on one wall, with the other on the second wall.

The third choice is a *parallel kitchen*. This is a kitchen that is basically open on both ends, with two counters opposite each other. Again, two of the areas are against one wall with the third opposite.

The least efficient design is when there is only one wall—or only enough width to put the three against one wall.

However the kitchen is designed, movement within the kitchen must be planned (FIG. 6-11). For maximum efficiency, the distance between the range and refrigerator should be between 4 and 9 feet; between the range and the sink, 4 to 6 feet;

and between the sink and refrigerator, 4 to 7 feet. The perimeter of the work triangle should be no less than 12 feet, and no more than 22 feet, with optimum being between 15 and 20 feet (FIGS. 6-12 and 6-13).

The idea is to have the major centers of the kitchen close to each other, but with sufficient space between them so you can get things done. This includes plenty of open counter space.

Traffic Between Floors—Stairs

If you have more than one floor, stairs will be needed to get from one level to the other. Sufficient height is needed to go up or down without having to duck your head, and enough width is needed to move. Space will be needed on both floors, much in the way that space is taken up by a hallway.

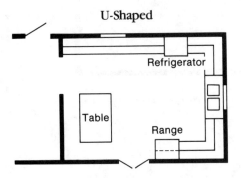

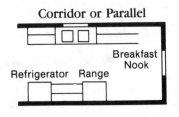

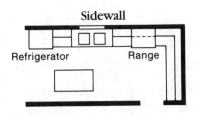

Fig. 6-10. *Standard kitchen shapes: U-shaped, L-shaped, Corridor, and One-wall.*

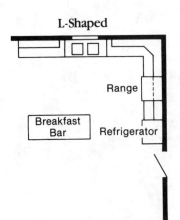

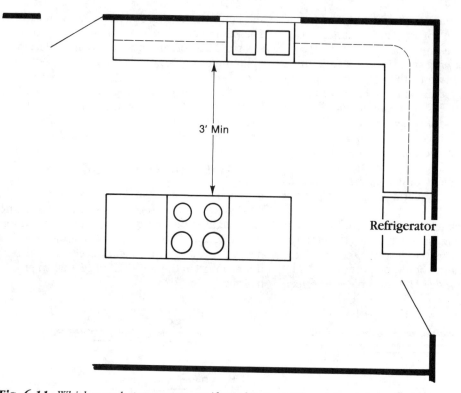

3' Min

Refrigerator

Fig. 6-11. Whichever shape you use, or if you have a kitchen island, be sure there is sufficient space between for easy movement.

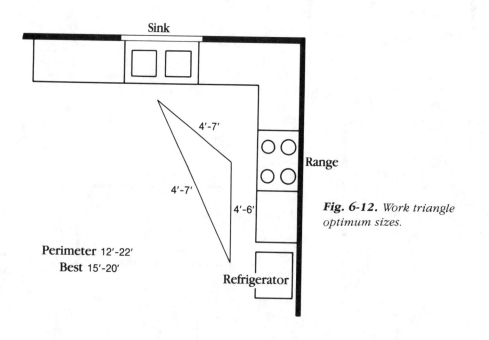

Sink

4'-7'

4'-7'

Range

4'-6'

Perimeter 12'-22'
Best 15'-20'

Refrigerator

Fig. 6-12. Work triangle optimum sizes.

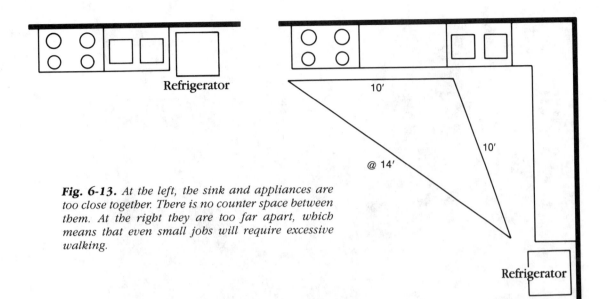

Fig. 6-13. *At the left, the sink and appliances are too close together. There is no counter space between them. At the right they are too far apart, which means that even small jobs will require excessive walking.*

Your two first choices are whether the stairway will be exposed or hidden. An exposed stairway can be dramatic and add to the appearance of the home (FIG. 6-14); however, it's not as safe as a hidden stairway (because of the lack of doors) and is always more expensive (since the stairway is there for appearance, it has to be somewhat fancy).

The next choice is the general shape. Will it be a straight stairway? Will it break along its length to make a landing? Will it turn? How many times? (See FIG. 6-15.)

No matter how you do it, there has to be enough headroom to get down the stairs. Absolute minimum is 6 feet, and 7 feet or more is much preferred.

Now imagine a stairway with 12-inch-wide steps (*treads*) and 6-inch-high *risers*. For every foot forward, you go down 6 inches. For just 6 feet of headroom, the stairs can't have a ceiling for at least 12 feet, and if the lower floor has a ceiling of 8 feet in height, the bottom of the stairs will be 16 running feet in length (assuming no landings) from the top.

This can be—and usually is—shortened by both reducing the width of the treads and increasing the height of the risers. Exaggerating to a ridiculous (and dangerous) degree, imagine the reverse, with treads that are 6 inches in width and risers that are 12 inches high. Now for every foot forward you drop 2 feet in height. You'll have 6 feet of head clearance after just 3 feet of linear distance and will reach the bottom after 4 feet.

The angle of the stairs means the difference between safety and danger. If it's too steep, the stairs will be treacherous. If too shallow, they'll waste space.

Realistically, most stairs use treads of about 10 inches in width, usually constructed of 2 by 10 planks. (If the builder wants to use 1 by 10's, insist that he use the larger size instead!) The risers are set under the treads so that there is a slight (usually 1-inch) overhang. This, in effect, gives you the comfort of a large tread, and saves 1 more inch for each step. This may not seem like much, but a foot is saved every 12 steps.

The riser is generally somewhere between 7 and 8 inches, with $7\frac{1}{2}$ inches usually being considered the standard. This provides enough rise so that the staircase isn't too long, while not being so high (or short) that using the stairs is difficult.

As mentioned earlier in the discussion on halls, some books list 30 inches as the minimum width for a staircase. This is fine if no more than one person will use it at a time, and you have no intentions of carrying any furniture up or down

Fig. 6-14. *A dramatic staircase takes up a lot of space but can add to the overall beauty of the home.*

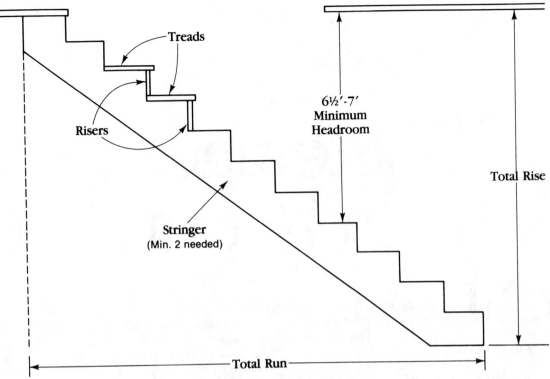

Fig. 6-15. *Parts of a staircase.*

the stairs. Better is to design for at least 36 inches in width, and more if large items will have to go up or down the stairs.

Stairs, by their nature, are treacherous enough. As mentioned above, you can lessen this by not making the stairs too steep and by not having the treads too narrow. Even so, every stairway should have a sturdy handrail on at least one side, and preferably on both.

If there is a door at the top of the stairs, it *must* open into the room and away from the stairs. The reason should be obvious. If the door swings open and bumps someone on a flat floor, there is less danger than if the door bumps someone on the stairs. (In my own home, we designed a pocket door at the top of stairs so no one on either side gets bumped.)

Storage, in & out

It has been said, justifiably, that no matter how much storage you have, you'll need and want more. Move into a larger home, and for a while the extra space will be luxurious. But soon it will be filled up and you'll wish there was more.

It's difficult enough to predict for all your needs and to design in sufficient storage. Once the house is constructed, it will be worse yet.

Try something simple. Draw a box to represent a 10-by-10 room—just the box, a space for the door, and a space for one window. Now try to fit in a 2-by-3-foot closet. At this point it's just a drawing. You can easily erase a line and redraw. If you've already designed the entire home (or that section of it), expanding one room to allow that closet will cut into adjoining rooms, which cut into adjoining rooms, which cut into . . . you get the idea; but, fortunately it's still on paper. Once the house is up, there are no lines to erase. You're dealing with the reality—real walls and real rooms.

Cabinets take space. Even a shallow pantry cabinet will cut a foot out of a room. Closets take even more. If planned for before construction begins, it's fairly simple. Afterwards, it may be too late.

It's best to at least try to figure your needs— present and future—as you're designing the home, and to figure the rooms, including the storage (rather than drawing in the 10-by-10 bedroom, and then trying to add the closet).

The same applies outside. Built-in (or built-on) storage can change the shape of a room or of the house. Without preplanning, the garage may suddenly no longer be large enough for your car once shelves are added. Or, you might find that the roof has to take an odd jog to cover an outside closet.

Virtually every room and area in and around the home needs some kind of storage. It's almost certain that any spot you miss will be regretted later. In some rooms this will mean closets. In others it will consist of cabinets. Shelving can be inside the closets and cabinets, or you can have open or recessed shelving. There are also special storage needs and solutions. One might be more appropriate in one area than another, but planning is still needed.

Closets

A hundred years ago many homes had bedrooms and bathrooms with little or no closet space. Clothing was kept in wardrobes, dressers, and other furniture-type units. Because of a lack of room, seasonal clothing was often boxed or placed in trunks, and transferred to the dresser when needed.

Although this scheme does work, it's not convenient. Instead, every bedroom and bathroom should have some kind of storage. This usually means built-in closets.

Size depends on need and what is to be stored, but take care that you don't design it too small or make it so that access is difficult. Generally, the opening should be no smaller than 2 feet in width. The inside should extend no farther than you can easily reach, which generally means no deeper than 6 additional inches on each side. (Thus, if the closet has a 2-foot opening, the shelving inside should be no wider than 3 feet total.) A fairly standard depth is 2 feet (FIG. 7-1). This is deep enough so that clothing can be put on hangers without interfering with the door or doors, while still not being so deep that items in the back are inaccessible.

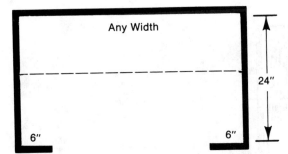

Fig. 7-1. *A standard closet is about 2 feet deep, and no more than 1 foot wider inside than the opening.*

If room allows, a standard hinged door can be used. If there isn't enough room for a swinging door to open, folding or sliding doors can be used (FIG. 7-2). Although the latter two block the opening (with a sliding door blocking as much as half), less space is needed inside the room. This can be especially important if the closet opening is large.

An exception is the walk-in closet (FIG. 7-3). This is like a miniature room. It can be left open or have a door to close it in. Either way, designing a walk-in is much the same as designing another room. There will be shelves or hanging rods or both on one or both sides, and possibly along the back wall as well.

A walk-in closet is a luxury as far as square footage is concerned. Ample room must be provided to get in and out, and to move around inside. Minimum for this is 2 feet. If the closet is only 6 feet long, that "hallway" represents 12 square feet, which doesn't do much of anything but allow you to move inside the closet. Putting

this in dollars; if the home is costing you $45 per square foot to build, that walk-in is costing you at least $540 more than two 6-foot-long standard closets.

To make the walk-in as efficient as possible, a width of less than 6 feet is usually impractical (FIG. 7-4). Such a closet with shelves and rods on one side only is little more than a very deep standard closet turned sideways.

A common failure is that of not providing sufficient light inside the closet (FIGS. 7-5 and 7-6). A ceiling light out in the middle of the room won't be enough except for a fairly shallow closet. (The same applies to any large storage area.) Even if the closet is shallow, care must be taken that enough incident light gets inside. Closets in hallways are often darker than they should be. Placing the light of the hall across from the closet serves double duty by lighting the hall and the interior of the closet.

The shelves in the closet can be fixed or adjustable. The latter requires nothing more than installing extra strips of wood on the walls of the closet. The spacing of the shelves inside is determined by the use of the closet. A bedroom closet meant for clothes will usually have just one shelf (fixed) about 5 feet off the floor. Higher makes the shelf inconvenient; lower means that long clothing will drag on the floor. Beneath that shelf will be the clothes rod for hanging clothes.

A linen or general storage closet will have more shelves at various spacings to allow storage of blankets, sheets, towels, and other items. A closet that is used for brooms, an upright vacuum cleaner, or other tall items should have no lower shelves for these items.

Pantries

A pantry is a specialized kind of closet. Its function is to store quantities of food and kitchen supplies that don't need refrigeration.

Although this varies on what and how you stock, generally the optimum shelf spacing is about 1 foot. At least some of the shelves should be farther apart to hold larger, taller items. An 8-inch depth is minimum, while 24 inches is generally considered to be too deep. More standard depths are 12 or 18 inches. Preferably, the lowest "shelf" should not be the floor but an actual shelf at least a few inches off the floor. This is especially

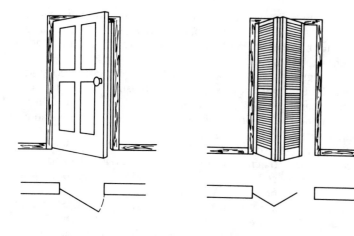

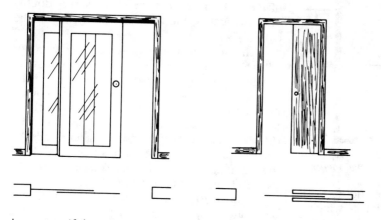

Fig. 7-2. *Swinging, folding, sliding, and pocket doors.*

important if there is any chance at all of water getting into the area.

The two basic choices for a pantry are walk-in and wall-mounted. If you're to have a choice at all, it has to be during the design stage. A walk-in pantry requires space (FIG. 7-7). To be at all efficient, it must have at very least a shelf along one side wall and one on the rear wall. If each of these is 1 foot wide, and if you allow yourself the bare minimum of 2 feet for movement, the smallest and least-efficient walk-in pantry is 3 by 3 or 9 square feet, of which almost half is wasted. Add a shelf on the opposite side wall, and the pantry becomes 3 by 4. Space needed for movement is still wasted, but it's a smaller portion of the whole at a cost of just 3 square feet.

Keep in mind that this *is* the bare minimum. Moving through a 2-foot-wide space is easy, but bending over to get something from a lower shelf can be troublesome. If you intend to have a walk-in pantry, try to allow yourself 3 feet between the shelves.

Cabinet-type pantries can be purchased with the rest of the cabinets so that everything matches. The amount of floor space needed is reduced because the room for access is already a part of the kitchen.

Either way, the pantry should be in, or very near, the kitchen. The only use of a pantry a distance away from the kitchen is for long-term storage of larger quantities that won't be needed often.

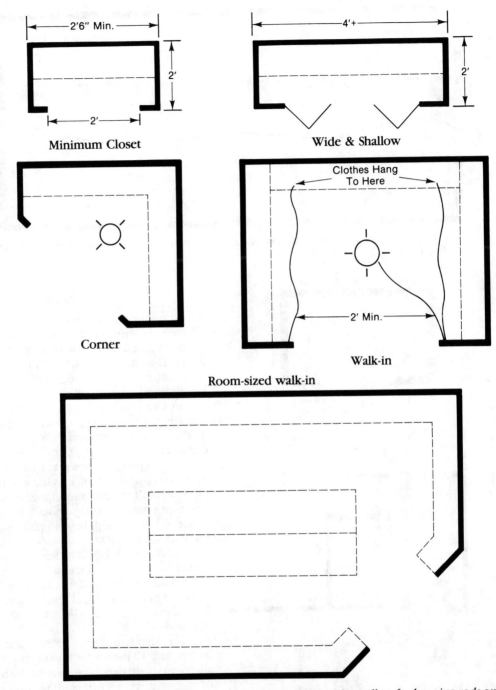

Fig. 7-3. *A minimal walk-in closet should be at least 6 feet wide to allow for hanging rods on both sides and about 2 feet of room in the center for movement.*

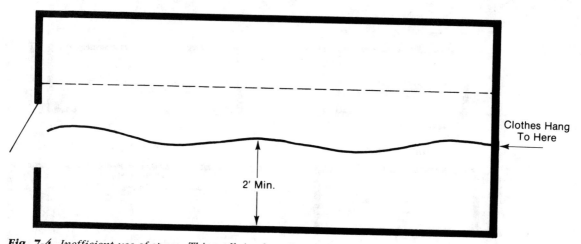

Fig. 7-4. *Inefficient use of space. This walk-in closet becomes little more than a too-deep standard closet with a door on the side instead of in front.*

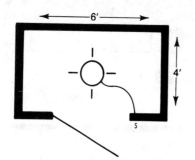

Fig. 7-5. *A deeper closet needs a light.*

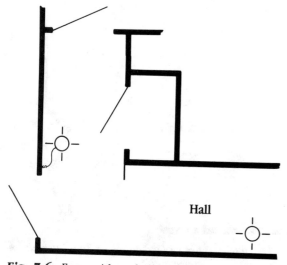

Fig. 7-6. *Even with a shallow closet, be sure that there will be enough light to see inside. In this case, the hall light serves two functions.*

Cabinets

It's extremely rare to find a kitchen without some cabinets. As with other kinds of storage space, it's almost as rare to find a kitchen with sufficient cabinetry. The same is true of other places where cabinets might be needed, such as bathrooms, laundry, and other work areas.

Just so much room is available. In whatever size kitchen you design, chunks of it are taken up by the three primary items: sink, stove, and refrigerator, at roughly 30 to 36 inches each.

In designing those areas that will have cabinets, you have two choices. One is to have custom cabinets built to the exact dimensions. This way you won't have to worry about a few inches here or there, but you will have to plan on spending a lot more for cabinetry.

The other choice is to keep standard sizes in mind (FIG. 7-8). There are a variety to choose from, often with widths of 12 inches to 48 inches in 3-inch increments, and spacers available to fill gaps, so it should be no problem to make use of the standards.

The standard depth of base cabinets is 24 inches, and 12 inches for the upper cabinets. This allows room on the countertop of the base. Height of the lower cabinet (including countertop) is 36 inches for the kitchen and 32 inches for vanities. The upper cabinets vary in height to meet the needs. You might use a 12-inch-tall cabinet over the range and refrigerator and 18-inch-tall cabinets

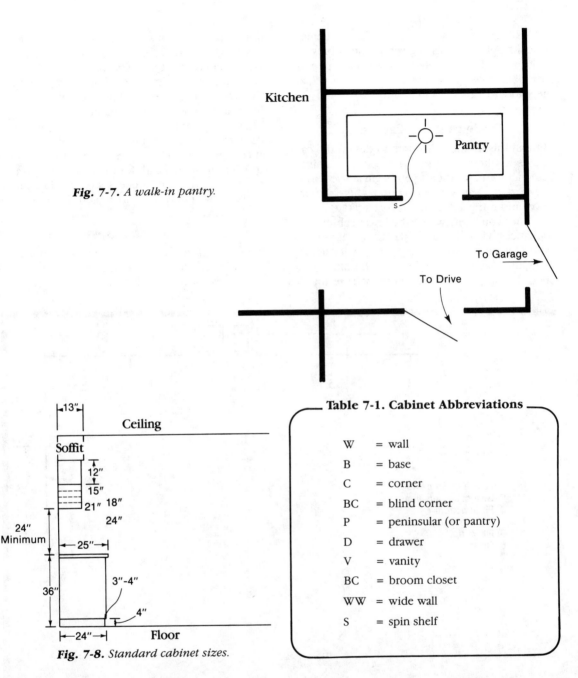

Kitchen

Pantry

To Garage

To Drive

Fig. 7-7. *A walk-in pantry.*

Ceiling

Soffit

13"

12"

15"

21" 18"

24"

24"
Minimum

25"

36"

3"-4"

4"

24"

Floor

Fig. 7-8. *Standard cabinet sizes.*

Table 7-1. Cabinet Abbreviations

W	=	wall
B	=	base
C	=	corner
BC	=	blind corner
P	=	peninsular (or pantry)
D	=	drawer
V	=	vanity
BC	=	broom closet
WW	=	wide wall
S	=	spin shelf

elsewhere. Both, and other heights, are readily available.

Standard dimensions are usually left out of the abbreviations used in the cabinetry catalog. For example, a standard base cabinet is $34^{1}/_{2}$ inches tall (36 with the countertop) and 24 inches deep. Since this is always the same, there is no need or reason to list it. A B24 means that the base cabinet is 24 inches wide and standard in both other directions. Likewise, a BD24 is a base cabinet with drawers only 24 inches in width with the standard height and depth.

As mentioned above, wall cabinets come in several heights, so this is given in the abbreviated description. For example, a PW3018 is a peninsular wall cabinet 30 inches wide, 18 inches tall, and the standard 12 inches in depth.

Designing the Cabinetry

With all this in mind, it's time to design the cabinets as a whole. Begin with the lower cabinets. You might find it easier if you begin at the corners and work outwards. Keep in mind where the sink, stove, and refrigerator will be located (FIG. 7-9).

After you know where the lower cabinets and appliances will be, you can design the upper cabinets. This time, start over the three major items.

Quite often the space over the sink is left open. If you put a cabinet there, be sure that it's fairly small in height so you'll have room beneath. The height of the cabinet over the refrigerator is also generally short to allow for a full-sized refrigerator (and ventilation needed by the refrigerator). The one over the stove is often modified to hold the venting pipe for the range hood.

For the sake of appearance, these three smaller overhead cabinets are usually matched and are most often 12 inches in height to allow for sufficient room beneath for the stove, refrigerator, and sink (FIG. 7-10). Since they are difficult to reach, things rarely used are stored there.

Countertops

The countertops can be any of a variety of materials. Take care to have them blend (or contrast) with the color of the cabinetry.

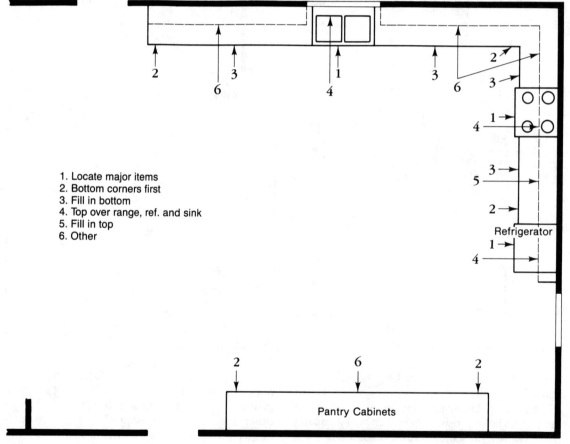

1. Locate major items
2. Bottom corners first
3. Fill in bottom
4. Top over range, ref. and sink
5. Fill in top
6. Other

Fig. 7-9. *Designing the cabinetry.*

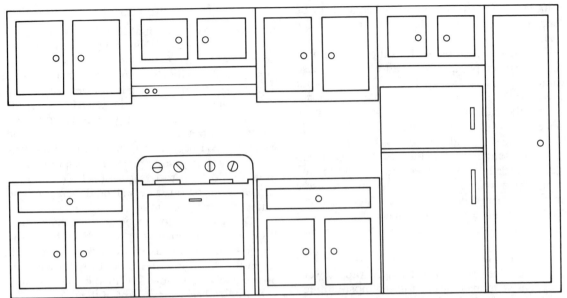

Fig. 7-10. *Cabinets over the stove and refrigerator are usually matched.*

In the past, most countertops were painted wood. Today most have a laminated hard plastic, such as Formica. (There are other manufacturers with similar products.) This kind of surface is durable and easy to clean. Because of its popularity, you'll have a wide choice of patterns and colors (FIG. 7-11).

Beware of the highly glossed surfaces. Despite the toughness of these materials, they will scratch rather easily. This won't show on a matt surface, but it can be very noticeable if the surface is shiny.

The plastic is bent over a base of wood and glued into place. The edges can be squared or

Fig. 7-11. *Plastic laminate countertop.*

rounded, they can have a lip to catch spills or be flat, or they can have a back or fit straight to the wall.

Stone countertops, such as those made with tiles, are very popular and sturdy, but are also more expensive, largely because of the labor involved. The two main keys for tile countertops is that the base be solid, and that the grout be sealed so as not to absorb spills.

Marble sinks and countertops have been popular for a long time. Trouble is, marble is expensive, especially when carved into a bowl for the sink. The easy and common solution is to use a man-made substance called "cultured marble." This is actually a plaster-like material that can be colored and then cast in a mold to any desired size or shape.

Another way to get a "marble" countertop is to use molded plastic. These range from the very inexpensive to materials that cost almost as much as real marble. The pattern, if any, is in the plastic material. With some of the more expensive types, the color is uniform all the way through, which makes taking care of scratches, burns, and other damages much easier.

Other Shelving

Shelving for closets and pantries was covered above, but these aren't the only shelves you might want. You might want built-in shelves to hold books, stereo equipment, photos, or maybe to display your collection of porcelain. Unlike the shelves of a closet or cabinet, these are in the open. If there are doors, they are generally of glass. (If the doors are solid, what you have is a cabinet.)

Of course, these needs can be taken care of by separate shelves. These are like furniture, and all you have to worry about is placement. If you plan to have built-in shelving, this must be taken into account during the design.

Your first choice is whether to have the shelves simply mounted to the wall, or to have the shelves recessed (FIG. 7-12). The first can be done just about any time, as long as you have enough room. The second requires definite planning since the wall must be built up at the ends of the shelves.

In the Garage

It might not seem like it at first thought, but storage in the garage is just like in other areas of your home with one exception: appearance isn't as important. The shelving can be less than perfect. The whole idea of shelving is storage, particularly in the garage. How will the shelves be used? Where can you place them without having them interfere with traffic (the car and you) in the garage? If you need 11 feet of width to pull your car into the garage and open the doors, the garage itself would have to be at least 12 feet wide to allow shelves on one side wall (and then you'll be cramped). (See FIG. 7-13).

Don't forget movement of the garage door. It's okay for the open door to partially block the upper shelf (as long as you can get at that shelf when the door closed). It's *not* okay for any part of the shelving to interfere in the slightest way with free and easy movement of the door.

Reinforcement of the garage shelving can be critical since at least some of them will probably be holding heavy objects. The shelves must be strong enough to hold what is placed on them without sagging or warping.

The need for variety is greater in a garage because of the diversity of things being stored there. One section might be used to store cans of paint and painting supplies. Larger, stronger shelves are needed for this. Another will hold oil for the car, lawn mower, and perhaps, snowblower, plus other miscellaneous parts. Since both the sizes and weights are smaller, these shelves can be smaller also.

Other things commonly stored in the garage are brooms, shovels, rakes, other gardening tools, bags of dog or cat food, and household tools. Somewhere in the garage there should be at least a small working surface. The complexity of the design depends on your own needs. (See Chapter 14.)

Try to keep the bottom shelves off the floor. This both protects the items on that lowest shelf and makes cleaning the garage floor easier.

Outside Storage

Outside storage isn't necessarily an afterthought or last resort. It can be designed as an integral part

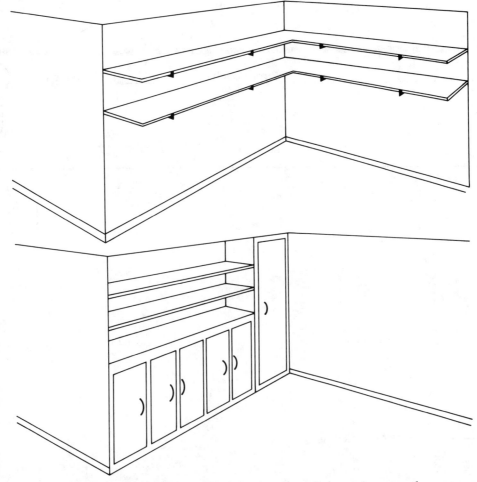

Fig. 7-12. *Shelves can be mounted to the wall or can be recessed.*

of the whole, even to the point that an outside storage building matches the appearance of the house (FIG. 7-14). Of course, this isn't necessary. A simple metal shell will serve to keep off the rain. Or, if you prefer, there are wood outbuildings in kit form or that can be built from hundreds of easy-to-follow plans. Your primary concern is that whether you build it now or later, there has to be sufficient room.

Outside storage can also be built into the outside walls of the home or as part of those walls. This doesn't mean that you have to give up space inside. If the house jogs in one place, it's fairly simple to have the wall extend another 3 feet. That space wouldn't be inside anyway. Put on a door

and it becomes an excellent and simple means of having a place outside (FIG. 7-15).

Whenever possible, put in a floor. Dirt is okay, and is considerably less expensive than a concrete slab or wooden floor, but everything stored inside is exposed to the ground. In some parts of the country, this can be a disaster. Rain, insects, a variety of vermin can all get inside too easily, causing damage to the building and to what is stored inside.

It's generally best to treat the construction of an outbuilding with the same care you would a home. It has to be sturdy and capable of withstanding the weather.

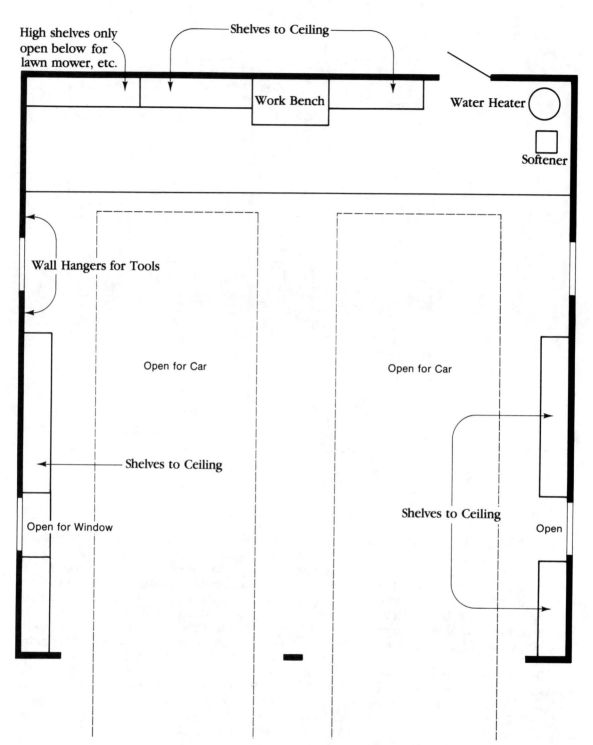

High shelves only
open below for
lawn mower, etc.

Shelves to Ceiling

Work Bench

Water Heater

Softener

Wall Hangers for Tools

Open for Car

Open for Car

Shelves to Ceiling

Shelves to Ceiling

Open for Window

Open

Fig. 7-13. *One way to design the garage shelving.*

Fig. 7-14. *This building serves for both storage and as a change room for guests coming to swim.*

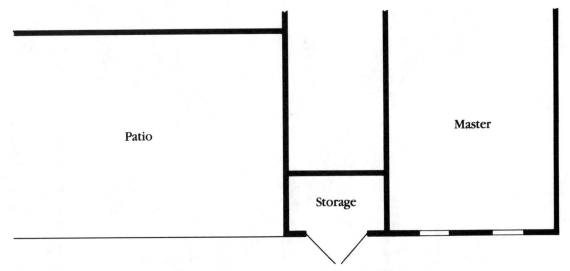

Fig. 7-15. *Outside storage can be a part of the house.*

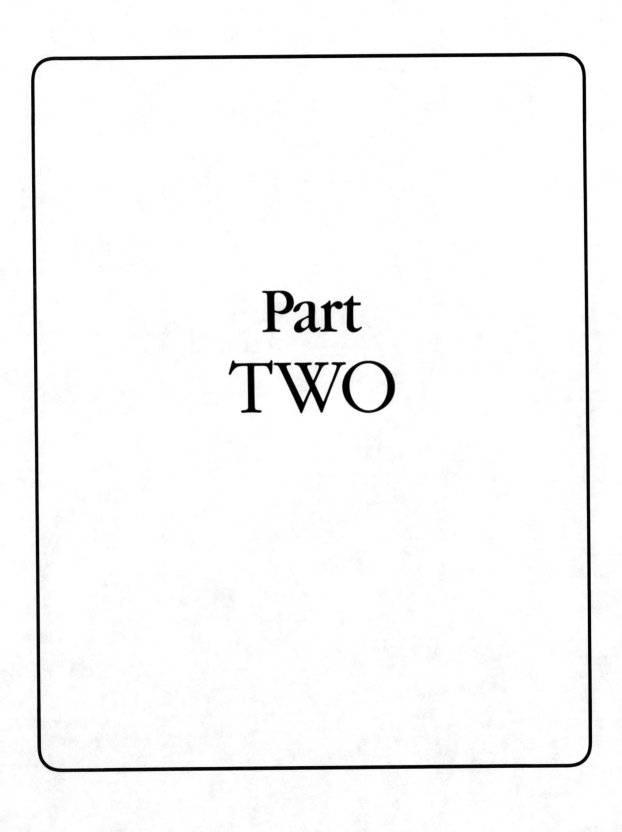

Part
TWO

8

The overall design

If you begin with little or no idea of how the end result is to be, you're guaranteed to waste a lot of time and paper. This might be a fine way to learn something ("The School of Hard Knocks—Trial and Error 301"), but it's not very efficient. You will make enough mistakes and false starts under the best of circumstances. Why make it worse?

With all the basics of Section I in mind, mingled with your own ideas, you should be able to come up with some kind of rough idea of just what the end result should be. The goal is to have a unified whole, both room-to-room and house-to-land. Although you might not have the landscaping done before you move in, this also has to be taken into account since it has a long-term effect.

There are many details to consider—before you begin your design, during, and afterwards. You *will* make mistakes, some of which may not show up for 10 years. Your goal is to minimize these errors, and to come up with the best-possible overall design.

Doing Things in Order

Your first job is to determine your budget. You *must* know this before you can even begin. How much can you reasonably afford? It doesn't make much sense to design and build a home that will be repossessed a year down the road—or one that you'll never move into at all.

Don't let your dreams get the better of your common sense. The lot will cost a certain amount. The structure will cost another amount. Add to this the interest charged for the loan, insurance, standard upkeep and maintenance, taxes, and a few other figures. You'll come up with the actual initial and monthly costs. Can you afford that monthly payment? If not, don't even begin.

Now you can start looking for the lot. You know how much money you can afford. This, in turn, lets you know roughly how large the house—and the lot—will be. Don't forget "hidden" costs, such as unusual preparation of the lot before it's suitable for construction.

With your financial status, and the lot, in mind, you can begin to determine the size and shape of the home.

Overall Size

The two primary considerations are financial and lot size. A larger home will cost more to build and more to maintain. While you might dream of a 5000-square-foot mansion on 25 private acres, can you afford that dream? It could be that even a 1700-square-foot ranch home on a quarter acre would be a financial strain for your present budget. Be honest with yourself! A home can be a wonderful thing. It can also be a crushing burden.

Size of the house is also determined by the size (and shape) of the lot, which, in turn, affects the overall costs. You can't squeeze a 60-by-90 home onto a 60-by-90 lot. The home will just fit, with the walls all around being right on the property line.

If the lot is 60 feet wide, as a general rule, the widest home on it should be no more than 40 feet. This allows 10 feet on each side. (Measure off 10 feet. It's not much.)

The same becomes even more important with a shallow lot. If the lot is only 60 feet deep, and you want a 20-foot-deep backyard, and allow only 10 feet in the front, maximum depth of the home becomes 30 feet.

Add the two together. To allow yourself even minimal room outside, the maximum home on a 60-by-60 lot would be 40 by 30. Anything larger is squeezing.

That same house placed in the middle of a 6-acre lot is very likely to look strange. Dwarfed. Or it will unless you plan the landscaping *very* carefully.

You don't have to use every available square foot of land to have an effective house. Balance of house to land is much more important. Overextending and squeezing can both be mistakes.

Shape

Most homes are square or rectangular. The reason is that this is the least expensive, and generally most efficient shape for a home. Every curve and corner adds to the cost, and also tends to bring structural and design problems that must be solved.

Your goal is to strike a balance—to blend the home aesthetically with the land and its features, to have a shape that is pleasing to you, and to do this while staying within your budget.

Homes can break in just one other direction, making a shape like an L. They can break in one direction on each side, forming a U, or go in two directions on each side to make an H. The home can also be a "cluster," with breaks in various spots and directions, depending on the terrain and landscaping ideas. (Refer back to FIG. 2-7 for basic house shapes.)

The key is always the same. If cost is a factor, keep the home as simple as possible while also matching it to the land (FIG. 8-1). For example, if the land slopes, a split-level home might be perfect, and less expensive than excavating the land

to hold a ranch-style home of the same square footage. Having the home bend around an existing tree could be more economical, while also providing shade and a nice appearance. Each situation is different. This once again emphasizes the importance of finding and knowing the site first, and designing the home second.

The shape of a home can be used to help create that balance with the surroundings. It can be made to bend around a natural large boulder, or to "waterfall" down a slope, or perhaps to hang out into space from the side of a mountain by a cantilever. A stream flowing through the property might give you the idea to build the home on piers with the stream flowing beneath.

Most homes aren't so dramatic. Shape is more often determined by necessity and budget than drama. Every corner, every break away from the basic rectangle, and certainly every "fancy" idea is going to cost extra.

Room Locations

Much has been written about using the sun to best advantage. Most of what you'll read is geared for the colder states, with the suggestion that the home should have "southern exposure." This means that important rooms in the house be located on the southern side where they'll get maximum sunlight. Often, larger windows are located on this side for the same reason. It makes the home more pleasant, while reducing utility bills.

In hotter climates, the opposite is true. In parts of many of our southern and southwestern states, the goal is to keep the sun out rather than letting it in (FIG. 8-2). The blistering sun of an Arizona desert summer coming through a picture window on the southern side of the house is going to put a strain on the air conditioner. It can also bleach drapes and carpets.

Either way, the idea is to place the rooms where it is more practical for you. If that's possible.

Almost always, the front entrance faces the front of the property. This, in turn, determines the location of the living room, which is often the largest room in the house. The backyard is usually off the kitchen and tucked behind the living room. In these matters, you may not have much

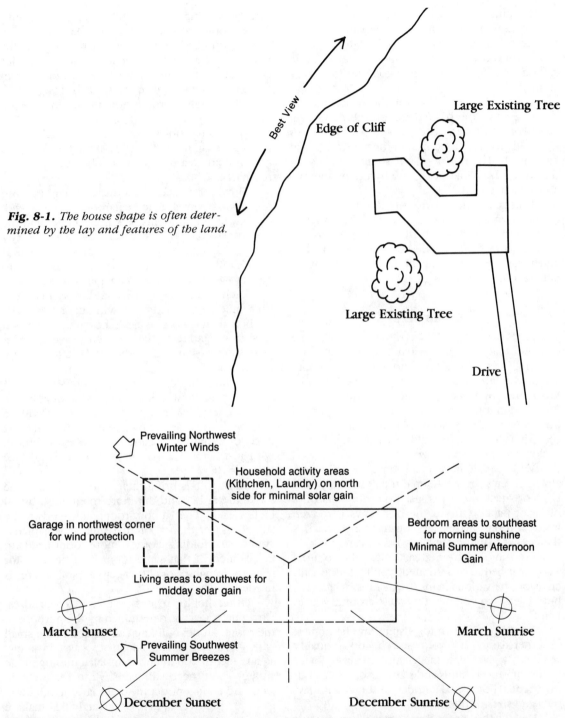

Fig. 8-1. *The house shape is often determined by the lay and features of the land.*

Best View

Edge of Cliff

Large Existing Tree

Large Existing Tree

Drive

Prevailing Northwest Winter Winds

Household activity areas (Kithchen, Laundry) on north side for minimal solar gain

Garage in northwest corner for wind protection

Bedroom areas to southeast for morning sunshine Minimal Summer Afternoon Gain

Living areas to southwest for midday solar gain

March Sunset

March Sunrise

Prevailing Southwest Summer Breezes

December Sunset

December Sunrise

Fig. 8-2. *Direction of the sun during various seasons can be made to add to a pleasant environment, or can end up costing you in larger utility bills.*

choice, unless you care to ignore tradition. The same traditions say that the home runs with the longest side to the front. In most neighborhoods, if you do otherwise your home will seem to be sideways on the lot, which is going to look very strange.

If you shop carefully for the property, you can determine the basic direction the home will face. For east–west roads, homes on the north side will face south; homes on the south side will face north. For north–south streets, homes on the west side will face east, and homes on the east side will face west.

Unless you depart from tradition, or have a "bent" home, your house will still be basically facing a certain direction. It's now up to you to decide how the house will be situated on the lot, and what goes where in the house, while maintaining a functional design.

Room Sizes

The types of rooms will be covered in the separate chapters that follow. In each case, certain rules and tricks are the same, and there are certain standard minimums. For example, a bedroom of less than 8 by 9 feet becomes a glorified closet. Put a bed in there, and about all you have space to do is crawl in and sleep. Minimum for a living room is 160 square feet, although 300 square feet is closer to the average size.

Many people have a hard time mentally visualizing room sizes. It's often difficult to know how large or small a room is just from numbers on a piece of paper. One of the best ways is to step inside a room of the size you have in mind. It's then easier to figure out just what can and can't be squeezed into such an area. Unless the room is also furnished and decorated, you'll still need to envision the various items (beds, tubs, whatever), but at least you'll have the walls around you to help.

This is one reason for visiting model homes. (Another is to aid your search for a quality builder.) It gives you the chance to see a lot of rooms of various kinds and sizes. Also, while visiting friends' homes, take notice of the various layouts and sizes of the rooms.

Lacking this, or for those times when you just can't go visiting, you can still mark off the rooms. For example, you can set up a "fake room" outside if you need to by marking off a spot on the lawn. This can be as simple as measuring the distances and scratching lines in the dirt, or you can go to the trouble of using stakes and string.

Visualizing the room from marks on the lawn might still be difficult. If so, setting up boards, boxes, or other objects as "walls" can help. Even placing a chair to mark each wall can be enough to give you an idea of what it will be like to be in a room of that size.

However you do it, always keep in mind those things that will go into that room. If it's a bedroom, the minimum inside will be a bed, and the smallest standard bed is just a little larger than 3 by 6 feet. (Adding a headboard will make it larger.) If there's only 2 feet left for movement, it's going to be a crowded, cramped room. (See Chapter 10.)

Each room has its own needs. A bedroom isn't much of a bedroom without a bed. The kitchen won't work as a kitchen unless it has a sink, stove, and refrigerator—each an average of at least 30 inches in width as a standard. (See Chapter 9.)

In the bathroom, a standard tub is roughly 3 by 5; a small shower is 3 by 3. Add a toilet (allow anything less than a 3 by 3 space and it will be cramped), and a sink (2 by 2 minimum). Leave just 2 feet of walking space and the smallest bathroom with just a toilet and sink will be 4 by 5. (See Chapter 10.)

Work rooms bring their own problems. The standard washer and dryer are roughly 30 by 30 inches each. The laundry-room sink tends to be slightly larger than a kitchen sink. If you plan a counter for folding clothes, more room needs to be planned. If that same room is to be used for ironing, sewing, or other tasks, still more is needed.

Other hobby rooms command other sizes. How much space is determined by the purpose of the room. Model building can be done on a small table. You can set up an artist's easel in a few square feet. If you intend to install a photographic studio, you'll need sufficient width for the subjects and sufficient depth to get far enough away to have some versatility. Other activities make a mess or require still other considerations.

Doors and Windows

Quite often, people inexperienced in home design will just mark spaces in the walls to represent doors and windows without giving any thought to size or scale. That's okay for the very first sketches. Your goal at that time is simply one of general layout. That includes locations of the windows and doors, but just about any kind of marking will suffice in those beginning stages.

After that, your specifications become more important. The final drawings—even your own final drawings that are handed over to a draftsman or architect—need to be accurate enough to take interior wall thicknesses into account. They certainly need to have the sizes of doors and windows drawn accurately. And before you can get an accurate bid from a contractor, you'll need to know not only sizes, but styles, types, materials, and other specifications.

As with so many other things, there are standard sizes for both doors and windows (see FIGS. 8-3, 8-4, and 8-5). Staying with these will be less expensive than having custom sizes made up. Fortunately, there are a variety of choices, not only in the sizes available, but in the styles you can choose within those standard sizes.

There might be local restrictions on the number and size of windows required. These are for light, ventilation, and safety (as secondary fire escapes). The sizes and styles you have to choose from are almost endless. Designation will be something like 2-0 × 3-4, for a 2-foot by 3-foot, 4-inch window. (The zero is usually said as "oh," so

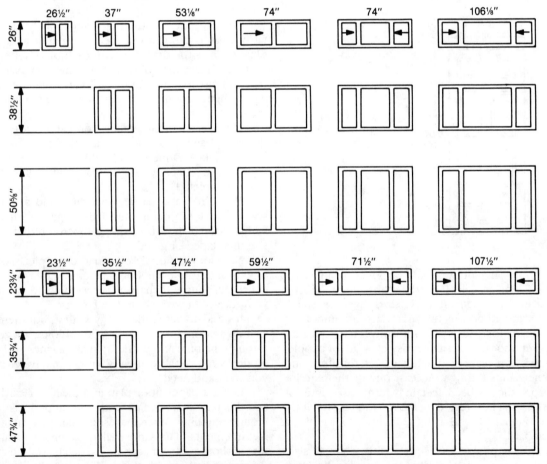

Fig. 8-3. *Standard window sizes.*

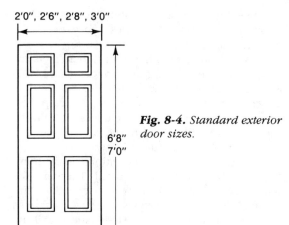

2'0", 2'6", 2'8", 3'0"

6'8"
7'0"

Fig. 8-4. *Standard exterior door sizes.*

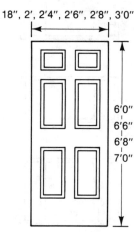

18", 2', 2'4", 2'6", 2'8", 3'0"

6'0"
6'6"
6'8"
7'0"

Fig. 8-5. *Standard interior door sizes.*

a 3-oh 4-oh window would be 3 feet by 4 feet.)

Doors are less restricted by code, mostly because they come in fewer sizes. Even the smallest standard door is utilitarian. A more important concern for you is size for convenience. A narrower door will still allow easy passage for people, but it can make it difficult to get furniture and other items through. At least one of the exterior doors should be 3 feet in width. Most interior doors will be 2 feet, 6 inches (30 inches) in width, although a 2-foot 8-inch (32 inches) door is also a standard.

Your primary concern at this point is size. With doors, you also have to consider the type.

(See FIG. 7-2.) Will it swing on hinges, fold, slide on a rail, or slide into a pocket? And don't forget about garage doors, which can hinge, swing upwards as a solid door, or swing upwards as smaller panels.

Garage doors and garage-door openers are a subject all in themselves. Quite often a company will specialize in this alone. At this point, once again your prime concern is size. Garage doors also come in standard sizes, with the most common being 8 feet in width, and 7 feet in height.

Model Homes

The simplest model home of all is a line drawing of the floor plan. Many people have trouble with this. Until you get used to what 9 by 10 really means, it can be difficult picturing the room in your mind.

One step of constructing your model is still fairly easy to do. Cut out pieces of paper to the same scale as the drawing, with each piece representing a particular object. You can then place these things in the rooms, and can quite easily move them around to determine proper placement.

If you have artistic talent you can do a perspective drawing of the rooms as you envision them (FIG. 8-6). Done to scale, this is an excellent way to have a preview of how the room will look when completed.

If you're enthusiastic, you can build a full-scale model of the home. This begins with a scaled floor plan. Pieces of cardboard are cut to size then taped or glued.

Not fancy enough? You can also use pieces of wood, and can even build a removeable roof, scaled furniture, then paint everything to meet your idea of how the home will look.

It's easy to get carried away with it, but there is little reason to do so. If you're going to go through the time and bother to make a fancy scale model, you probably already know exactly what you want and need.

Using a paper floor plan and pieces of cardboard taped to it is fast and easy and doesn't require anything other than some fairly accurate measurements. The same scaled paper for furniture and other objects can be used. The only real difference is that with the cardboard walls you'll

Fig. 8-6. *A perspective drawing, done to scale, can give you a very good idea of how the room will look.*

also have some height to the rooms, which is often helpful if you're not used to envisioning such things in your mind.

The Overall Design

The important thing to keep in mind in the overall design is to be sure that everything works the way you want it to work. Is your design livable, or is it merely dramatic but not very practical? Do the rooms work together as a whole, or have you ended up with a hodgepodge of sections with no unification between them? Can you get into, out of, and around inside the home? As you're making your sketches, don't forget placement of the doors and windows.

Your first step is to determine which parts of the house are most important to you and your lifestyle. This is usually the best place to begin. For most people, the kitchen and dining areas are the centers of home life. This, and the fact that the kitchen is one of the more complicated areas (plumbing, special electrical and ventilation needs, and so on) makes it a good place to start. If you leave it until last, you're very likely to find yourself making false start after false start.

There is still one other reason to begin with the kitchen, and to give it priority. It may not seem important to you now, but the kitchen is the most important room in the house when it comes to keeping or losing resale value.

Now you have a choice. As a rule, the bedrooms and bathrooms complete the length of the living areas of the home, while the living room or family room will "fill up" the width (FIG. 8-7). The advantages of going to the bedrooms next is that these tend to be the second in importance for most people, and because the bathrooms tie in with the plumbing from elsewhere in the home (FIG. 8-8).

The advantage of going to the living room next is that it usually completes the width, while the private areas only partially complete the length. (The garage or carport will usually go on one end of the home, adding to the overall length.)

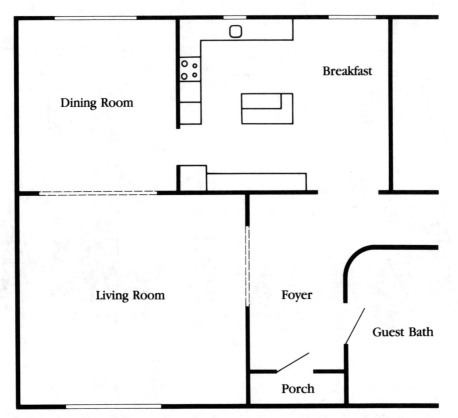

Fig. 8-7. *The kitchen, dining room, and living room often "fill up" one end of the home.*

When these areas are completed, the other parts can be designed: a laundry room, any other work areas, the garage or carport and other outside areas.

If the home you have in mind will have two floors, the order might need to be juggled slightly. The size and shape of the lower floor will determine, at least in part, the size and shape of the floor above, and vice versa (FIG. 8-9).

Unless you have a specific reason to do otherwise, care must be taken to have the walls line up. This is least expensive and most efficient. For example, if the main floor is 30 feet wide, the second floor should generally also be 30 feet wide.

Not only should the outer walls line up, any interior supporting walls on the upper floor must line up with supporting walls below. (If they don't, that upper supporting wall isn't, itself, being supported.)

The lining up of the outer walls isn't a hard-and-fast rule that can never be broken. You might want one floor to be a little smaller—or a little larger—than the other. This is very common with basements. Many homes have a basement under only part of the home (FIG. 8-10). This is no problem since the part of the main floor that "overhangs" the basement is supported by the ground.

As mentioned in Chapter 5, multilevel homes bring with them the need to "stack" plumbing if the design is to be practical and economical. If both of two floors have a bathroom, for example, placing one over the other allows an easy, efficient, and relatively inexpensive connection.

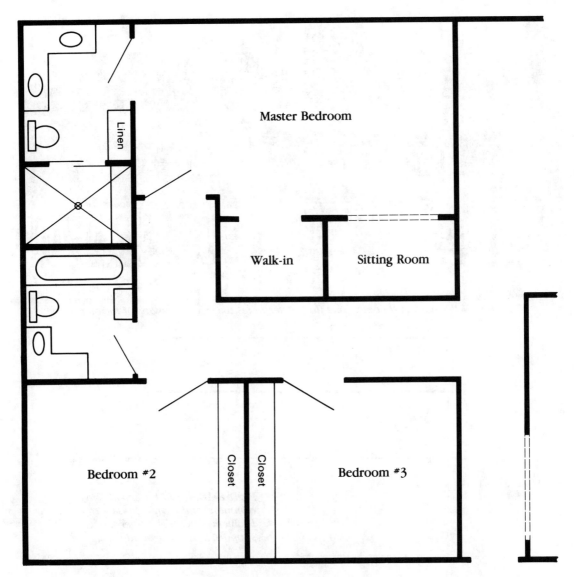

Fig. 8-8. *Or, you can design the private areas of the home next to help determine length.*

Master Bedroom

Linen

Walk-in

Sitting Room

Bedroom #2

Closet

Closet

Bedroom #3

Fig. 8-9. *With multilevel homes, one floor determines the size and shape of the others.*

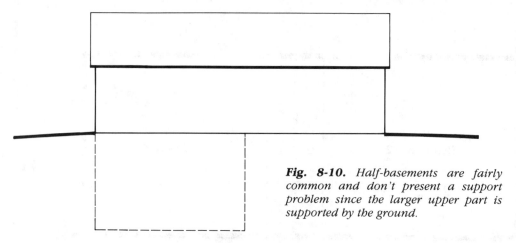

Fig. 8-10. *Half-basements are fairly common and don't present a support problem since the larger upper part is supported by the ground.*

9

Kitchens & dining rooms

As mentioned in the last chapter, the kitchen is often considered to be the most important room in the house for two reasons. First, in many homes the kitchen is where the family gathers together most often. (All too often, this is the only time when the entire family is together.) Second, the kitchen is often what prospective buyers look at first and last. In many cases, it determines the resale value of the home more than any other room in the house. You might have the most glorious master bedroom ever made, but if the kitchen is poorly designed, that buyer is likely to go down the road to find something else.

The kitchen also represents one of the more complicated areas in the home. In it you have all the things that make up a home. There is hot and cold water, waste disposal, and very possibly, other special plumbing, such as for a dishwasher or icemaker.

The kitchen also has electrical needs, both standard and special. There are a variety of smaller kitchen appliances that need to be plugged in, which means there must be plenty of outlets. Some might be dedicated, such as for the refrigerator or for a microwave oven. If the range is electric, it will have its own 220-volt outlet.

The Basic Design

The basic function of a kitchen is preparation of food. This begins with storage (cabinets and the refrigerator). You'll need counter space to prepare the food.

For ease of movement, the refrigerator should be off to one side, and never between the range and the sink (FIG. 9-1). (If it is, you'll find yourself having to move around the refrigerator too often.)

Next to each should be counter space. The counter by the refrigerator is used both for putting groceries away and for getting food out for the meal. The one by the stove is used during cooking. Counters by the sink—preferably with room on each side—are used for preparing food and for cleaning up afterwards.

These requirements are the minimum. The more you can plan (within reason), the more convenient the kitchen will be. Equally important is the consideration of distance. Imagine an absurd case in which the refrigerator is in one room, the stove in another, and the only sink down in the basement. There will be a lot of walking to get anything done. The idea is to make the kitchen efficient, with the major points (refrigerator, stove, sink) not too close and not too far apart. (See "Shapes for the Kitchen" on p. 92.)

Proper lighting and ventilation are extremely important for a kitchen (FIG. 9-2). There should be an abundance of both. Without proper lighting, working in the kitchen can be even more of a

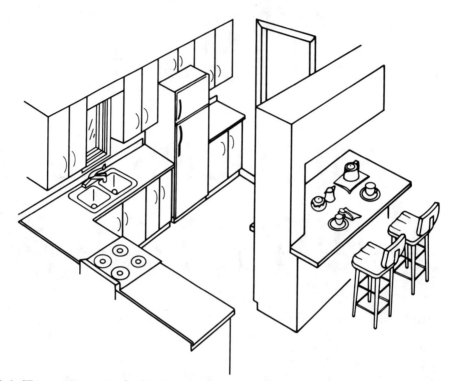

Fig. 9-1. *The arrangement of cabinets, counters, and appliances can make or break your kitchen.*

chore than it already is. And since you're sometimes handling hot, sharp, or otherwise dangerous things, too little light is risky.

There should be at least one window (usually located by the sink) of fair size to provide both light and ventilation. A ceiling light (or more than one) is the usual solution for providing general lighting for the area. Individual lights can be located directly over key areas, such as a light over the sink and another over the stove, with the latter often being incorporated into a hood fan unit. This same unit will aid in ventilation by helping to remove odors, smoke, and so on, where such removal is most needed—over the stove. The problem comes when the ventilation concerns in the design stop with this one small fan.

The kitchen window can help. Not only will the window provide light, it gives you a way of ventilating the kitchen by bringing cross-ventilation into play. Even a gentle breeze (*preferably* a gentle breeze) coming in from one window will tend to vent out through another on the opposite side of the home. In addition, proper placement

of vents for the heating/cooling can help, especially at those times when you don't want to have the windows open. Ceiling fans are also a solution and can be especially valuable when used in conjunction with the other schemes.

Electrical Needs

The kitchen has special electrical needs. In it are at least two major appliances: the stove and the refrigerator. Although the refrigerator is usually operated from a 110-volt circuit, that circuit is generally either dedicated to just the refrigerator, or is set up on a limited branch circuit (in other words, with perhaps only one more outlet).

The oven/range is always on its own 220-volt circuit. Both the oven and the top burners can draw a lot of current, as do all devices that use electrical heating elements.

The same applies to other places in the kitchen. You might consider, for example, setting aside an outlet on an open spot on the counter as a limited circuit for using plug-in appliances that

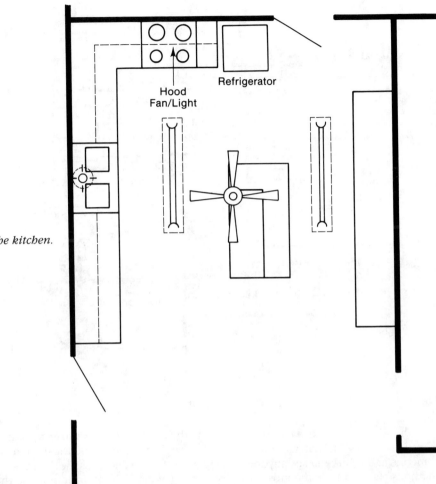

Fig. 9-2. *Lighting in the kitchen.*

Hood
Fan/Light

Refrigerator

tend to draw heavy current. Very definitely call out for a dedicated outlet for a microwave (preferably a 20-amp circuit). Even if you don't have a microwave yet, you might one day. And in any case, this gives you one more feature for resale, and meanwhile, gives you a dedicated circuit for other uses, should you want or need it.

An outlet under the sink is usually standard. It's used for the garbage disposal. Quite often it is split-wired, with one side "hot" all the time and the other side switched. Be sure to specify this.

There are two basic types of disposal. One operates off the wall switch. The other is activated by a switch in the top of the unit, so that the unit is turned on by putting the cover in place and giving it a turn. This second type is much safer than

the first, since you *cannot* operate the disposal without the cover in place. However, even if you have this type, you should still have that side of the outlet switched. That allows you flexibility in the future.

Not exactly an electrical consideration, but be sure to call out a telephone outlet in the kitchen (and in any part of the house where you'll spend any time).

Placement of the Kitchen

Most often, the kitchen is placed in the back of the house, with the window over the sink looking into the backyard. This allows whoever is at the sink preparing a meal to keep an eye on the kids playing outside (FIG. 9-3).

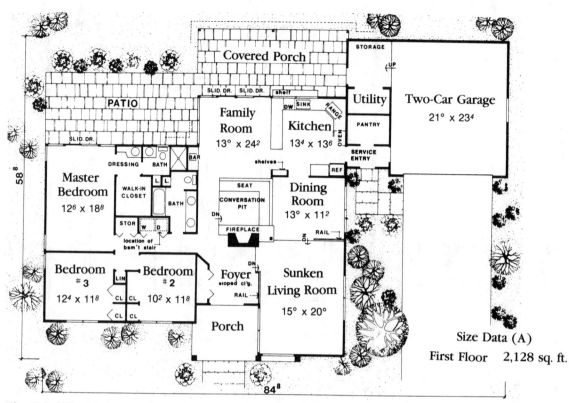

Master Bedroom 12⁶ x 18⁸

Bedroom #3 12⁴ x 11⁸

Bedroom #2 10² x 11⁸

Family Room 13⁰ x 24²

Kitchen 13⁴ x 13⁶

Dining Room 13⁰ x 11²

Sunken Living Room 15⁰ x 20⁰

Two-Car Garage 21⁰ x 23⁴

Foyer

Porch

PATIO

Covered Porch

STORAGE

Utility

PANTRY

SERVICE ENTRY

WALK-IN CLOSET

DRESSING BATH BAR

BATH

STOR W D

location of bsm't stair

CONVERSATION PIT

FIREPLACE

SEAT

shelves

REF

RAIL

RAIL

SLID. DR. SLID. DR. shelf

DW SINK

RANGE

HOOD

SLID. DR.

LIN

CL CL

CL CL

DN

DN

DN

UP

58⁸

84⁸

Size Data (A)

First Floor   2,128 sq. ft.

Fig. 9-3. *"The kitchen can be placed in the rear . . ."*

Also common is to have the kitchen in the front (FIG. 9-4), with that window placed so that someone at the sink can see anyone coming up to the house (and can see the kids if they're playing in the front yard).

A part of the decision is made by the scenery. Since a fair amount of time is spent in the kitchen and at the sink, it's nice to have something pleasant to look at. Placing the kitchen and the window so that the only view is the wall of a garage might be sufficient for ventilation purposes. It might even still provide enough light. But the view is going to be rather boring.

Just as you can locate the kitchen in the front or in the back, you can also place it on either end, in the middle, or almost anywhere you wish (or at least you can as long as you keep in mind how the house is arranged overall).

Such important considerations are another reason to begin with the kitchen as you design the home. Then the choice is yours; it is not forced

upon you because a particular spot is the only space available for the kitchen.

The usual solution is to have the kitchen at more-or-less one end or the other, generally by the garage or carport. The reason is obvious. You'll be bringing in groceries on a regular basis. Having the kitchen or other food storage areas near the place you park your car is a distinct advantage. Otherwise you'll have to carry those groceries through at least a part of the house.

The reverse is also true. The kitchen creates garbage—sometimes messy garbage. Having a door to the outside close at hand is essential. Having it near the spot where garbage is placed outside is handy. That usually means towards one end of the house.

Shapes for the Kitchen

As with most rooms in the house, the kitchen is usually rectangular in shape. It's highly functional and allows you maximum flexibility for internal

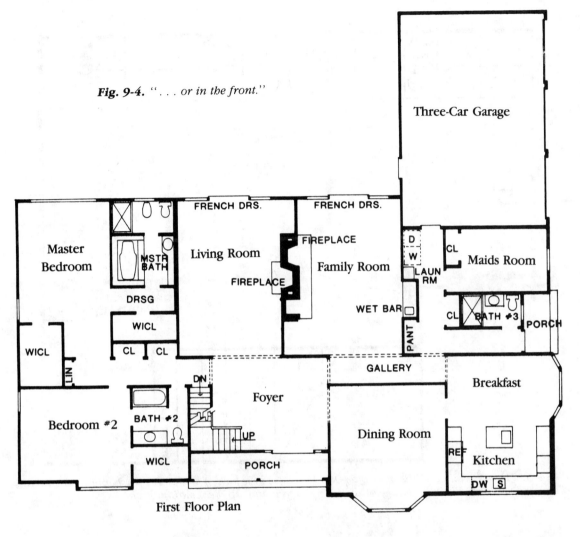

Fig. 9-4. *". . . or in the front."*

Three-Car Garage

FRENCH DRS.   FRENCH DRS.

Master Bedroom

MSTR BATH

Living Room

FIREPLACE

FIREPLACE

Family Room

FIREPLACE

D

W

CL

Maids Room

LAUN RM

DRSG

WICL

WET BAR

PANT

CL

BATH #3

PORCH

WICL

CL   CL

LIN

GALLERY

Breakfast

DN

Foyer

Dining Room

Bedroom #2

BATH #2

UP

REF

Kitchen

WICL

PORCH

DW   S

First Floor Plan

design. Within the rectangle you can have the cabinets, counters, sink, and appliances arranged in any of the four basic patterns (as appropriate to size).

Chapter 6 concentrated on traffic flow in and around the home. This becomes particularly important in the kitchen, where work is done at least two or three times per day. The shape of the kitchen and the arrangement of the things in it determines the efficiency.

As mentioned earlier, the four basic shapes are one-wall, parallel, L-shaped and U-shaped. (Refer back to FIG. 6-10 for examples of each.) The one-wall design is sometimes thought of as being a "forced" kitchen. You've run out of room, or space is given elsewhere as more important, leaving you with a very narrow kitchen, and with the sink and appliances in a straight line so that there is no real work triangle (FIG. 9-5).

A step forward is the parallel, or corridor, kitchen. This kind of kitchen can be efficient both for working and for access to the rooms on both sides.

One of the more popular designs is the L-shaped kitchen. This allows another wall of counters and spaces over the one-wall design, while still allowing an open space for an eating area.

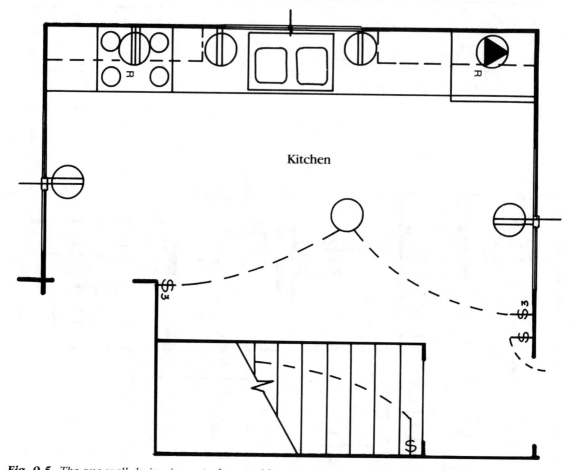

Fig. 9-5. *The one-wall design is most often used because of a lack of space. The kitchen working area is along one wall, usually with storage or an eating area taking up the remaining space.*

The U-shaped design provides a "wrap-around." There are counters and spaces on three sides. This makes working in the area highly efficient because of maximum flexibility. However, it tends to close in the area, and some people don't like that feeling. (This also reduces traffic flow in and out.)

There are any number of variations to the four basics. For example, one quite common possibility is a basic L-shape for the major parts of the kitchen, with a breakfast bar and counter to make a broken U (FIG. 9-6). This island can have its own range top, if you wish. It can be all one level, or can be at two levels. It can have cabinets beneath, or be open. It can be an island, or the added counter can connect to the wall (FIG. 9-7).

Cabinets and Counters

Cabinetry and storage was covered in detail in Chapter 7. Review this chapter. It is an important consideration throughout the house. In the kitchen, where a variety of different items must be stored, such as dishes, pans, utensils, and food, it can be the critical difference between a kitchen that works and one that encourages you to eat out often.

As mentioned in Chapter 7, unless you pay the cost of having custom-made cabinets, there

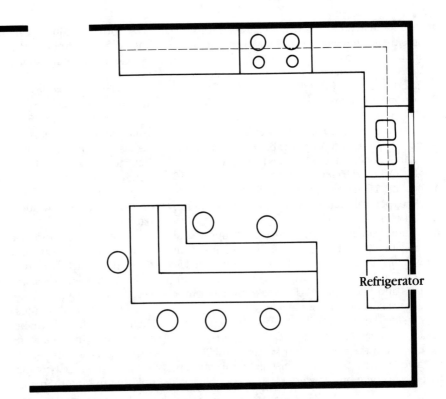

Fig. 9-6. *A bar can make the* L *into a broken* U.

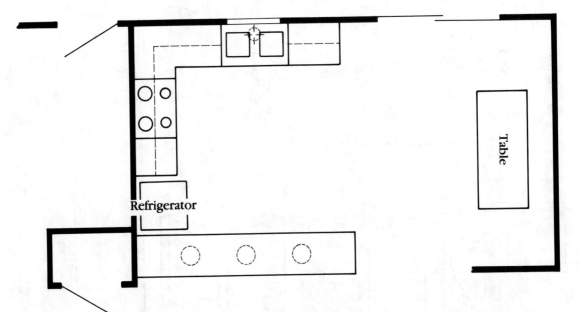

Fig. 9-7. *This is actually an* L*-shaped kitchen, but the counter makes it appear to be* U*-shaped.*

Kitchens & Dining Rooms   95

will be standards to follow. For example, for most people the ideal height from floor to countertop is 36 inches. Most base (lower) cabinets are therefore $34^1/_2$ inches in height. Once the countertop is installed, the top of it will be 36 inches from the floor. Other heights are available (30 inches, 32 inches, 34 inches).

Standard depth for the lower cabinets is 24 inches. The standard upper cabinet will generally be 12 inches deep and 30 inches (actually $30^1/_8$) in height. Over a refrigerator the height might be 12 inches or 15 inches. Also readily available are stock upper cabinets with heights of 18 inches and 24 inches.

Widths are more variable for both upper and lower cabinets, usually in 3-inch increments from a 12-inch minimum up to 48 inches (i.e., 12, 15, 18, 21, 24, 27, 30, 33, 36, 39, 42, 45, and 48). Spacers and fillers are used to make up any other differences needed in the total length.

Inside the cabinets are shelves, drawers, turntables, and special storage racks. Quite often, except under the sink, each base cabinet will have a drawer at the top. (You can also get base cabinets that are nothing but drawers.)

Corner cabinets can be square or have an angled front. Either way, getting back into the corner can be difficult, so many corner cabinets have built-in turntables.

Colors and styles are available in just about anything you imagine (FIG. 9-8). Fancy, plain, dark, light—your goal is to pick what you like best, and what you'll like 5 years from now. A common mistake is to choose a color that is too dark. It's deep, rich, and dramatic; however, it can have a tendency to make the kitchen seem dreary (depending on what else is in the kitchen, and what other colors you use), and quite often people tire of the darker colors.

Plan for the future. Don't design a "bare minimum" kitchen to save money on cabinets. Try to find other places to save, if you need to. Otherwise, it's likely to be a savings you'll regret before very long.

FHA-HUD minimums call for 30 square feet of shelf space for a one-bedroom home; then 38 square feet, 44 square feet, and 50 square feet, respectively, for two-, three-, and four-bedroom homes. These are bare minimums. It's easy to "use up" that minimum in a hurry.

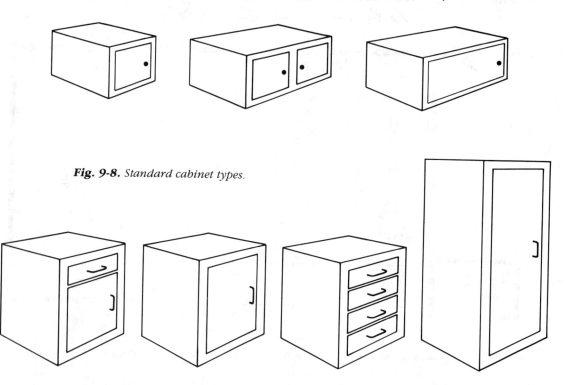

Fig. 9-8. *Standard cabinet types.*

For example, a 24-inch-wide base cabinet might have only two shelf areas, each 24 inches deep. Such a cabinet provides 8 square feet of shelf. Three of these —just 6 feet of base cabinets (measure out 6 feet on the floor; it's not much)— gives 24 square feet of shelving. With upper cabinets usually being 12 inches deep and containing two shelves, each 2-foot length gives 4 square feet of storage space. So, to meet the minimum requirements for a one-bedroom home, you need only 3 feet more of upper cabinetry.

For the 8 additional square feet required for a two-bedroom home, add one more base cabinet or two more upper cabinets. You don't need even that much for the next step upwards.

The requirements of 40 to 50 square feet may *seem* like a lot, but think of it in reverse. The standard sink and appliances will take up roughly 7 to 7^1/$_2$ feet of running length. However, the sink can have a shelf beneath, and the refrigerator and stove can have a shelf (even two shelves) above. That comes to something like 14 square feet, leaving 16, 24, 30, and 36 square feet of additional shelving for one-, two-, three-, and four-bedroom homes. Just two 2-foot base cabinets will provide 30 square feet and satisfy the requirements for a one-bedroom home; one more base cabinet, or two upper cabinets, would take care of the minimum requirements for a two-bedroom home.

In short, my advice, and the advice of most professional designers, is to give yourself as much storage space in the kitchen as you can get, and afford. Minimums just aren't enough.

The countertops are an important part of the kitchen's efficiency and an important part of the kitchen decor. Neutral tones give the greatest flexibility, but also the least dramatic flair. A medium-toned woodblock look is going to fit with almost any decor, without causing any big "splash." A bright blue counter is going to add distinctive color, but could be disastrous if the other colors in the room aren't chosen correctly. (See Chapters 7 and 19.)

Most countertops these days are plastic laminate, such as Formica. This surface provides extremely good durability for relatively low cost. The choices in this kind of counter are many, from the look of wood, to the look of stone, to the look of leather, to almost anything you can imagine.

Natural surfaces, such as wood and stone tile, are popular, but are more expensive and carry with them some disadvantages. (Wood absorbs and can stain, while also having the tendency to show wear in a relatively short period of time. Stone surfaces are very slick and can chip or crack if something heavy is dropped on them.)

You also have to decide if the counter will be straight or will have a backsplash to help in the event of spills. Will the fronts be squared or rounded? Will the corners be squared or rounded? Chapter 19 contains the details and considerations you'll have to consider before "finalizing" the kitchen.

Meanwhile, in the overall design, your main concerns are the number of cabinets, the amount and location of counter space that this will give you, and where you will locate the major items of the kitchen.

The placement of the major items can be creative, but must still follow certain rules of common sense. As mentioned earlier, don't put the refrigerator between the stove and sink. Its height causes a block to the flow of work being done. You should be able to move between the sink and stove without having to step around anything. Have counter space (at least 18 inches, and larger if possible) beside each major item, and preferably space on both sides of the sink. Don't allow any two items to come up directly against each other. Remember: The overall arrangement should provide maximum efficiency.

Pantry

Pantries were discussed in some detail in Chapter 7. The focus at that point was of storage. Now the main concern is placement.

Pantries are special storage areas in or near the kitchen, used to hold quantities of food—almost like miniature grocery stores. A pantry can be a separate room—like a large closet—or it can be a section of cabinets set aside for this purpose (FIGS. 9-9 and 9-10). The first requires some distinct preplanning because of the space it takes up. Often it will be a part of an entry room between the garage and kitchen. The latter also needs preplanning, but to a lesser extent. Most pantry cabinets are only 12 inches deep. That cuts a foot out of the room, though. If you've allowed only 3 feet of open space for movement, even a shallow pantry is going to cause a problem for traffic flow.

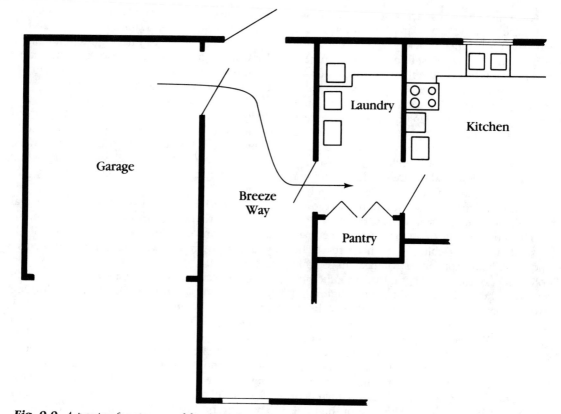

Fig. 9-9. *A pantry for storage of food can be a separate room. (Note the minor traffic-flow problem.)*

Rooms Off the Kitchen

The most common room off the kitchen is the dining room (as detailed below). Some kind of eating area is a necessity. And it should be located immediately next to the kitchen (FIG. 9-11).

It's also common to have the living room adjoin the kitchen area, usually through a pass-through or by way of a door (FIG. 9-12). (See Chapter 11.) This makes entertaining a little easier. As a hint, if you decide that you want to design your home this way, with either a separate dining room or living room next to the kitchen, provide the means of closing off each from the other.

Another room very often placed next to the kitchen is a laundry room. It might seem impractical to have a laundry room off the kitchen because that means that the place where dirty clothes gather—the bedrooms and bathrooms—are usu-

ally farthest away. However, there *are* reasons for having the laundry room near the kitchen.

One reason is that it can be used as an entrance. Since there is (or should be) a sink, you have a place to clean up if you, or the kids, have gotten dirty outside, so that you won't be tracking dirt through the house (FIG. 9-13). (In some plans, you'll see the room with the label, "Mud Room," which is sometimes an apt description.)

Another is that it makes it much easier to be doing two household chores at the same time. Once the washer or dryer are going, no further attention is needed until the cycle is through. You can be in the kitchen preparing a meal or cleaning up after one, and still be able to hear if something goes amiss.

Still another is that, by placing the laundry room away from the bedrooms, the noise created by the machines is also isolated. (Don't forget to

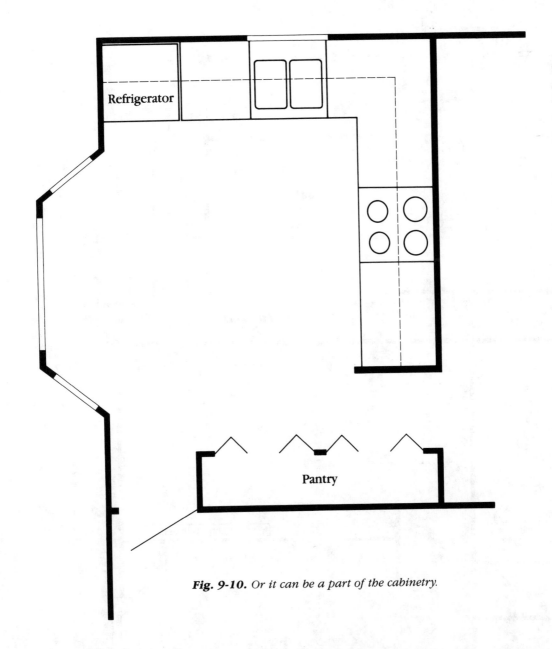

Fig. 9-10. *Or it can be a part of the cabinetry.*

have a door between the kitchen and laundry room, if at all possible, to keep out the noise.)

The Eating Areas

You have three basic choices concerning the eating areas. The first is to have a totally separate din-

ing room. The second is to have it separate from the kitchen, but combined at least partially with the living room. The third is to incorporate it into an overall kitchen/dining area, with the living room separate.

A separate dining room is nice if you can afford the space (FIG. 9-14). For many people it rep-

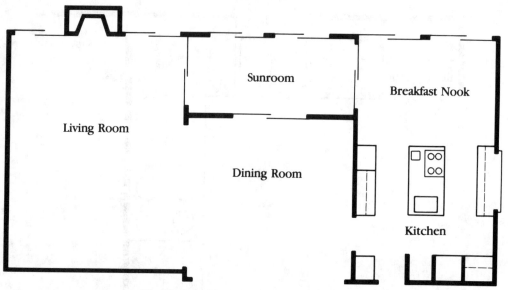

Fig. 9-11. *A dining room off the kitchen.*

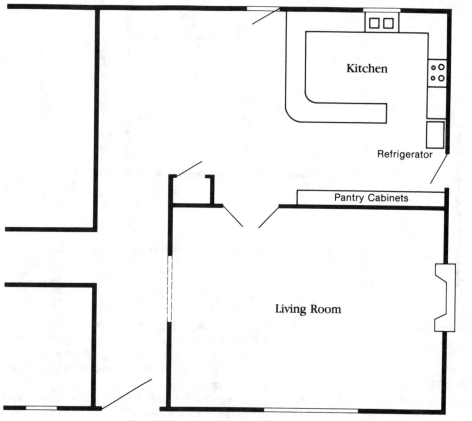

Fig. 9-12. *A living room off the kitchen.*

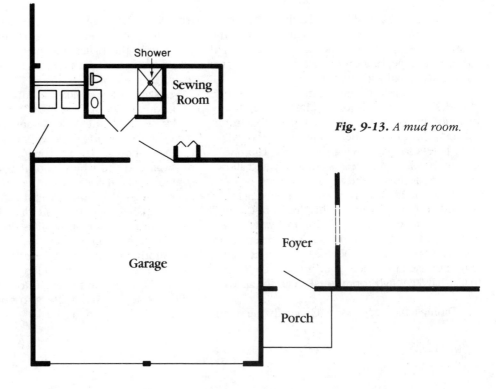

Shower

Sewing Room

Fig. 9-13. *A mud room.*

Garage

Foyer

Porch

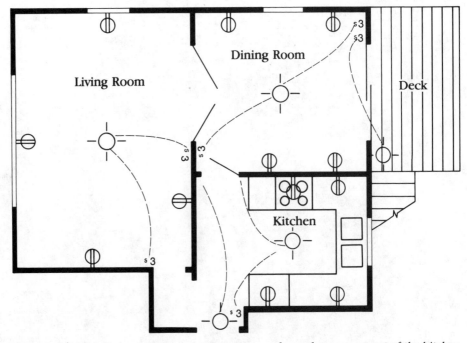

Living Room

Dining Room

Deck

Kitchen

Fig. 9-14. *The dining room can be separate, as shown here, or a part of the kitchen.*

resents a room that will be used only occasionally. Having it attached to a living room increases the possible uses, but only if the two can be opened to create a single, larger room (although one that is usually separated with a door).

If you entertain often, or if your lifestyle includes some more "formal" dining (even if only one meal per day), consider having a dining room separate from the kitchen. However, if your lifestyle is less formal, having the dining room as a part of the kitchen increases efficiency and allows an "open" feeling in the design.

Most kitchens will have at least a small area set aside for family eating. This "breakfast nook" gives you an efficient place for many, or most, family meals. You may not care to entertain in such an area, but it *can* be used for that as well if you're pressed for space. Your primary concern is that it have enough room to take care of all your needs.

Dining tables vary in size. Generally the small-est will be 3 by 3, which is suitable for four people, but doesn't leave much room for anything other than the plates and utensils. Larger tables measure 4 by 6 and sometimes larger, especially in length.

A standard chair takes about 2 by 2, but this is misleading. When in use, it's tucked partially under the table, but to allow someone to sit down, the chair has to slide back far enough. That means that you should plan for roughly 3 feet between the wall and the table. More if you can, so that someone can move past a person seated at the table. Ideally, then, the smallest room for a 3 by 4 table will be 9 by 10—and *that* is going to be crowded. If one or more sides don't have walls, the planning is a little easier.

Another reason for predetermining the size of the table is to locate the ceiling lights. Normally there will be one in the center of where the table will be placed. That might also be the center of the room—but it might not.

10

Bedrooms & bathrooms

How you design your bedrooms and where you place them depends on two things: the size of the house and your personal lifestyle. (Obviously, you can't have six bedrooms of 15-by-20-foot dimensions in a 1700-square-foot house. And, you probably don't want the only bathroom in the house to be inside the master bedroom.)

On the whole, bedrooms and bathrooms are set away from the main living areas of the home. This is to provide privacy. Even if *you* don't need privacy, having the bedrooms too exposed can greatly injure the chances of resale of the home.

The smallest house needs at least one bedroom, and one that is more than just a fold-out couch in the living room. Better is to have two bedrooms. Even if you, yourself, use only one of them as a bedroom, the other can serve as a den, hobby room, or whatever, and will definitely add to the resale value.

On the other hand, once you get past four bedrooms, you're once again dealing with a limited market for resale. Obviously, if you really need those rooms, design them into the house, but be aware of what you're doing. It's not as easy to find a buyer for a six-bedroom home. However, if you plan properly, and make sure those extra rooms can be converted to be used for other things, you can have the best of both. For example, my own home is officially a five-bedroom home, with three bedrooms upstairs and two in

the basement. A future buyer *can* use them all as bedrooms, but the two "bedrooms" in the basement aren't really bedrooms. One is my office, the other is an adjoining library. The design is perfect for someone who works at home, and the space can be easily converted into either a basement gameroom or into one or two bedrooms.

In any case, you'll need one bedroom for yourself and your spouse, and, if you have children, at least one each for the boys and girls. Once they get past a certain age, they will want—and deserve—some privacy. It might be okay for a very young boy and girl to share a room, but before long, they should be separated into their own rooms.

The other private part of the home is the bathroom. For obvious reasons, no home should be without one. (The days of outhouses are long past, and they're illegal in many areas.)

One bathroom *is* the minimum, and if there is only one, it should be more or less centrally located, at least from the bedrooms. A step up is $1^1/2$ baths. This odd term means that you have one bathroom complete with a bathtub or shower stall, and another (usually located in or near the living areas of the home) with just a toilet and sink.

You may want more. A two-bedroom home can get by with just one; a three- or four-bedroom home should have at least two, and maybe two full baths and a half elsewhere in the home. Local codes might affect this. (For example, in many areas, if you have a four-bedroom home, you'll have to have at least two bathrooms.)

Ideally, if your home is on more than one level, there should be at least a toilet and sink on each floor. The standard is to have a full bath located by and connected to the master bedroom. If this is the only bathroom in the house, there will have to be another door so that others in the house can use the bathroom without walking through the bedroom. That, of course, means that there needs to be secure locks on both doors.

Bedroom Sizing

You might hear that the accepted standard minimum for a bedroom is 8 by 9 feet. That will work, but just barely. Once the bed is in there, not much space remains for anything else.

The smallest standard bed, the twin, is a little over 3 feet wide and 6 feet long. Put this in the room so that there is just 18 inches of space on the one side, and there will be just a little more than 3 feet left for getting into and out of the room, and only about 3 feet of space at the bottom of the bed. Now add a dresser of any kind and moving around is going to be difficult (FIG. 10-1).

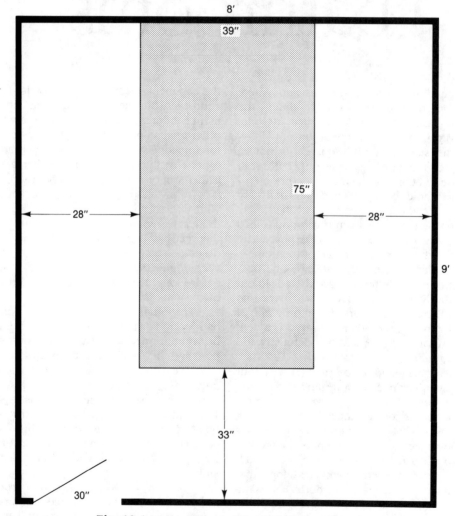

Fig. 10-1. *A minimum bed in a minimum room.*

Trying to squeeze in any other bed makes matters worse yet (FIG. 10-2). A full-size bed is the same length, but adds another 15 inches to the width. A queen is another 6 inches again in width and close to 7 feet in length. A king-size bed will fit in that room, but at this point, you might as well have a wall-to-wall mattress. (Refer to FIG. 10-3).

It's not just the bed. For example, if you want a dresser or bedstand, those take up space. The room will also have at least one window. You must also be sure that there is enough space for the doors—both the door to enter and exit the room and the one to the closet (FIG. 10-4).

Figure out what furniture you intend to have in the bedroom other than the bed itself. Even if

Table 10-1. Standard Bed Sizes

(in inches)

Twin	39 × 75
Full (Standard)	54 × 75
Queen	60 × 80
King	76 × 80
California King	72 × 84

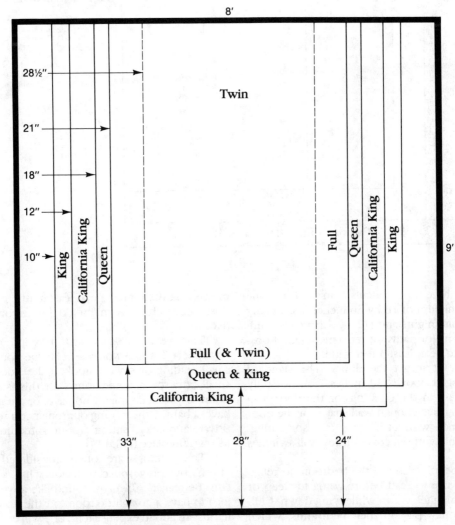

Fig. 10-2. *Other beds in that same room.*

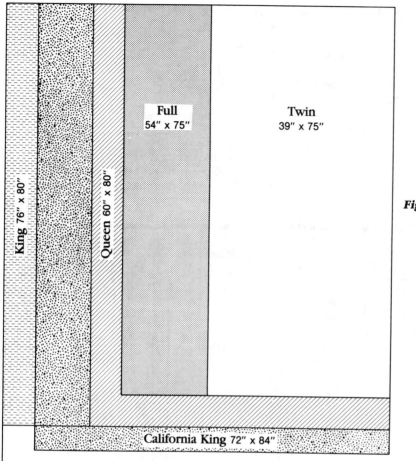

Fig. 10-3. *Standard bed sizes.*

King 76" x 80"

Queen 60" x 80"

Full 54" x 75"

Twin 39" x 75"

California King 72" x 84"

you don't have one, calculate in at least one dresser (minimum of 18 by 36 inches is generally best) and one nightstand (12 by 12 inches minimum). Any major paths for movement (all, if possible) should be at least 3 feet wide.

And don't forget the doors. The standard interior hinged door is 30 inches. You not only have to figure in the opening for the door, you also have to leave enough wall space for the door to swing open without banging into something, and preferably without covering any wall switches (FIG. 10-5).

Many people also use the bedroom to relax. Maybe you like to read before going to sleep or enjoy watching television while lying down. Children very often play in their bedrooms, which

means that there must be at least a little room for this. Older children might do homework there (FIG. 10-6).

The overall size also has to take into account any special features you want. Maybe you want a small reading or sewing nook at the side—like a small extra room. Some homes use this as a selling point to young couples who have, or are going to have, a baby. Others bring out romance and have a private and cozy "sitting" room, sometimes with its own fireplace (FIG. 10-7).

These things are often considered to be "fluff," but only *you* can decide what is important. Be realistic. It might sound like a wonderful idea to have a cozy little room off the master, but it's just an added expense if no one will ever use it.

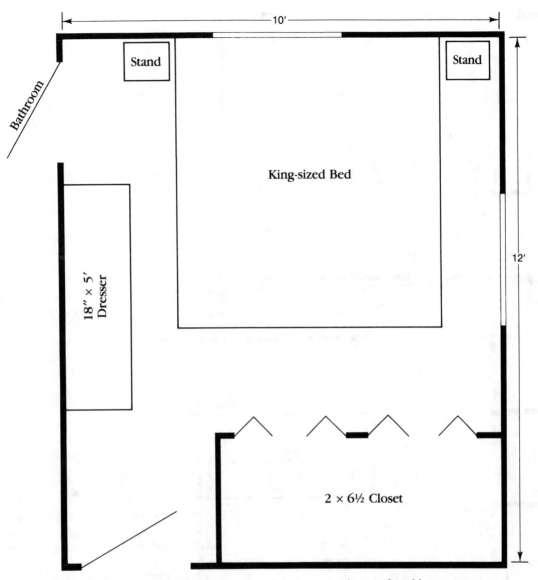

Fig. 10-4. *An over-filled bedroom doesn't leave space for comfortable movement.*

Usually, the master bedroom is the largest. There is a valid reason for this. In that room there are, usually, two grown adults. Quite often both are employed and have wardrobe needs.

Other rooms that are to be shared by two or more children likewise need to be larger than a room meant for just one individual. Two twin beds take up more width than a king-sized bed. Look again at FIG. 10-2. A king-sized bed in that 8-

by-9 room leaves only 10 inches on the sides. Two twins in that room will leave only 9 inches on each side, or if shoved against the two walls, will have just 18 inches between them (FIG. 10-8).

One solution, of course, is to use bunk beds, where the beds are stacked one above the other. But some people, and especially some children, don't like bunks. For them, sleeping up in the air can be disconcerting.

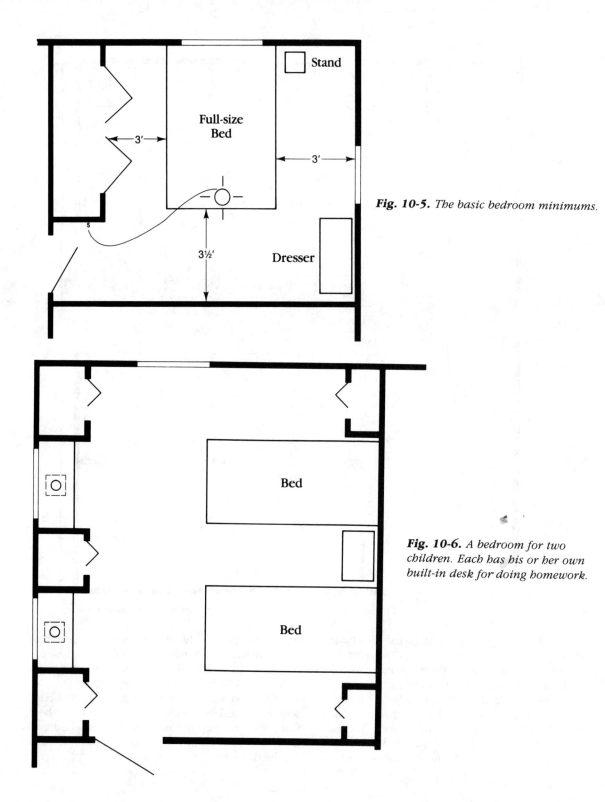

Fig. 10-5. *The basic bedroom minimums.*

Fig. 10-6. *A bedroom for two children. Each has his or her own built-in desk for doing homework.*

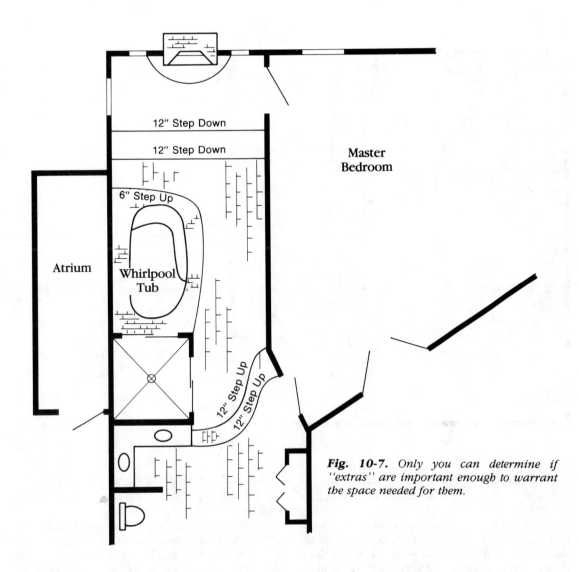

12" Step Down

12" Step Down

6" Step Up

Atrium

Whirlpool
Tub

12" Step Up

12" Step Up

Master
Bedroom

Fig. 10-7. *Only you can determine if "extras" are important enough to warrant the space needed for them.*

Closets

Closets are important enough to deserve their own subsection. I would urge you to review Chapter 7 on storage areas. These considerations become very important when designing a bedroom.

Years ago, a bedroom with a closet was a luxury. Clothing was stored in dressers or wardrobe cabinets. Both have their uses, but a closet is still essential.

A standard bedroom closet will have one shelf at roughly head height, a clothes rod beneath, and sufficient floor space for miscellaneous items. The standard depth is about 2 feet, and width is whatever you can afford—generally the larger the better (within reason).

The inside of the closet can be modified to suit, either during construction or afterwards. For example, you might want a shoe rack rather than putting shoes on the floor. All this is, really, is a compartmentalized unit, with each spot wide enough to hold a pair of shoes.

Wide closets usually have either sliding or folding doors. These doors can be an advantage

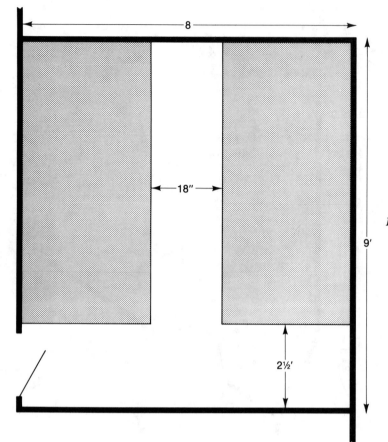
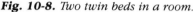

Fig. 10-8. *Two twin beds in a room.*

even for smaller closets since you don't have to contend with the room taken up by a swinging hinged door.

The advantage of a hinged door is that it tends to be more durable and secure. The disadvantage is, again, that it requires sufficient floor space to swing open. In addition, it's difficult to find doors wider than 36 inches—and 30 inches is more standard (FIG. 10-9).

Sliding and folding doors can be made to cover almost any width. They're not as durable nor as secure as a hinged door, but they are generally good enough for a bedroom closet and don't require floor space to open.

Bedroom Placement

In most homes, the bedrooms are separated from the rest of the house. That usually means a hallway, which, in turn, means some wasted space useful only for traffic flow; however, for most people the privacy allowed makes the cost worthwhile (FIG. 10-10).

Also usual is to group the bedrooms. This simplifies construction, especially since the bathrooms are usually in the same area, but not so much that you can't separate the bedrooms if you wish. Having all the bedrooms together keeps the functions together—and the people together. However, having them separated gives extra privacy (FIG. 10-11).

A part of the decision is dependent on your lifestyle. If part of the family is going to be awake and making noise, while another part will be trying to sleep, separation of those bedrooms and the living areas is important. At the very least, if there are shared walls, consider investing in extra soundproofing in those walls.

When we designed our home, we were

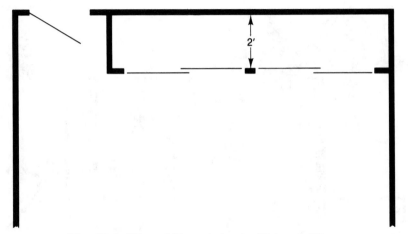

Fig. 10-9. *His and Hers. A closet with two sections.*

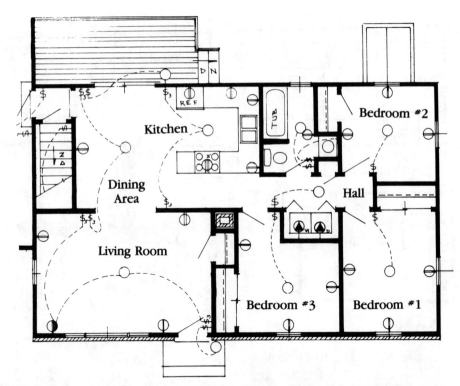

Fig. 10-10. *Bedrooms are usually set to one side of the home, with the living and eating areas on the other.*

expecting a new baby. We wanted his room separated as far from the rest of the house as possible so that his sleep wouldn't be disturbed, yet close enough to our own bedroom so we could hear him well enough in the night to wake us. (We may regret this closeness later, as he becomes older—and noisier.) An added problem was that I have the tendency to work late into the night and sleep in the next morning.

His room is in the most distant corner, but

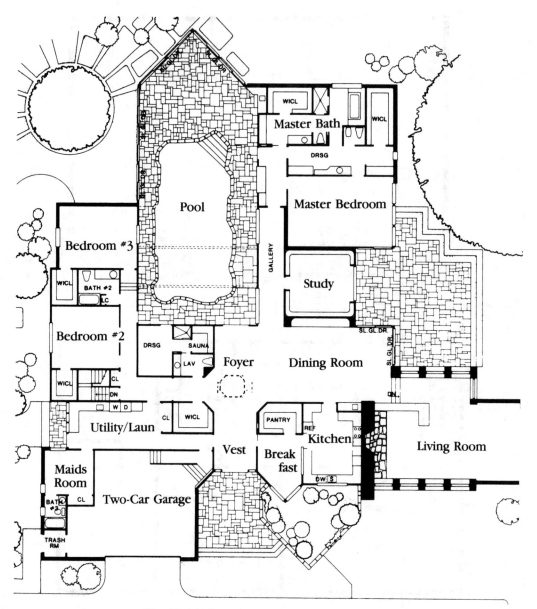

Fig. 10-11. *Some homes separate the bedrooms.*

just down a short hall from our room. The shared wall between our room and the kitchen/dining area has extra insulation to help block out the sound from that area (FIG. 10-12).

Another factor in placement is the position of the sun. Homes with the bedrooms on the east side will get the morning sun. Homes with bedrooms on the west will get the afternoon sun. Those bedrooms on the south will get more sun than those on the north. (If you like to wake to the morning sun, set your bedroom on the southeast side.)

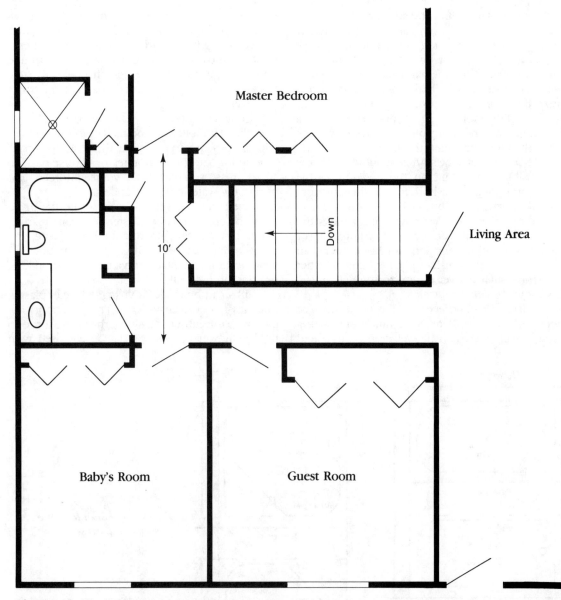

Fig. 10-12. *The baby can sleep undisturbed, while still being close enough to disturb* us *if need be. And* I *can sleep without being disturbed by the rest of the house.*

Bathrooms

A friend of mine called to ask my advice on a problem he was having. The guest bathroom in his home was beginning to take on a bad smell. I'd been to his home and suspected what was causing the trouble. Although the bathroom was properly located as far as convenience, it was small and poorly ventilated. The bathroom was almost dead center in the home, with no windows. Ventilation was provided by a small ceiling fan.

That left him a couple of choices. Use that

bathroom less to reduce the amount of moisture. Install a more powerful ventilation fan (which may or may not have required larger ducting). Leave the existing fan on for longer periods and leave the door open when the bathroom wasn't in use.

Proper design of a bathroom doesn't stop at providing sufficient space for the functions. Because of the moisture and odors, ventilation is a real concern. The more often the room will be used, the more important this becomes.

There must also be sufficient light. A window (if possible, depending on the location of the bathroom) will provide both light and ventilation, but it's not enough by itself for either. There should be sufficient general lighting for the entire room. This is usually done with a ceiling light (or lights if the bathroom is large or has corners). In addition, strongly consider placing lights in other key spots, such as over the mirror (which is usually mounted behind the sink).

As stated earlier, every home needs at least one full bathroom. Bare minimum is one with a shower stall, but you'd be well-advised to spend the little bit extra to have a tub with a showerhead for the extra versatility. (A very small shower stall will measure about 30 by 30 inches; a standard tub takes up about as much width and only about 2 more feet in length.) Refer to FIGS. 10-13 through 10-15 for standard bathroom fixtures and sizes.

Concerning fixtures, you have many choices to make. The toilet can be made of china or certain plastics. It can be standard, or a "low-boy." The action can be siphon-jet or reverse-trap. In some areas, you may find yourself forced into using only water-efficient models.

What kind of sink do you want? It can be made of china, enameled steel or iron, marble, cultured (man-made) marble, molded plastic, and a few other materials. The sink can mount in a vanity cabinet, be placed on a pedestal or on legs, or hung on the wall.

Tubs can be made of enameled steel, plastic, fiberglass, or even custom tile. They can be as simple as a basic tub with a showerhead and a rod to hold a shower curtain, or can be enclosed with

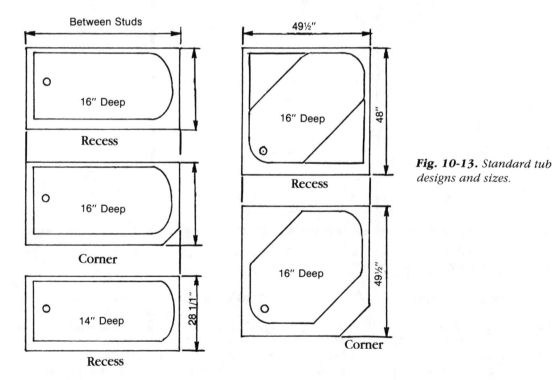

Fig. 10-13. *Standard tub designs and sizes.*

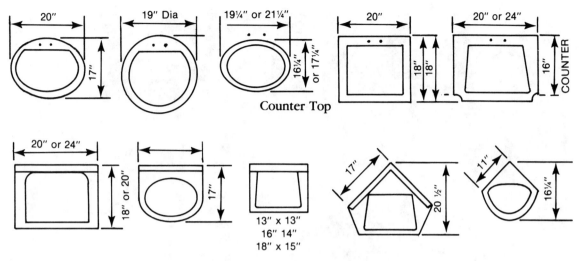

Counter Top

Wall Hung

Fig. 10-14. Standard basin designs and sizes.

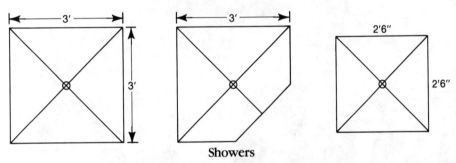

Showers

Fig. 10-15. Standard shower stall sizes.

sliding doors. You might prefer a corner tub, a sunken tub, or perhaps one that incorporates a whirlpool.

For versatility if no other reason, whenever possible plan the tub as a tub/shower. If done during construction, the additional cost is very small. The plumbing is easy and inexpensive while the walls are open. You'll need a way to protect the wall from splashes anyway, whether you do it with plastic or fiberglass panels, or with custom tile. The first two come in stock sizes for a "surround" and are often less expensive to install as full surrounds than to cut them down for a tub alone. The extra tile to bring it up for a shower is relatively minor in cost. And you have the option to use it as a tub or as a shower.

Having a tub available becomes even more important if you have young children (and makes resale of the home easier for the same reason). The versatility of being able to use it as a shower is an inexpensive investment.

A tub or shower stall is a major item. They're large and difficult to move. Generally, they'll be put in place before the framing is complete. A lot of construction will be going on afterwards, and the builders will be standing in the tub to do the finish work. Be *sure* that the effort is made to protect the tub, and make this one of the places you inspect carefully during the walk-through.

A tiled tub or shower is a little different (FIG. 10-16). Since the tiles can be easily moved in at any stage, they're often left until last to avoid any pos-

Fig. 10-16. *The bathroom can be as fancy as you wish, but it must still contain the basics: a sink, a tub and/or shower, a toilet, some storage, sufficient counter space, and plenty of light.*

sible damage. The two general tiling methods are "glued" and "mudded." The second is preferred.

Glued tile is placed directly to the drywall with a mastic. It's quick, easy, and inexpensive. It also means that a minor leak is going to seep into the drywall—a material highly prone to water damage.

The better method requires more planning and more work. As a consequence, it's also more expensive, but not by all that much. A lath is put up to hold a plaster-like material. In a sense, you end up with something like thin concrete walls (usually about $1/2$ to 1 inch thick). The tile is attached to this with waterproof mastic, creating a nice bond and a fairly waterproof wall behind.

It might sound unnecessary, but be *sure* to specify that the grout in a tiled bathroom be waterproof. Most of the time, this is a given. Other times, the tile subcontractor will use whatever grout is at hand—and is cheapest. By clearly specifying it in writing (signed by the contractor), *if* something goes wrong and the grout starts washing out, there can be no excuses.

Other Bathroom Considerations

The faucets for a tub, shower, or sink can be dual or single—with the former having a separate faucet for the cold and hot sides, and the latter with a single combined faucet for both. Whichever you choose, you'll have a variety of looks, styles, and materials, such as plastic, chrome, brass, wood, or crystal. You can create any variety of decors. Happily, swapping faucets is a simple job. You can do it yourself, usually in a matter of minutes. This makes it one of those things you can put off until

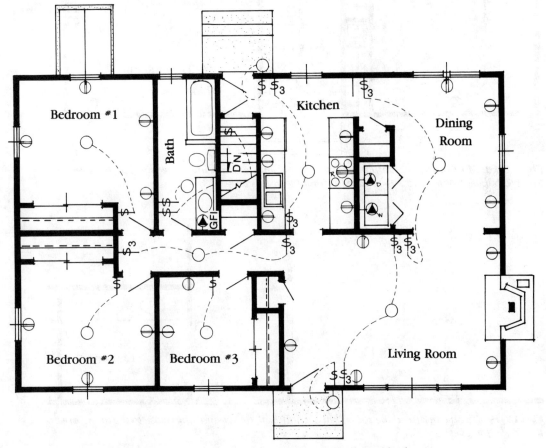

Fig. 10-17. *A smaller home might have one shared bathroom.*

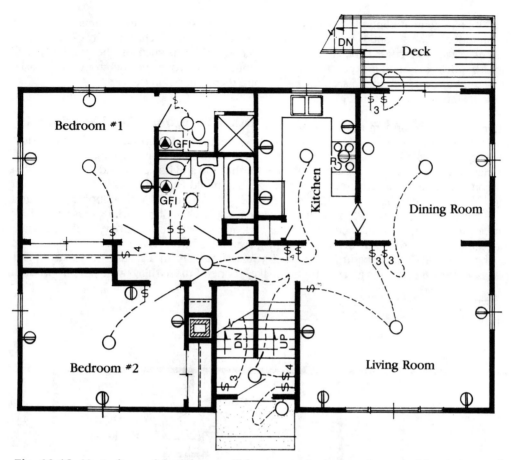

Fig. 10-18. *Most often, a 2-bath home will have a master bath and a second located central to the other bedrooms. Note the shared plumbing in this case.*

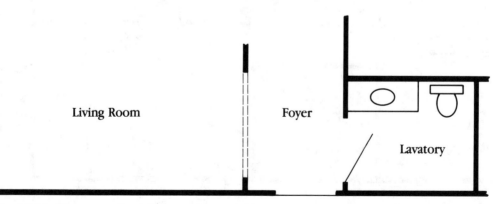

Fig. 10-19. *If you can afford the room, have a half-bath (toilet and sink) close to the living area of the home for guests.*

later, if you wish. (As usual, though, it's silly to have the contractor put in cheap fixtures if you're planning to swap them out in a month or two. You'll already be paying for the installation, whether the fixtures are cheap or expensive, and you'll be paying for the cheap fixtures you'll be yanking out and replacing.)

The vanity cabinets, if any, aren't quite the same. Although replacing them isn't terribly difficult to do, even the least expensive cost quite a bit. More, they have a very real effect on the "feel" of the room.

Medicine cabinets are often recessed into the wall, which provides plenty of storage inside and the cabinet does not stick out into the room. Surface-mounted units are also available. The cabinet may have a mirror or it may not. There is more variety and more choices than most people real-ize. Take the time to find out what is available, and what best suits your needs and tastes.

Bathroom Placement

There are two general places for a bathroom. The most obvious is where the bedrooms are located. This is the "private" area of the home. Having a full bathroom, or bathrooms, is essential here. You can increase construction efficiency (and thus reduce costs) by designing the bathrooms for shared plumbing (Refer to FIGS. 10-17, 10-18, and 10-19).

What is often forgotten is that visitors will have to use a bathroom now and then. If you can afford the room, have at least a toilet and sink somewhere in the living area of the home. It doesn't have to be fancy—just a place for guest to "freshen up."

11

Living rooms & family rooms

Some families gather around the kitchen table. Friends come over and gather around the kitchen table. The day begins, ends, and centers around this table. Other families stay out of the kitchen as much as possible. Guests may never even see the kitchen. Meals are taken in the dining room, and afterwards the family gathers in the living room.

Between are the majority. Sometimes the kitchen table is the appropriate location for gathering; sometimes the best place is a living room or family room.

How you design your home depends on your own tastes and lifestyle (but don't forget that designing the home just to fit your lifestyle might hurt the chances for later resale). Is the living room important to you? Do you need both a living room for more formal entertaining *and* a family room for less formal occasions? Perhaps you have children and want a place for them to play, but also don't want them to use the living room.

In addition to these decisions are those rooms set aside for special purposes. Some of these are covered in Chapter 12. This chapter concentrates on what are generally larger areas. Maybe you like to play pool, which is an activity that can easily take up an entire room. Such "game rooms" come close to fitting into the "family room" category and are thus covered in this chapter.

Size

It might sound like a given, but the living room should be designed to be as large—or as small—as you need it to be. You know your needs. (But don't forget to take resale into account. A home with an overly large, very small, or nonexistent living room is going to be harder to sell.)

The smallest should be sufficient to hold at least one couch, two chairs, some kind of coffee table, and still have enough space so that the furniture is not crowded into the room and people can move around comfortably without stepping on each other (FIG. 11-1).

The absolute minimum for a living room is 10 by 12 (120 square feet). Find such a room, or mark the dimensions off. You'll soon see why this is the bare minimum. Especially if the room is enclosed, those in it are going to feel cramped. For this reason, many professional designers discourage anything smaller than about 160 square feet, and sometimes suggest living rooms closer to about twice that (FIG. 11-2).

Before determining the size, consider how the room will be used. Is it just for the family and occasional guests? Or do you often have groups of people gather in your home? Even if you have to bring in chairs from other rooms, there has to be enough floor space to put them down. And if those gatherings require card tables and the like,

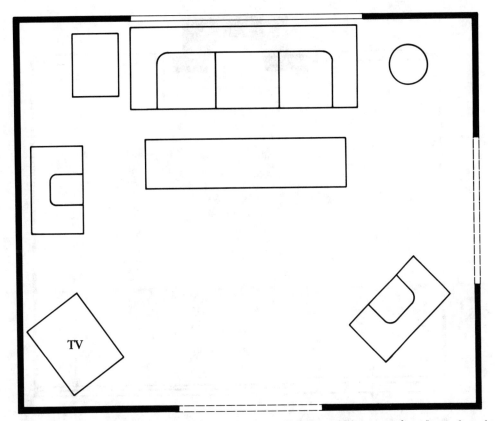

Fig. 11-1. *Even a minimal living room should be no smaller than 120 square feet. It needs to be large enough to hold a couch, two chairs, and coffee table, and still have space for people.*

sufficient space has to be planned for this as well—preferably with a minimum of furniture movement.

The living room also needs sufficient light for the size, both during the day and at night. This means allowing room for at least one window—preferably a large one—and for floor lamps if you don't want ceiling lights.

Ventilation is another concern. (See also Chapter 4.) Ventilation is important in any case, but becomes more so if you, your family, or your guests are smokers, and you allow smoking in the house. You won't always be able to just open the windows (FIG. 11-3).

A smaller room won't require as much light, but it will require better planning for ventilation, especially if the room is enclosed. A larger room will still bring concerns with ventilation, but even greater ones with lighting.

When planning the room, think over placement of the windows carefully. This can make a difference in the needed size. The window sill should be roughly at a height equal to the eye-level of a person sitting down. With rare exception, it should also be high enough so that a couch or chair won't come over the top of the sill. A larger window—one closer to the floor—will preclude placing anything in front of it. That means that the couch, for example, will have to go elsewhere, and the room will consequently have to be larger.

Room Shape

As is so often the case, rectangular living rooms are easier to handle—both in design and in decorating—than odd-shaped rooms (FIG. 11-4). At the same time, the rectangular rooms are more diffi-

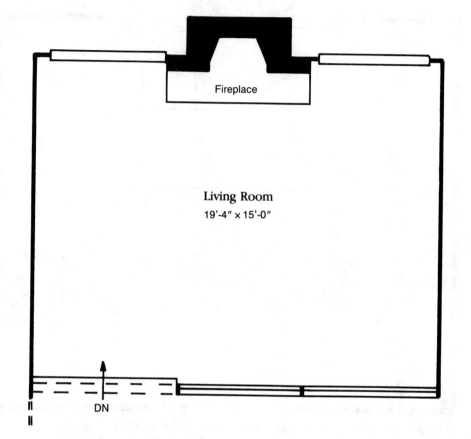

Fireplace

Living Room
19'-4" x 15'-0"

DN

Fig. 11-2. If the living room is to have a fireplace, be sure that there is enough space for it, and for the heat. A fireplace in a too-small room can be uncomfortable.

cult to make dramatic. They're versatile, which is why they are so common, but they are not unique in appearance unless you do something else to them, such as decorating.

A living room will usually have one focal point, or center of attention. This might be a television, or perhaps a fireplace. (Don't have more than two such centers. If there are two many, the room will be too "busy" and disjointed.) Usually this center is at one end of the rectangle, and the rest of the room faces it. With an odd-shaped room, you may find it more difficult to have a center (FIG. 11-5).

Then there is the cost factor. Building a room with curves or angles is more expensive. The more complex the shape, the more expensive it will be. And it will be more expensive to put down a floor covering, since this also has to be cut to fit the shape.

On the positive side, a properly planned room of a shape other than rectangular can add a sense of beauty that might, for your tastes, outweigh the negative. Imagine yourself entering the living room in FIG. 11-5. It would add a distinctive flare to the inside of the home, while doing the same for the outside.

One popular and relatively inexpensive way to change the apparent shape is to use a bay window. They can be large or small—just deep enough to create a window sill capable of holding a number of plants, or deeper yet to create a window seat.

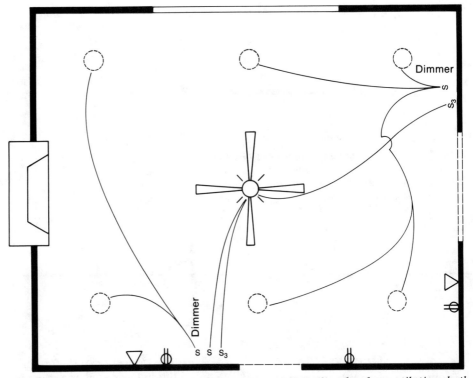

Fig. 11-3. *This living room has a large window and a ceiling fan for ventilation, both of which are made more effective by the openings into the living room. For lighting, in addition to the central ceiling light (a part of the fan) there are 6 "can" lights recessed into the ceiling, all on dimmers to help create whatever mood is desired. Note that the pair by the fireplace are on one dimmer and the other four are on another.*

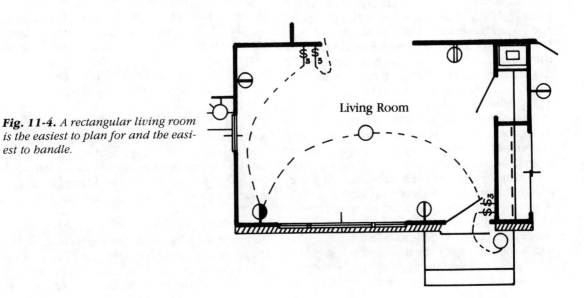

Fig. 11-4. *A rectangular living room is the easiest to plan for and the easiest to handle.*

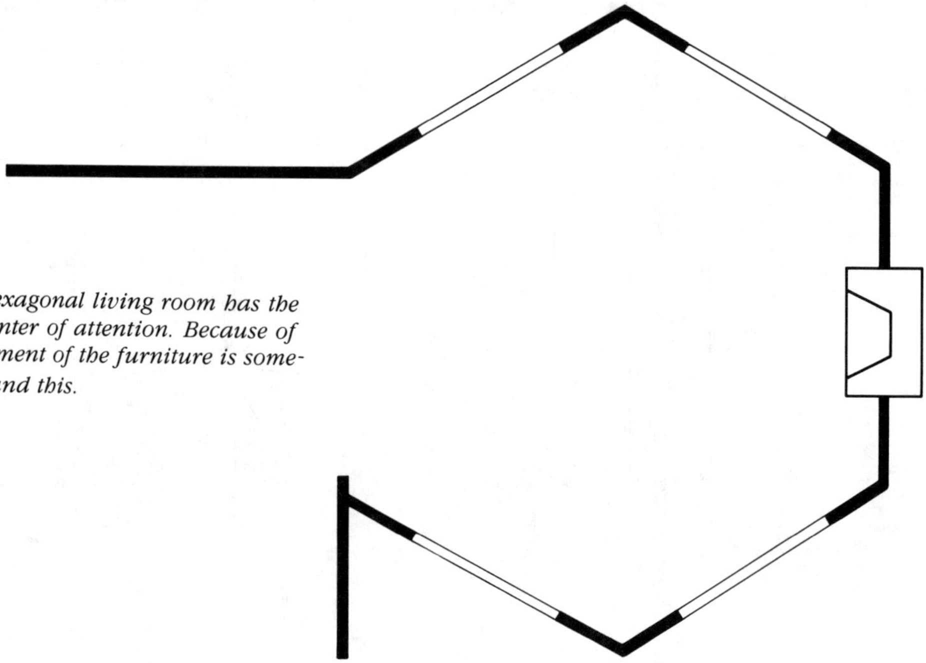

Fig. 11-5. *This hexagonal living room has the fireplace as the center of attention. Because of the shape, arrangement of the furniture is somewhat circular around this.*

Open vs. Closed

A completely closed design would be like a bedroom, with doors that can shut off the room from the rest of the house. While this is common for private areas of the home (the bedroom), it's generally something to avoid for a living room. What's meant by "closed" is simply that there are some walls to at least somewhat isolate the room. The "open" design has few if any walls (see FIGS. 11-6 and 11-7). "Closed" living rooms are more common because they are easier to handle. The second is more dramatic. Perhaps the ideal, if there is such a thing, is somewhere between.

A "closed" living room can still be open to the rest of the home. Use large openings. If there are doors at all, be sure that they can swing or slide out of the way without interfering with the room arrangement.

Many people are used to seeing furniture, televisions, and so on placed up against a wall. With an open design, there are no walls (at least none in two directions). It then becomes more like placing furniture in the middle of a room. The rest of the space has to be designed to reduce this effect. For example, you might use half-walls (partitions that come up just a few feet from the floor).

This concept can be further increased by sinking the living room area, thus leaving it open while still setting it off on its own (FIG. 11-8).

You'll notice that both are heading towards a middle ground. The "closed" living room is opened, while the "open" design is closed. There are many varying degrees of each until they meet in the middle with a design that isn't either open or closed. It's extremely rare to find a purely closed or open design—and usually neither works very well.

You have to decide which factors are more important to you and plan accordingly.

Living Room Placement

As mentioned in the last chapter, the living room can be separate or integral to the dining room. It can be located off the kitchen or set off on its own. Each scheme has its own advantages and disadvantages. Most of these are determined by your lifestyle.

With most homes, the living room is located very near the front door. The reason is obvious. If the main entrance is in the front and the main area for guests is in the back, everyone is forced to walk through the house when they come to visit.

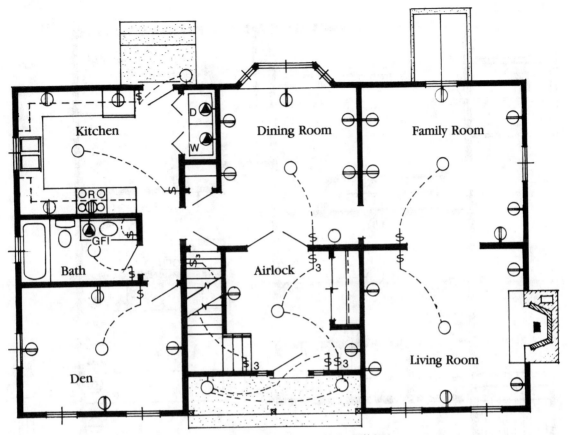

Fig. 11-6. *A first floor plan with a "closed" living room.*

(See "Family Rooms" below, where the condition is reversed.)

As mentioned in Chapter 6, smaller homes often have the front door open directly into the living room. With fewer square feet, it's difficult to afford the space for an entry hall.

If you *can,* it's best to have some kind of entry area. This might be a foyer or simply a short hall that splits to lead into the living room and other areas of the home.

Even if the living room is separate (closed design), it is a part of the whole house. The inter-relationship between rooms determines its location. The living room is often connected to the kitchen, which makes it easier to bring coffee, snacks, or whatever to the guests. If the home will also have a dining room, it's more important to connect the dining room to the kitchen. Because both the living room and dining room tend to be large, it takes careful planning if both are to be accessible from the kitchen (see FIGS. 11-9 and 11-10).

As mentioned in Chapter 9, the kitchen is usually the center of the home. Placement of the dining room, if you have one, takes priority. It doesn't make much sense to have the living room connected directly to the kitchen at the expense of having the dining room isolated from the kitchen.

The Family Room

Is there a difference between a living room and a family room? Yes and no. Traditionally, a living room is for entertaining guests more formally, while a family room is less formal (and often messier)—a center for family and friends, and a place for the kids to play. Usually the same room

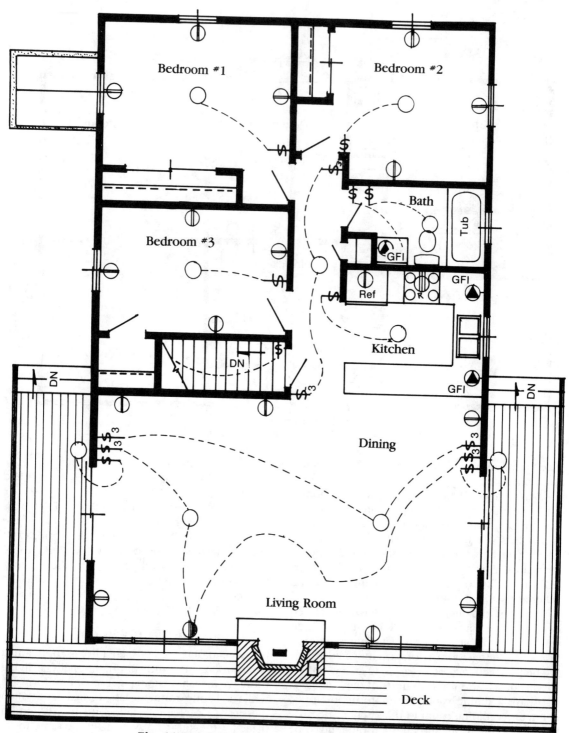

Fig. 11-7. *A floor plan with an "open" living room.*

Bedroom #1

Bedroom #2

Bedroom #3

Bath

Tub

GFI

Ref

R

GFI

Kitchen

GFI

DN

DN

DN

Dining

Living Room

Deck

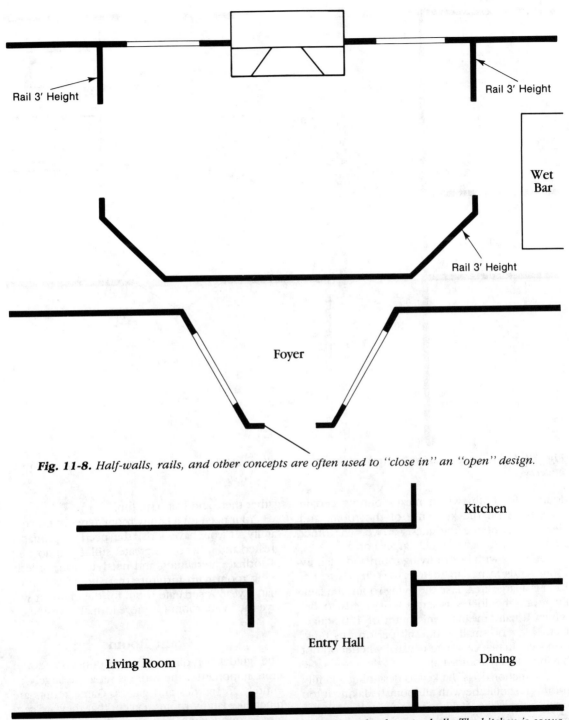

Fig. 11-8. Half-walls, rails, and other concepts are often used to "close in" an "open" design.

Fig. 11-9. This design separates the dining room and living room by the entry hall. The kitchen is convenient for both. Transition for guests between the living room and dining room is easy.

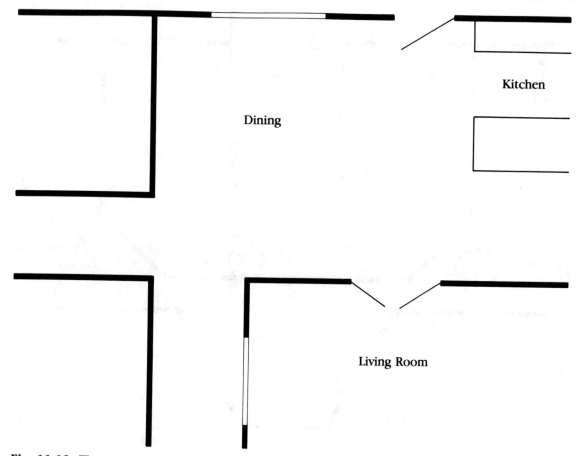

Fig. 11-10. *The open design of kitchen/dining areas allows the living room to also be connected to the kitchen.*

doubles for both, which means putting certain restrictions on the kids' use of the room, and cleaning up before the guests arrive. The other alternative is to have a much larger home.

A home with both a living room and a family room tends to be large (FIG. 11-11). It has to be. Each is a large area. Like the living room, the family room should be as large as it needs to be, which usually means a minimum of 120 square feet. If it's too small, it doesn't perform its function well. In that case, you're usually better off not having a family room at all.

"Functional" is the key to designing a family room. (It should be with all rooms!) Making it too small is a mistake. Making it too formal—with too many "You can't do that's"—also defeats the purpose. The family and friends should be able to

gather there and just have fun.

Your need for a family room depends on your family. If you have kids, the need is probably greater, and it becomes greater still if you do a lot of formal entertaining and need a clean, orderly living room with furniture that should last more than a year. A separate room for the children will save the living room for more formal occasions.

Game Rooms

The guidelines discussed above become even more important if the room is set aside largely or entirely for parties and games. Game rooms are much like family rooms, except that they are centered around games and often around just one—a pool table, for example.

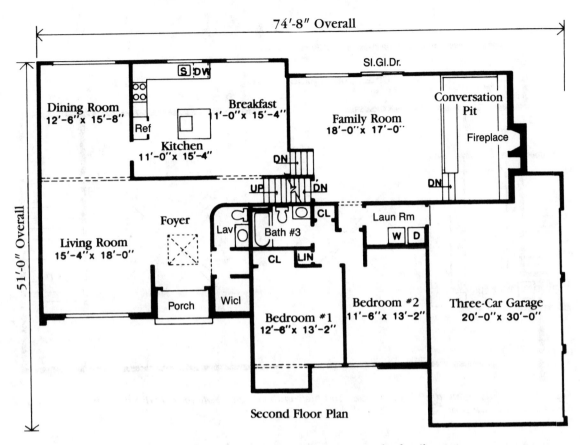

Fig. 11-11. *A home with both a living room and a family room.*

A 4-by-8 pool table, with just 3 feet of room for movement around it, requires a 10-by-14 room. That provides just enough room for use of the table and nothing else. If you want room for chairs, still more is needed (unless those seated don't mind ducking while the players make their shots). In addition, most pool tables are too heavy to move easily.

Other games might take less room. A 4-by-4 card table with chairs will take up half the room and can be moved more easily. (A collapsible table can even be tucked into a closet—if the closet is large enough.)

You can even find special "game-room carpet," with a variety of games as the pattern. One part might be a chess/checker board, another backgammon, still another might be Parcheesi. There are a number of board games, and many of

them can become a part of the floor.

It's fairly common to have the living quarters on the main floor, and the "game" area in a basement. (See Chapter 13.) This keeps the noise away from the rest of the house, which comes in handy if the adults are upstairs in the living room and the kids are in the basement with the pool table or games (FIG. 11-12).

A Very Special "Game" Room

This book has concentrated, and will continue to concentrate, on practical and functional ideas. This one time it will "splurge" on a dramatic and expensive idea—an indoor pool.

When I was growing up in Minneapolis, I always regretted that there were just a few months out of the year when we could go swimming.

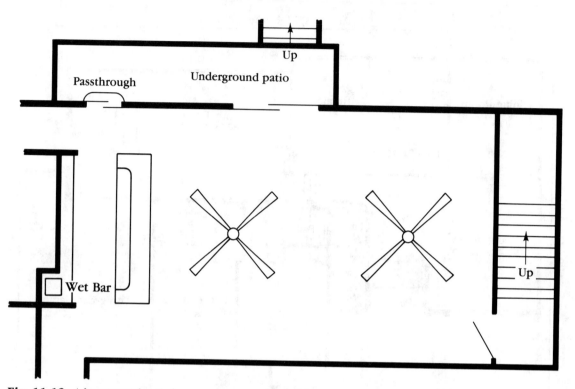

Fig. 11-12. *A basement family/game room, complete with wet bar. Note the arcadia door and ceiling fans for increased ventilation.*

Up

Passthrough

Underground patio

Wet Bar

Up

There weren't many indoor pools and almost all required a membership of some sort. In one of the suburbs a man had designed a home with a pool room. More, the room had a balcony, which was the access to the high board.

The cost of such a room is high (even without a board off a balcony). The cost of the pool itself is a given. Then comes the structure around it. Because of the extra moisture, proper ventilation is of extreme importance. Even then, you have to take the moisture into account. And if the pool is to be of any use year round, heating and cooling are crucial.

Having such a room is a luxury. If you intend to resell the home and property and recoup the costs, you'll require a special type of buyer. You'd get back some of it in lower maintenance costs for the pool. (Being inside, it won't get so much dirt and debris in it.)

One compromise is to have the pool located in a central area, with the home built around it. This makes it very difficult to access the pool for heavier maintenance, however. A better idea is to have one side open, of course with sufficient room allowed for the workers to gain access (see FIGS. 11-13 and 11-14).

A pool—inside or outside—is a "game room" with special concerns. There has to be plumbing to and from, which becomes even more complicated if you install a heater. The entire area has to be waterproof, and if enclosed, the increased moisture level is of concern.

Topping the list is that of security. Accidental drowning is one of the biggest killers of children. Any pool area, regardless of where it is, *must* be secure to protect children. Kids have the ability to defeat the best of systems. A locked gate is sometimes no more than a challenge to climb the fence. Still, it's your duty to do as much as you can.

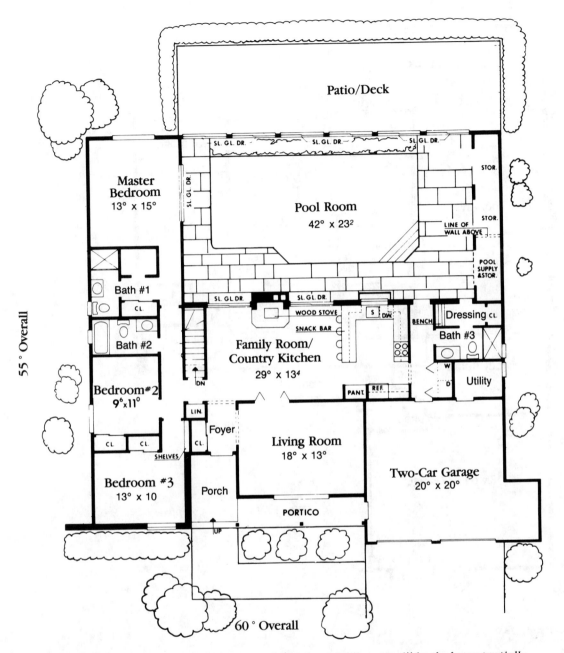

55° Overall

Patio/Deck

Master Bedroom
13° x 15°

SL. GL. DR.

Pool Room
42° x 23²

STOR.

LINE OF WALL ABOVE

STOR.

SL. GL. DR.

POOL SUPPLY & STOR.

Bath #1

CL.

SL. GL. DR.

SL. GL. DR.

WOOD STOVE

S

DW

Dressing

CL.

BENCH

Bath #3

Bath #2

SNACK BAR

Family Room/
Country Kitchen
29° x 13⁴

DN

Bedroom#2
9⁶x11⁰

PANT.

REF.

W

D

Utility

CL.

CL.

SHELVES

LIN.

Foyer

CL.

Living Room
18° x 13°

Two-Car Garage
20° x 20°

Bedroom #3
13° x 10

Porch

PORTICO

UP

60° Overall

Fig. 11-13. *To reduce dust and increase privacy, the pool can be "wrapped" by the home partially . . .*

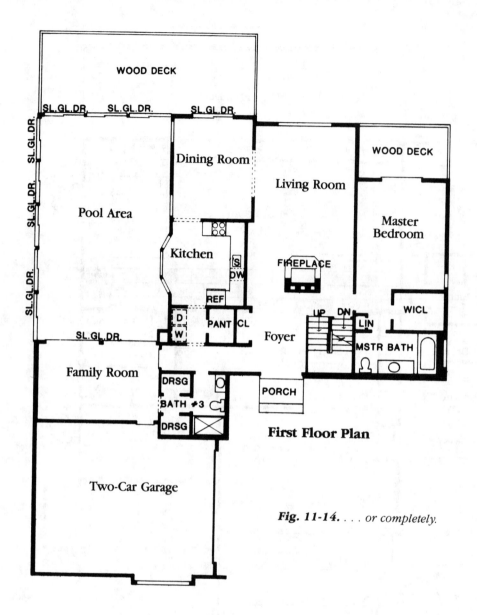

WOOD DECK

SL.GL.DR. SL.GL.DR. SL.GL.DR.

SL.GL.DR.

Dining Room

WOOD DECK

Living Room

SL.GL.DR.

Pool Area

Master
Bedroom

Kitchen

S

DW

FIREPLACE

SL.GL.DR.

REF

WICL

D
W

PANT CL

UP   DN

LIN

Foyer

MSTR BATH

SL.GL.DR.

Family Room

DRSG

BATH #3

PORCH

DRSG

First Floor Plan

Two-Car Garage

Fig. 11-14. . . . *or completely.*

12

Rooms for work & relaxation

There are many things people do, some from necessity and others just for the fun of it. You might want a room for sewing, painting, building, repairing and tinkering, operating amateur radios or computers, kit- or model-making, photography, or you just might want a room for displaying a collection to use as a library and/or study.

Quite often this room is meant to do "double duty." What serves as a study for you might be used as a spare bedroom by the next owner. (Maybe it will serve both for you.) Or perhaps a corner of an existing room is set aside for this other function, such as having a counter installed in the laundry room for sewing.

Some of your needs might bring special requirements. A darkroom *must* be sealed against light and have a source of water (and a drain to take the water out again). The floor should be, at very least, linoleum to reduce dust and to make cleaning up chemical spills easy. A room for computers or other electrical equipment will need enough electrical outlets. Any room where you will spend a lot of time should probably have at least one phone outlet as well.

Then there are those activities that are potentially messy. Sawing wood is going to leave sawdust on the floor and in the air. Working with ceramics is not only messy, if you have a kiln you'll need special wiring and a way to vent all that heat away. Working on a car is messy and requires plenty of room and ventilation.

Functionality is the key. Will the room do what it's supposed to do in the way you want it? Usually, an existing room is adapted to the need. But because *you* are designing the home, you can also design the rooms so that they don't have to be adapted.

Location

Where you place the room depends on several things, primarily on the purpose of the room. If the activity will be noisy, messy, or fumy, you will probably want to locate it outside, or at least near an end of the home.

Other times you'll want the room to be integral to the rest of the home, or to a certain part of the home. A sewing room is often a part of, or attached to, the laundry room, which in turn is often attached to the kitchen. If someone does a lot of sewing, you may wish to be more centrally located.

Then there are various special needs to consider. A weight room needs to be located where the floor is solid enough to withstand some occasional accidents. A room with a spa or pool will need plumbing, special electrical circuits, a floor and walls that can tolerate the moisture, and extra ventilation. The combination *could* dictate the location. More so if you also wish to have the area accessible to guests, or if you want complete privacy.

If you want an artist's studio, you might want to locate it where there can be a lot of windows, both for light and for the scenery (FIG. 12-1). A darkroom requires just the opposite and, therefore, should have some degree of isolation.

Electrical Needs

As mentioned elsewhere, the standard is to have an electrical outlet for every 12 feet of running wall. Unless you specifically call out something different, each branch circuit will handle a mixed batch of outlets and lights. For ordinary uses this is fine. It may not be if you have special needs.

Some things draw more current. If you like ceramics and want your own kiln, that special oven is almost certainly going to require special wiring (and special ventilation for the heat). Some power tools also require special wiring or dedicated circuits. Other hobbies don't require circuits capable of carrying a lot of current, but *do*

need a lot of outlets to plug in various things.

It's a common failure not to plan ahead. Code calls for one outlet every 12 running feet, but you might find yourself using outlet cubes or extension cords to provide enough places to plug in. Try to determine the number of outlets and the current draw while designing these areas of the home. If you need to plug in a number of items, plan for extra outlets. If one or more of those pieces draws heavily, think of *at least* providing dedicated circuits, of the proper amperage.

Lighting

Most people prefer natural light whenever possible. That's accomplished with windows of one sort or another. These can be standard windows, large picture windows, wraparound windows like in a greenhouse, or skylights (FIG. 12-2).

What natural light doesn't do must be done by artificial light. This can be incandescent or fluorescent, mounted to the ceiling or wall, or set on a table or the floor. Such guidelines hold true of

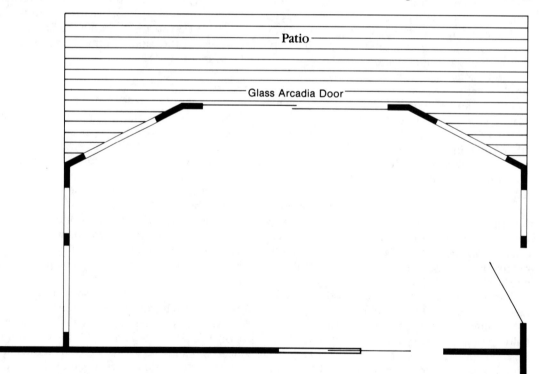

Fig. 12-1. *This location and design might be perfect for an artist's studio. It's not at all suitable for a darkroom.*

Fig. 12-2. *Skylights are windows in the roof.*

any room in the home. It's stressed here because hobby rooms and home offices are some of the most important areas as far as effective lighting is concerned. These are rooms where work is being done.

In a shop, especially if power tools are to be used, there has to be light and plenty of it. "Shop lights" are one name used for overhead fluorescent lights (FIG.12-3). Their purpose is to provide a general, diffused lighting for the area.

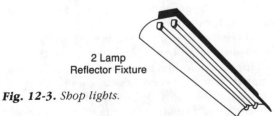

2 Lamp
Reflector Fixture

Fig. 12-3. *Shop lights.*

15"

15"

12"

Fig. 12-4. *Task lighting provides light exactly where it is needed.*

In addition to the general lighting, there may also be a need for task lighting. Task lighting provides light to a specific area (FIG. 12-4). For example, light from a ceiling fixture isn't always the best to use for sewing, reading, or performing any detailed work.

View the room and its purpose. What will be done and where? Only then can you design the lighting that will be needed. (And keep in mind that even if some of the lights are to be portable, they'll still need electrical outlets.)

Ventilation

As with lighting, the basic principles of ventilation apply to all rooms, including any special areas you design. As with lighting, ventilation can become very important under certain circumstances.

A darkroom is going to have chemical fumes. While only a few of these are dangerous, if the fumes are allowed to build up, being in the darkroom isn't going to be pleasant. An exercise room without proper ventilation has "fumes" of its own that will build up, too.

In some areas, proper ventilation can mean the difference between life and death. Working on an engine in a closed area is inviting disaster. It becomes, almost literally, a gas chamber unless the carbon monoxide and other fumes are vented outside. The same is true of the use of certain solvents.

In still other areas, inadequate ventilation won't kill you, but it can make the room much less pleasant—especially if there are smokers around.

The overall ventilation begins with the heating/air conditioning system, but it only begins there. A common mistake is to give the room an adequate air inlet, but allow no way for the air to get back out. (Having a return vent in the hall just outside doesn't do much good when the door is closed.)

Windows are of great help, especially when working in conjunction with other windows to create cross-ventilation. However, you can't rely totally on this. There will be times when you won't want the windows open.

The solution depends on the circumstances. Adding a ceiling fan might be all that's needed. (Maybe you can even get by with using a portable box fan when extra ventilation is needed.) The circumstances could also dictate the need for an extra air-return duct in that area. Yet another solution—more common because it's easier—is to have outlet ducts or ports installed. These can be as simple as a baffled hole through a door or wall, or as complex as a duct with its own fan. (This latter solution is little more than a modification of

the standard bathroom venting fan—that alone might be enough.)

Communications?

These days, almost every home in America has at least one phone, and many have two or three. Three key (and common) spots are living room, kitchen, and bedroom. Don't forget, though, that there are other spots where having a telephone, or at least a telephone jack, can be advantageous.

Just as the telephone can keep you in touch with the world, an intercom can keep you in touch inside the home. There are many times when that special room needs to be in communication with the rest of the house. This becomes more important depending on the amount of time you'll spend there and on the degree of isolation.

Perhaps the studio you intend to use in the afternoons while the baby is napping is in the opposite corner of the house. By having an intercom in both rooms, you can hear if the baby wakes. By having one at the front door, you can answer the door on the first ring, without having to leave your studio. (Having a telephone in the studio gives you similar benefits.)

During construction, it's very easy and relatively inexpensive to install extra wires for telephone outlets or intercoms (or for connection to a stereo). Doing so later is considerably more difficult.

During the designing stage, think carefully about any place you *might* want a telephone, intercom, or other device requiring wiring. Consider both communications with the world outside the home (telephone) and within the home (intercom). Where appropriate, don't forget about cables to televisions.

Even if you're not sure if a telephone or intercom will ever go into a particular room, think of where you'd locate them in the room *if* you wanted them. It's a simple matter during construction to run the wires to that spot, then to another accessible spot (such as the attic). The lower end doesn't have to come through the wall. All you need is to know where you can get at it if you want to. Neither end has to be connected to anything at all (FIG. 12-5).

The cost of wire for such a scheme is low.

Fig. 12-5. *The best time to run wires for a telephone or intercom is during the framing and before the drywall is installed.*

You can get by with even less by running sturdy twine instead. This would later be used as a pull cord for the real wire *if* you decided that you wanted it. (Here's a hint: *If* you do this, and *if* you use the twine to pull a wire, pull through another length of twine at the same time. That way, if ever another wire is needed in that spot, you can pull it through without disturbing the existing wire.)

Laundry Rooms

Unless you take all of your dirty clothes to a cleaner or laundromat, you'll need some place in the home for a washer and dryer. The area can range from a laundry closet to an actual laundry room (FIGS. 12-6 and 12-7).

A laundry closet is usually just large enough to hold the two appliances. This saves space but makes maintenance difficult. It also brings with it a greater risk of water damage to the home if the "closet" is located inside.

If you can afford the space, have a separate laundry room. It will make doing the laundry much less toilsome and maintenance or repairs will be easier. If designed properly, you can avoid causing water damage to the rest of the home should the washer overflow or leak.

The most common location is off the kitchen (see FIG. 12-7). There are several reasons for this. First, it allows you to monitor the clothes washing while working in the kitchen. Second, it isolates the noise from the rest of the house. Third, it allows shared plumbing.

Another common place for the laundry room is outside the main part of the house, often as a part of a storage area, one that may also hold the water heater. This is unsuitable in colder areas unless the room is heated and the pipes placed where they won't freeze.

A minimum of 5 feet is needed to hold the standard washer and dryer. That squeezes them

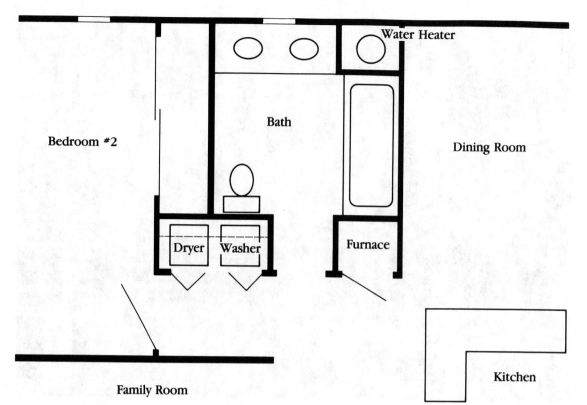

Fig. 12-6. *The simplest laundry room isn't a room at all, but a glorified closet.*

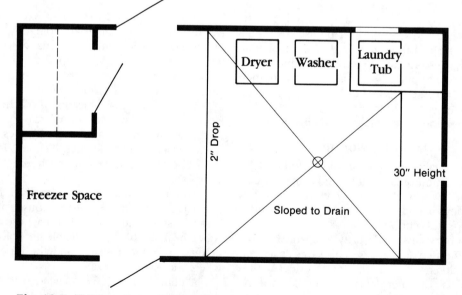

Fig. 12-7. *This laundry room is sunken and sloped to a floor drain. Note the large laundry tub and the desk-height counter.*

together with no extra room. It's normally better to plan the space to be just a little larger so that maintenance and repairs can be performed more easily.

Sufficient space must also be allowed to move comfortably in the room. If you allow 3 feet in addition to the approximately 3 feet needed for the appliance and its hookups, you'll have enough space to move, and enough space to pull out either appliance for servicing. Thus, the smallest practical laundry room is 5 by 6.

By adding just 2 more feet in length, you can also add a tub and a counter. This minor bit of extra space greatly increases the utility of the room. One foot more will allow a larger tub or some extra space to make servicing the appliances easier.

It's fairly simple to also add a corner (or larger area) to make the room a combined laundry/sewing room. In the room shown in FIG. 12-8 there is 3 feet of counter space. If set at "desk height" (as in FIG. 12-7), a portable sewing machine can be placed on the counter for use. (You can also design a section of the counter to swing a sewing machine up for use and down when you need the counter.)

The greatest disadvantages of this are noise and lack of room. If you or someone in your

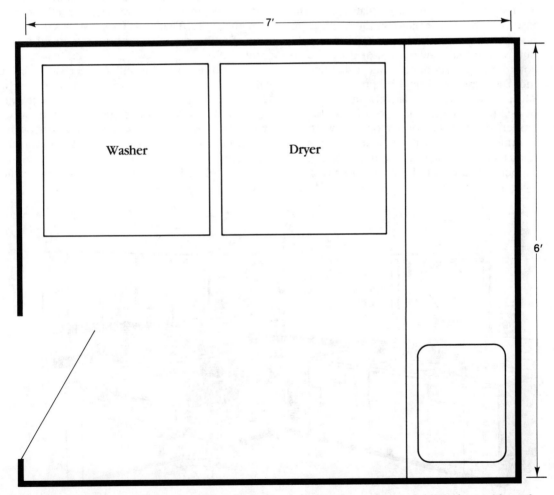

Fig. 12-8. *A laundry room that measures 7 by 6 can squeeze in the washer and dryer along with a tub and counter, and still provide room for movement.*

household intends to do a lot of sewing, it's sometimes better to provide a separate room for this. At very least the laundry/sewing room should be larger to accommodate the needs of the person working in it (FIG. 12-9).

Another direction the laundry room can take is as a "mud room." A sink and usually a toilet are added, along with a door to the outside. This then becomes an entrance when someone has been working in the yard or has otherwise gotten dirty. There's no need, then, to track dirt through the house, or water, if you have a pool (FIG. 12-10).

Dens and Sitting Rooms

A den or sitting room is usually isolated. Its basic purpose is to be a quiet and subdued place to relax. Depending on your choice, it can be bright and sunny with lots of windows, or it can be an interior room with subdued artificial lighting to enhance the sense of privacy and peace.

Most often, a den is relatively small. It isn't meant as a place to entertain a lot of people. It's more often a quiet place for just one or two people. For this purpose, it will have at least one comfortable chair, or perhaps a sofa if you prefer to stretch out. It will usually have a shelf or two for books or a stereo. It might also have desk. If you

decide to make the den larger, it can also serve as a spare bedroom.

How you design and decorate the interior of the room is entirely up to you (FIG. 12-11). Through the rest of the house, utility has to be taken into account. The den is more of an individual retreat and can be furnished to taste. As such, the traditional den will be fairly well isolated, with the walls insulated against sound.

One step up from this is a den that doubles as an entertainment center. Such a step puts it halfway between being a den and being a family room. A step to the side and the room can double as an office. In many cases all you need do is to add a desk and perhaps a filing cabinet. Either way, you begin to move away from "den" and into something else. That's just fine. It shows the versatility of such a room. Its purpose is to be what *you* want it to be.

A "sitting room" is still another variation. It can be a quiet place for one or two people, or it can be more like an enclosed patio (and there's no *absolute* reason for it to be enclosed) with lots of windows. The former is sometimes a part of the master bedroom, to become a private and romantic place for a couple. The latter might be more centrally located and accessible to general traffic flow.

Fig. 12-9. *By making the laundry room just a little larger, one side can be used as a sewing center.*

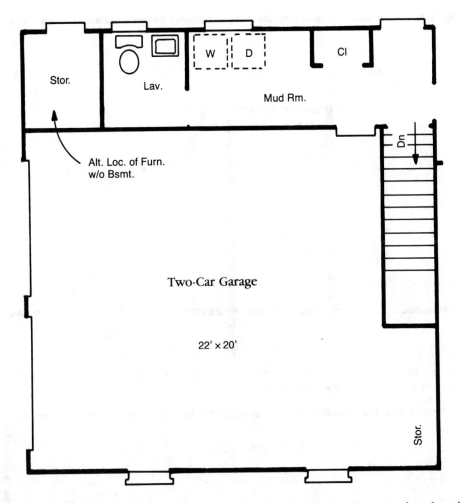

Fig. 12-10. *The mud room in this partial floor plan is a part of the laundry room but doesn't have an attached sewing room, as does Fig. 12-9.*

Library

Almost every home has a variety of books, some more than others. If your own collection will fit on a single shelf, or even in one bookcase, there is probably no need to have a library in your home.

Quite often dens and libraries are very much the same. The focus of a den is to have a quiet place to relax. More often than not the den will have shelves of books, at least one comfortable place to sit, and perhaps a desk as well. The focus of a library is the books. However, it will usually have at least one comfortable place to sit and perhaps a desk as well.

As you can see, the difference is the focus of the room. A den concentrates on being quiet and comfortable, but usually has books in it; the library concentrates on books, but usually is quiet and comfortable.

The easiest room to make into a library is rectangular and fairly large (depending on how many books, how many shelves, and many other things). Unlike many dens, a library doesn't have as much window space because much of the wall space is used for books. However, at least one window should be provided for light and ventilation and also to prevent the room from seeming too dreary (FIG. 12-12).

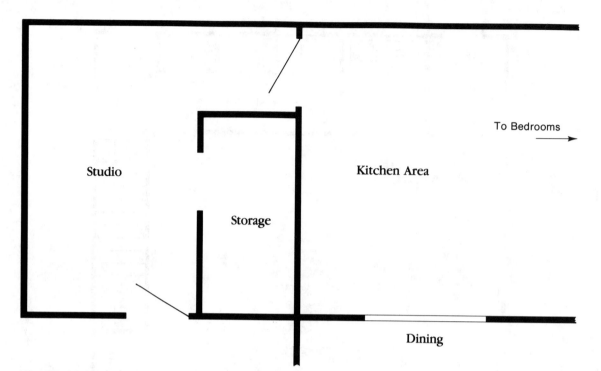

Fig. 12-11. *This studio is attached to the kitchen and has its own private entrance. This makes it easy to convert, either to an office or to an eating area.*

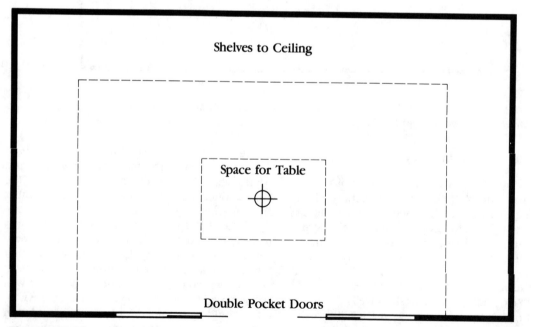

Fig. 12-12. *The easiest room to build into a library is rectangular with plenty of wall space and few windows.*

The shelves generally line the available walls. If the room is large enough (and you have enough books to warrant it), there may also be a central, usually double-sided, shelf. (See FIGS. 12-13 through 12-15.)

Home Office

Another room much like a den is the home office. Add a desk to what was a den, and it can serve nicely as an office. One difference is that while the den tends to be designed and decorated with a subdued approach, the office is usually brighter and more open in tone. If clients will be coming, the home office will usually have its own entrance, or at least an entrance that can be used without disturbing the rest of the household.

The location and size depends on your needs (FIG. 12-16). If you work there day by day as your sole income, you owe it to yourself to make it nice. This becomes less important if the office is being used for a few hours per week and only at night. In any case, it needs to be large enough for you to do what is necessary. It makes little sense to have a room called an "office" when it's too small for anything to be done in it.

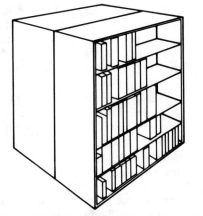

Fig. 12-13. *A central shelf can be double-sided, like two bookcases placed back-to-back . . .*

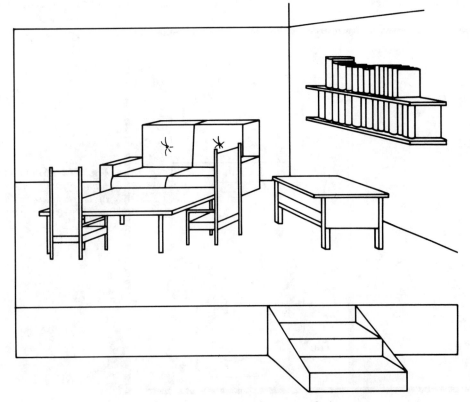

Fig. 12-14. *. . . or it can be of an open design . . .*

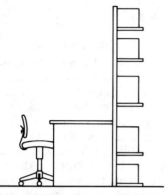

Fig. 12-15. . . . *or it can be one-sided, with the other set for other purposes.*

Darkroom

A darkroom, by its nature, has some special requirements. First, it's supposed to be just what the name says—dark. *All* light has to be blocked out. Simply closing a standard door and turning off the light isn't enough. Not only can this be troublesome as far as design and construction is

concerned, it brings with it another problem—ventilation.

A darkroom creates fumes. Those fumes can build up in a sealed room. It's fine to have a window in a darkroom (as long as it is light tight), but it's of no use when you need it most. And if vent ducting isn't designed just right, it can let in light while taking out the fumes. In addition, there are the usual problems of being sure that the electrical needs of the darkroom are met, and that there is plumbing.

Making the room dark can be done in any number of ways. It's easiest if you begin with an isolated room in a fairly dark part of the home (or one that can be made dark). This reduces the amount of light that has to be blocked. You can create your own "isolation" by building a maze of sorts for the entrance—like a bent hallway. The inside is painted flat black. This in conjunction with doors or at least lightproof curtains on both ends of the trap will do a fairly effective job of keeping out the light (FIG. 12-17). The disadvantages of this are that it takes up space that could be

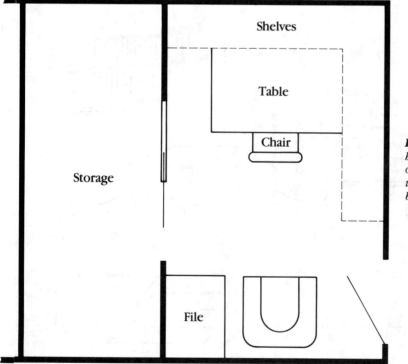

Fig. 12-16. *A minimum home office needs some kind of work space, storage, and usually some shelving for books.*

put to better use, and it makes getting in and out of the darkroom, especially with any equipment or supplies, much more difficult.

Easier and more efficient is to seal the doors. The classic method is to make an oversized door stop with generous weatherstripping to create a seal. If you use a pocket door, as I did, the job is easier and more effective since the seal is on both sides of the door.

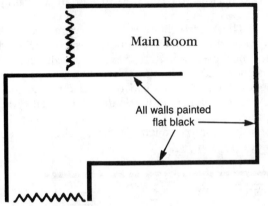

Fig. 12-17. *A light trap as an entrance.*

The usual way of handling ventilation is to use either active or passive light traps, either in the door or in a wall. The active kind has its own fan, which means that it will need electricity. The passive kind relies on the incoming air from the heating/air conditioning system to push the air in the room out.

In my case, the darkroom is in the basement, which makes venting through the wall difficult. I have pocket doors, which makes using door mounted vents impossible. Besides, I didn't want to vent the fumes into other parts of the basement. Instead I had ceiling vents with fans installed. These blow the air into flexible ducting that goes up through the roof. To be *sure* that no light could find its way in, the inside of the ducting was sprayed with flat black paint, and it was made into two loops before exiting through the roof.

The shape of the darkroom is determined much like that of a kitchen (FIG. 12-18). There is a work triangle to consider between enlarger, trays, and sink. In addition, an effective darkroom will

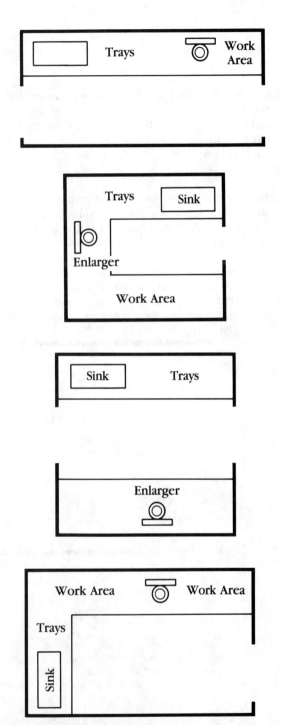

Fig. 12-18. *Darkroom shapes are similar to those used in kitchen design.*

have "dry" and "wet" areas, with sufficient space between them that contamination doesn't become a problem.

The smallest darkroom should be no smaller than 5 by 5. That just barely gives you enough room for a sink, counter space for the minimal three trays, room for the enlarger and just enough left over for turning. If you can afford the space, consider a room 8 by 8 as the smallest.

Gym

The exercise craze has reached across America. Slowly but surely we are becoming a healthier nation. More and more people are doing aerobics and other exercises regularly. Many are doing so at home.

Some exercise programs can be done within just a few square feet. Others require much more room (FIG. 12-19). You can do most aerobic exercises in a space just large enough for you to lie down, and to swing your arms and legs freely. However, if your "thing" is dancing or martial arts, you'll need the space for it.

However you design it, the room should be large enough to be airy. There is a need for good ventilation, but without creating obvious or strong breezes. The room shouldn't be too hot, too cold, too humid or too dry. Keep in mind that the purpose of the room is too help you develop good health. You can't do that in an unhealthy room.

The kind of floor can be very important. A very hard floor, such as concrete, is to be avoided for most exercises. It's too easy to sustain damage to your ankles. The floor should have some resiliency. Exercise mats can be used for small-area exercises; carpet (indoor/outdoor is usually the preferred type) with decent padding might be the solution. Or you might prefer a polished wood floor.

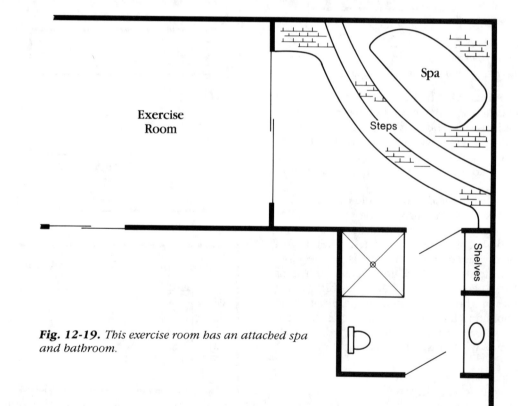

Fig. 12-19. *This exercise room has an attached spa and bathroom.*

Shops

Almost every home has some kind of workshop—if you can call it that. Often it's a disorganized section of the garage where some basic tools are stuffed in a box and some scattered, miscellaneous materials for maintenance of the home and car are piled onto a shelf.

With just a little effort, you can have an area that will serve its purpose much better. Instead of taking up room, it can save room. This is the most basic, and will be discussed in more detail in Chapter 14. However, this brief preview is important since a more complex home workshop begins with this basic.

The key is organization. "A place for everything and everything in its place." Even if you're not interested in building things, there will still be some basic household tools and supplies, both for the house itself and for the yard. These have to be stored somewhere (FIG. 12-20).

A separate storage area might be used for the lawnmower, snow blower, and so on, or these might be assigned to one part of the garage, or to a part of the shop. The latter two are often the same, since the most common shop is in the garage.

The location and size, once again, depends on what you intend to do, and how much space is required. You might be able to squeeze all your needs into a portable "shop" of some kind that can be tucked into a closet when not in use. Or you might need sufficient room to store and handle sheets and planks of wood, or space enough to have an engine hoist lift the engine from a car.

The basic workbench is 24 inches to 30 inches in width, 4 feet to 7 feet in length, and 30 to 34 inches in height. You can modify this to suit your needs. This bench can be a part of the shelving, can jut out from the shelves and counters as a peninsula, or can be an island of its own (FIG. 12-21), perhaps with casters on the legs so it can be easily rolled. The first take up more space and require preplanning. The last can be built almost any time.

The first two can also be a part of the storage. Counter space along the walls is a natural for having cabinets above and below. Designed carefully, the combination of shelves, cabinets and counters can provide all the storage you'll need.

You have the advantage in designing your own home—and your own shop—in that you can design the space just as you want it without it interfering with other activities or needs. You don't have to do what most people are forced to do—that is, to sacrifice a part of the garage. Since you are designing your own home, you can either plan for a larger garage to allow for the shop, or you can plan for a separate (or attached) shop area of the appropriate size (FIG. 12-22).

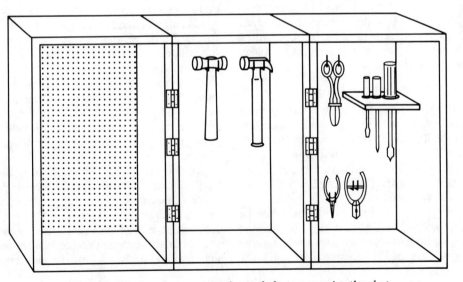

Fig. 12-20. *A tool storage rack can help to organize the shop.*

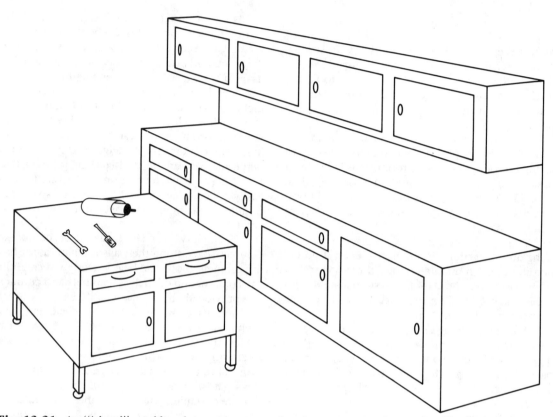

Fig. 12-21. *An "island" workbench provides access from all directions. By putting casters on the legs, it can also be moved.*

A good way to begin is with an ideal, tempered with realism. Your dream might be to have a 30 by 40 shop, but can you afford it? Your option will be to cut it in size, with a design that makes maximum use of the space.

Other Hobby Rooms

Once again we return to the adage of how a room should be as large as it needs to be. There are thousands of different hobbies. Some take very little room, while others can fill a warehouse if given the chance. Some can be done in a very small area, and others will require a very large room if they are to be done correctly.

If your hobby is amateur radio, you might be able to get by with as little as a 2-by-3 counter and enough room for a chair. (Such a spot will need to be located so that the cables can pass through the walls to the antennas.) Or you might like to make quilts and will need to have the space to set up the form for long periods of time. Model or kit building will require sufficient counter and/or table surface area for all the parts.

There are nearly as many variations and possibilities as there are hobbies. What there isn't is one single solution. In short, there is really no such thing as a "hobby room." The closest is a spare room that happens to be adapted to the hobby.

Once again, by designing your own home, you can make the room into whatever you wish it to be. Determine (realistically) what your needs are and design accordingly. Don't forget the possibilities that more than one person might be using the room at the same time or that more than one activity can be planned for the same room.

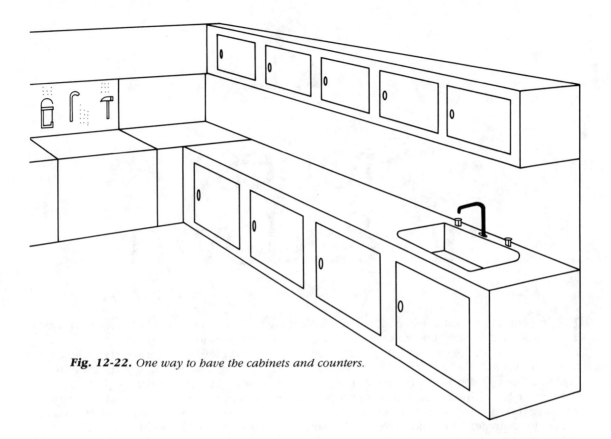

Fig. 12-22. *One way to have the cabinets and counters.*

13

Stories, up & down

If you want more floor space, it's generally less expensive to build up or down than out. This is true in three ways. First, the more your house sprawls out, the more land you'll need to hold it. A 30-by-40-foot home represents roughly 1200 square feet of space. To get 2400 square feet you can either increase the dimensions (60 feet by 40 feet, for example), which means that the lot has to be considerably larger, or you can build a full basement below or a full second level above. Same lot, twice the living space.

Second, a larger single-level home requires a larger roof. For each square foot, you're building a complete home. However, when floors are stacked, only one smaller roof is needed. That reduces expenses considerably.

The third way concerns ongoing costs of heating and cooling. In either direction, up or down, one floor helps to "protect" the other. An upper floor makes heating and cooling the main floor easier. A basement is underground (at least in part). As such it tends to maintain a fairly steady temperature. At worst, the insulative value of the ground makes heating and cooling of a basement easy and relatively inexpensive.

Up or Down?

There are two basic considerations to take into account when deciding which way to go. Both

have to do with cost, and both are determined by a number of factors.

Building upwards is almost always less expensive. Building downwards requires excavation. In some areas this can be outrageously expensive. For example, if there is bedrock 2 feet beneath the surface, digging down for a basement is going to be costly—maybe impossible.

Second, a basement often requires some special walls if the basement is to be free from leaks. You could be in one of those areas where the water table is just a few feet beneath the surface, in which case the walls have to hold back an almost literal pool of water. Ground also tends to be somewhat corrosive. Untreated wood, for example, will rot away quickly in almost every area.

However, if the ground (and local restrictions) allows it, a basement is generally less expensive in the long run due to the lower utility bills (FIG. 13-1). The ground acts as an insulator. The basement is like a home underground.

Meanwhile, there is the simple matter of physics: heat rises. Especially in the warmer states and almost everywhere during the summer, trying to keep an upper floor cool is more costly than keeping a basement cool. For that matter, keeping an upper floor warm during the winter is more costly than keeping a full basement warm.

In a hot climate with lots of sun, try to avoid building upwards. You'll pay for it over and over

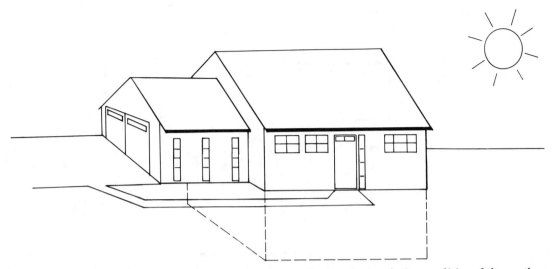

Fig. 13-1. *Building downwards is more expensive initially, but the insulative qualities of the earth can greatly reduce utility bills.*

again in the long run. In a cold climate at least consider the potential savings. In a cold climate the insulative value of a buried level might still be worthwhile if the excavation can be accomplished without great expense.

Although building up means extra maintenance (painting, for instance) on a regular basis, building down *can* bring some very costly maintenance (such as having to dig up a buried wall for repairs, and backfill it again). The insulative qualities of the earth are wonderful, but as mentioned above, the deteriorative effects can be disastrous. The outer walls are often kept damp almost constantly, which can wear away at those walls. *Hydrostatic pressure* (water sitting in the soil next to the walls) makes matters worse. Leaks are possible, maybe inevitable. And if there is also freezing of this water, those leaks might appear in a short time.

Waterproofing is *always* needed. If extensive waterproofing is needed, the cost goes up. In some areas, digging a basement and keeping it dry is more expensive than it's worth.

Then there's the appearance factor. Building a second story is dramatic to the eye. Two visible floors of 1200 square feet each appears to be a fairly large home. A basement home of the same dimensions is going to *appear* to be half the size. A basement can't be seen from the street. You

might have that same 2400 square feet of glorious house, but to the eye from outside, it seems that you have a considerably smaller home. By building upwards, the home is more showy.

Your own likes and dislikes are also a factor. You might hate the idea of being underground, even if there is plenty of ventilation and windows. Or you might be one of those who enjoys the sense of seclusion and even safety. (Storm cellars have been traditional in areas where tornados strike often.) It's a balance of factors that are determined by where you live and what you want.

Halves and Partials

There's no absolute reason to have either a full basement or a full second story. Partial basements are fairly common, even to the point of the "cellar" being little more than a single underground room.

A partial basement is often done for economic reasons (FIG. 13-2). It reduces the cost of excavation, and the cost of the underground walls. Other times, the way the land lies will only permit a partial basement.

A partial second story is sometimes done for the visual effect (FIG. 13-3). No matter what the basement is like, it usually doesn't much change the external appearance of the home. However, a

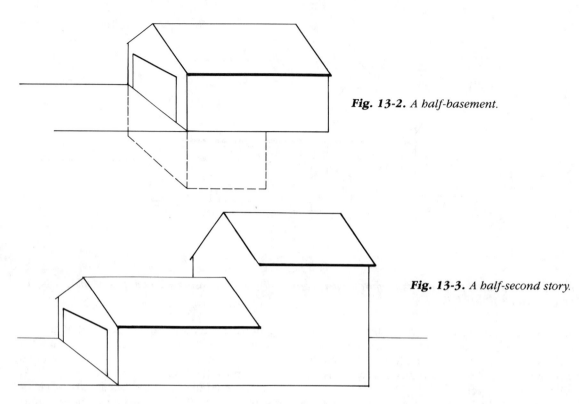

Fig. 13-2. *A half-basement.*

Fig. 13-3. *A half-second story.*

partial upper floor will dramatically change the appearance of a home. Architects and designers are often fond of this method for adding a personal and dramatic touch to the appearance of the home (see FIGS. 13-4 and 13-5). You can do the same, if you're careful.

There are possible structural problems that will have to be overcome. Two-stories is more weight, and the supporting members have to be appropriately larger. You could find yourself with one size for the supporting floor joists and foundation on one side of the home, and another size on the other. That's fine, as long as you take it into consideration.

Then there is the simple matter of appearance. Without proper care for design, it's easy for a wanted sense of the dramatic to become a sense of confusion. The home might end up looking strange and awkward instead of beautiful.

It's easy for a novice to get carried away with fancy lines, and easier yet if that novice lacks the ability to envision the final results. It would be a great benefit to learn how to make at least crude elevations (see Chapter 15) from all four sides.

They don't have to be gorgeous, just a fairly accurate rendition of what your "dream house" will look like if you have the roof splitting off in three different directions. (See FIG. 13-6.)

Stairs

Getting from one floor to another is generally accomplished by stairs. A few ritzy homes might have an elevator, but this is rare (and expensive).

As mentioned in Chapter 6, there are certain minimums and maximums if the stairway is to be functional and safe (FIG. 13-7). In most cases, a stairway should be no narrower than 3 feet. If you can afford to allow 4 feet in width, so much the better. There should be minimum headroom of $6^{1}/_{2}$ feet.

Stairs that are too steep are more dangerous. Stairs that are too shallow waste space. To achieve a fair compromise, the risers should be between $6^{1}/_{2}$ and $7^{1}/_{2}$ inches. (The treads should be between 10 and 14 inches in depth. Narrower makes walking up the stairs difficult, deeper is wasteful.)

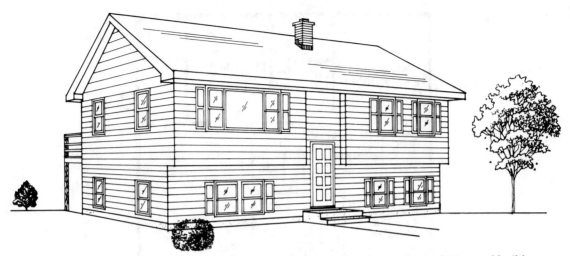

Fig. 13-4. *A home with equal floors tends to look boxy, but it is easier to design and build.*

Fig. 13-5. *Notice the difference when there is a break in the roof caused by different levels.*

All the treads should be the same, as should all risers, on any given stairway. If you've decided that 12-inch treads are the best, have *only* 12-inch treads all the way down (or up). The same applies to risers. If they're to be 7 inches, *all* should be 7 inches. Even a 1-inch difference in either can cause a person using the stairs to misjudge.

All stairs should have some kind of handrail for safety—one that is securely mounted. The usual distance between the stair treads and the handrail is 3 feet.

Calculating the space needed for the stairs isn't difficult, but it can be tedious. You need to know several things to do so. How far is the total drop from one level floor to the next? How wide are the treads? How tall are the risers?

Assume that the drop is an even 9 feet. You want risers of a median 7 inches and treads of 12 inches. For every foot you move forward, you drop 7 inches in height. Now all you have to figure are how many 7 inch risers are needed to take care of the 9 foot total drop.

The 9 feet equals 108 inches. Divided by 7 comes to 15.4. That is the total length of the stairway, including the top and the bottom. In other words, at "0" you'd be standing on a level floor, 15.4 feet forward you'd be standing on another level floor.

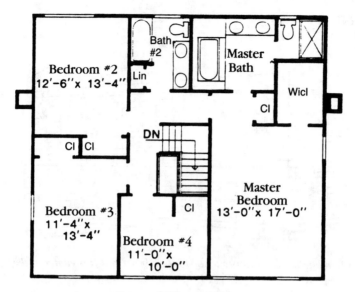

Second Floor Plan

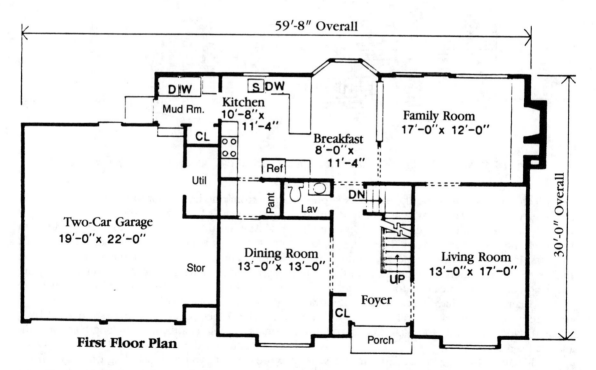

First Floor Plan

Fig. 13-6. *This is the floor plan for a home with a partial upper floor. Can you envision or draw how the house will actually look?*

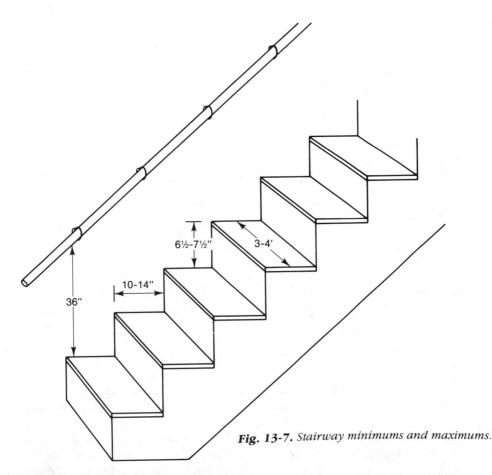

6½-7½"

3-4'

10-14"

36"

Fig. 13-7. *Stairway minimums and maximums.*

If you don't like math, you can do it graphically. Quadruled paper is excellent for this. Mark where the level floor is above, then measure straight down, using an appropriate scale, to show the drop. That is the next lower level floor. Draw a line there to represent that floor.

From the upper floor, measure down for the riser, then out for the tread, until you reach the bottom floor. If your measurements are accurate, you'll be able to measure the drawing with a ruler to determine the actual length (run) of the stairs.

Both methods are for straight staircases only. If you bend the stairs and have a landing somewhere in the total run, that landing also has to be taken into consideration. Another kind of "bend" is one that is more gradual, such as with a spiral staircase.

Of course, the easiest way is to come up with a rough calculation—to within an inch or so—and

let the draftsman or architect do the hard work of exact planning. An average stairway between two level floors is going to be roughly 14 feet in length. After about 11 feet of run, the top of your head will be roughly even with the floor above. This means that you'll need to allow for about 12 feet taken out of the upper floor to provide headroom for the staircase.

No matter how you do it, stairs are like sloped hallways. They serve little use other than to get you from one area to another. And because of the slope, the area beneath the stairs is of less general use (see FIG. 13-8). This is further complicated if you do the smart thing (for safety reasons) and have more than one stairwell to an area.

If you have more than one level—an upstairs, a main floor, and a basement, for example—you can "stack" the stairs so that the "wasted" space of one is the headroom for the one beneath. (This

Stories, Up & Down **155**

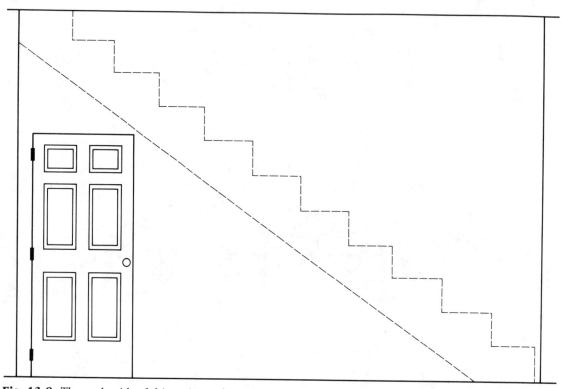

Fig. 13-8. *The underside of this stairway became a closet, but that closet slopes, just as the stairway does.*

will be covered in more detail later in the chapter in "More Than Two Levels?" and "Split Level.")

Second Story

The typical ranch-style home is all on one level, with the private areas (bedrooms, for example) separated from the rest of the house by a hallway. Now imagine slicing that ranch house with a very large knife and stacking the bedrooms on top.

When a home has a second story, traditionally the private areas are on the upper level, and the living areas are on the main floor. It's fairly rare to find the reverse—that is, a main floor of living area and the private areas in a basement (FIG. 13-9).

As mentioned above, the simplest, least expensive way to build a two-story home is to go straight up, with the floors matching (as far as overall external dimensions) exactly. The disadvantage is that this kind of a home looks like a large box. To get away from this, the roof is made to "break" in one of several ways.

A common place to make a break is over the garage (FIG. 13-10). The home itself is then two levels, while the garage is just one. The roofs are also at two levels. This can be made to be more dramatic by having the garage at an angle to the home (FIG. 13-11).

Another easy way is to have something on one floor that the other floor doesn't have. In FIG. 13-12, the home has a covered porch on the first level. Such a roof is relatively inexpensive to build since it doesn't have to be insulated. (You may even like the looks of having the rafters exposed.)

Any kind of break to the roof will change the appearance. Coming back into popularity are dormers (FIG. 13-13). These break from the main roof, usually at what appears to be right angles, for the windows to the rooms inside.

The number of designs and solutions are limited only by your imagination—and by how much you can afford. Keep in mind that every time you make an angle or break, it's going to cost.

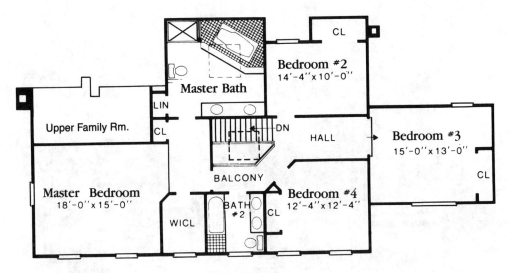

Second Floor Plan

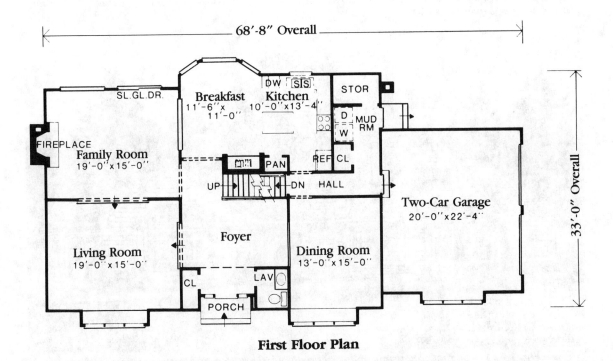

First Floor Plan

Fig. 13-9. *A fairly typical two-story home. Note that the plumbing is stacked.*

Fig. 13-10. *One way to make a two-story home less of a box is to cause the roof to "break." A common place to do this is over the garage.*

Fig. 13-11. *The roof can also be made to break off in a different direction at some point.*

Fig. 13-12. *Another easy way is to add an outside porch to the first floor. It's not only utilitarian, it causes the upper floor to indent.*

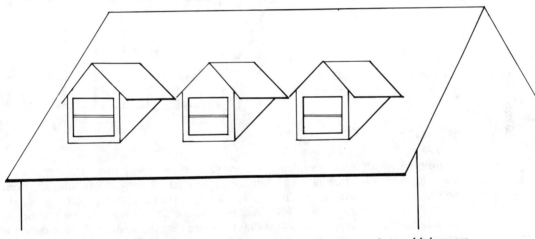

Fig. 13-13. *Another way to get rid of the box appearance is to add dormers.*

Basements

Basements can be full, half, underground, partially underground, finished, or "raw." Which one you choose depends on your desires and even more on the conditions.

A sloping lot is a natural for a partially buried basement, with one side open to yard (FIG. 13-14). If the ground is flat, you won't have this option without great expense. To do it, a tremendous amount of earth has to be excavated and moved. Consequently, a basement for a home on level land almost demands to be straight down.

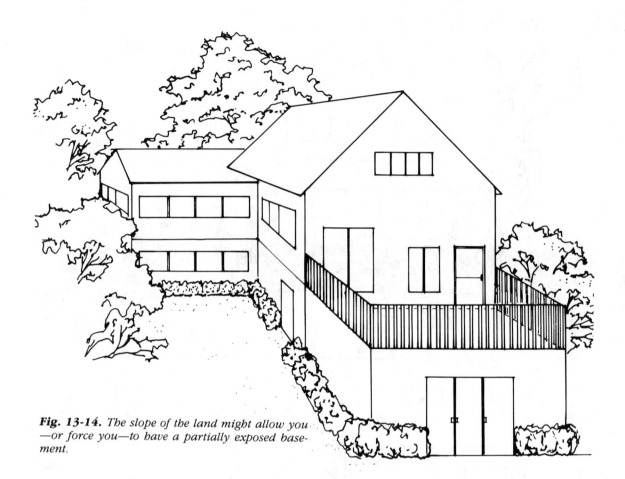

Fig. 13-14. *The slope of the land might allow you —or force you—to have a partially exposed basement.*

There are two problems with a basement of any kind, and especially with one that is completely buried. The first is moisture; the second is ventilation.

Moisture in the ground doesn't evaporate easily. In addition it tries to spread out as more water comes in. The combination creates hydrostatic pressure, which is a fancy way of saying that water is trying to get into the basement. Steps must be taken to prevent this from happening.

The outer walls are usually coated with a waterproof substance before the backfill is done.

Concrete—the usual way that basement walls are made—is porous. Water can get through, even if only slowly. Special concrete can be used to reduce this, but don't assume that it will be. Also don't assume that the sealing of the exterior will be done properly. This is one day you'll want to be there.

Inspect the concrete work before the coating goes on. Are there holes or honeycombs? Any flaws at all? If so, these should be taken care of *before* the sealant goes on.

There should be a minimum of two coats of

the sealant, preferably three. Once the basement is backfilled, putting on more will be very expensive. If the contractor is going to charge you a little extra, fine. It's money well spent.

The same applies to a moisture barrier beneath the floor. This is often nothing more than a layer of polyethylene plastic, which is fine if there are no breaks or holes in it. Some areas—and some contractors—will try to pass off a "slurry" as a moisture barrier. This kind of process is just barely tolerable. It's a very loose mixture, somewhat similar to concrete in nature, and is still porous.

The more moisture there is in the ground, the more important these considerations become.

Ventilation is also important. Although an underground room or collection of rooms are easier to keep cool and warm, the area can get stuffy in a hurry.

Providing windows for the basement isn't as easy as providing them for the floors above. A window above ground only requires a hole through the wall. A window in the basement needs more. It needs a permanent excavation up to ground level, and a means to hold back the dirt so it doesn't collapse.

This in turn means that there is an open hole in the surface. That presents a danger—and an opportunity. Leaving it open makes it possible for someone to fall in. And a large hole that extends beyond the roof is going to gather the rain and snow that falls. (Even a small window well has these disadvantages.) A rail grate over the window well can prevent accidents. It should be sturdy enough for at least one grown adult to stand, even jump up and down, without danger.

Plan the window well locations carefully. Be sure to place them where the roof overhang is largest. (You might be able to locate one or more of the wells in covered areas, such as in a roofed patio.) Removeable covers can also help keep out the weather (FIG. 13-15). These can be made to be as sturdy as needed. In areas with little or no snow and ice, not much is needed. In areas where the snow is going to build up 4 feet around the house every winter. . . .

There are, as always, a number of solutions. The easiest place to begin is to determine where the weather problems will be least and, if possible, locate the largest window wells there. From

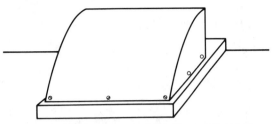

Fig. 13-15. *One way to keep the weather out.*

there, what you do depends on the problem. In dry areas with little rainfall and no snow, there is no problem. If the problem is rain, a partial "roof" can catch what rain isn't diverted by the roof of the house and carry it away.

Snow is one of the worst problems. It tends to stay, then to build up. That will block ventilation during those months (even if you did want to open the window during the cold weather). More, in the spring the snow that is allowed to fill the window well is going to melt.

One way to help handle any water problem is to be sure that the well has good drainage. This might mean adding a drain, or the solution could be as simple as digging down a few feet and filling to level with small rocks.

As to the advantage of a larger window well, it can be used as a fire escape. All you need do is specify the grating to have a hinged section, and that the well has a ladder. Both are fairly inexpensive (and local codes might require it—or should). While the fire escape provides you greater safety from fire, having a hinged section increases the threat of break-ins. The *wrong* solution is to lock the section. That makes it useless as an escape unless you happen to have the key with you.

Just as effective for security, and much more effective for escape, is a lockless-lock (FIG. 13-16). There are several ways to do this. One system uses a long rod with a pin at the bottom. Our own solution was to use a length of chain welded to the top and clipped to the bottom with a heavy spring-loaded clip. Trying to get in from the top is almost impossible. Getting out from the bottom is as easy as flicking the clip to release the chain.

There is one more matter to take into consideration when designing a basement. If there is to be plumbing, you have to know where the sewage lines are. If they are above the lowest point in the basement, you'll need a sump pump to lift that

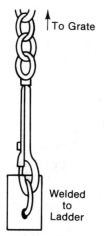

Fig. 13-16. *A lockless-lock for the fire escape ladder.*

waste water out (FIG. 13-17).

An alternate solution, but an expensive one certain to cause serious problems sooner or later, is to have a septic system installed beneath the basement floor. If this is your choice, be *sure* to plan for an easy way for clean-out. The tank will

have to be pumped out on a regular basis (generally ever 5 years is sufficient).

You might also consider having floor drains installed, with an underfloor system of pipes to carry water to the sewage lines, to the sump pump, or to the septic tank. There is always the chance that the basement will become flooded. If there are floor drains, this isn't a serious problem. Without floor drains, taking care of basement flooding is both troublesome and expensive.

More Than Two Levels?

It's not uncommon for a home to have more than two floors. A 2-story home will often have three floors: main, second, and basement (FIG. 13-18).

The advantages and disadvantages are the same for each of the floors. Building upwards is less expensive and usually causes fewer structural problems. It's also more difficult to cool. The basement costs more, is relatively temperature-stable, but can cause problems, such as leaks, if not built properly.

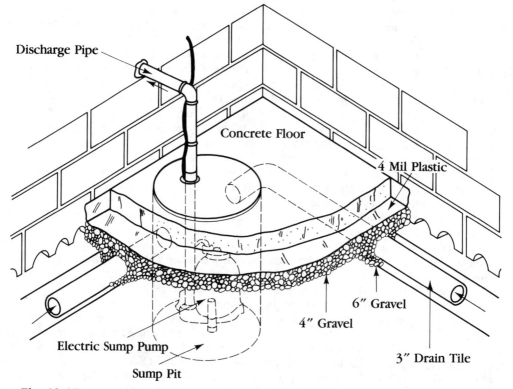

Fig. 13-17. *A sump pump lifts the waste water upwards and into the main sewage pipes.*

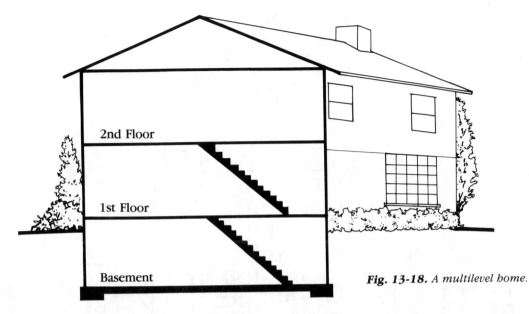

2nd Floor

1st Floor

Basement

Fig. 13-18. *A multilevel home.*

The reason for building in either direction, up or down, is to have more living space without having a sprawling home. As mentioned early in this chapter, imagine a 1200-square-foot home, with dimensions of roughly 30 by 40. To get 2400 square feet you can extend the dimensions of the home (to 60 by 40, for example), or you can build either a complete upper floor or a complete basement. If you want a 3600-square-foot home, you can expand a single level (to 90 by 40, for example), or you can have two 1800-square-foot levels, which may or may not fit properly on the lot, or you can have three levels of 1200 square feet each. The "footprint" of the home remains the same 30 by 40, but by building both upwards and downwards, you can triple the living space without tripling the cost of the home.

For figuring what goes where on what floor, you can basically follow the same guidelines as given above. As with a two-level home, the living area is usually on the main floor, with the private areas on the second floor. The basement, if it has rooms, very often becomes the informal area, with family room, party room, space for hobbies, and so on.

That doesn't mean that *your* home has to be that way. You might prefer a mixture—perhaps with the family bedrooms upstairs and a guest room in the basement. Or perhaps you'd like the master bedroom on the upper floor and the rooms for the children in the basement. Also, as with any home with more than one level, you should try to "stack" the plumbing for efficiency and cost savings.

Another thing you can stack are the stairs. You'll have about twice the number of stairways—and potentially twice the problems. As mentioned above, stairs are like sloped hallways; they have certain minimums and maximums. They will take up a certain amount of space that is pretty much useless for anything else.

By placing one stairway over the other, the wasted space from the slope of the upper stairs becomes the headroom for the stairs going down (FIG. 13-19). While you give up the possibility of a closet, you actually gain because of less wasted space.

Split-Level

One type of multilevel home is the *split-level,* and the variation on it called a *split-foyer.* The usual reason for building a home like this is to fit the lay of the land. The property might have a small hill, for example, forcing a splitting of the levels. The split-level can have just two levels. Also common are three levels. The floor plan and placement of rooms is much like that of a more standard two-story (or multilevel). A little extra care is needed,

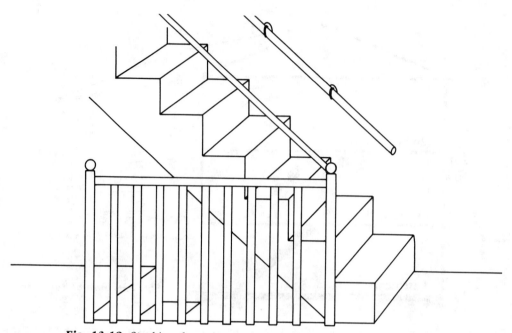

Fig. 13-19. *Stacking the stairways in a multilevel home can save space.*

however, because the levels are often fairly small individually and are not completely separated.

Note in FIG. 13-20 and FIG. 13-21 how the split works. The ceiling height is achieved by having a "half" floor to one side (and its ceiling appropriately higher). The levels go up like steps.

A variation on the split-level is the split-foyer. (FIG. 13-22). With this design, the entrance is at one level and then splits in two directions for the floors.

You might like one type over another, but the final choice may not be your own. A split-level is totally unsuitable for level land. In fact, each home really needs to be designed specifically for the land on which it will sit.

You need to know where the slope is that is causing the split and how large it is. If it's right on the edge of the property, building a split-level might put part of your house outside the property line, or so far to the edge that it will look strange.

Some slight modifications to match the home design to the land are possible—and often expensive. Excavation and land moving might be needed to match the house to the property. The

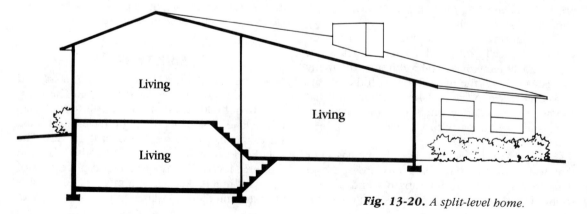

Fig. 13-20. *A split-level home.*

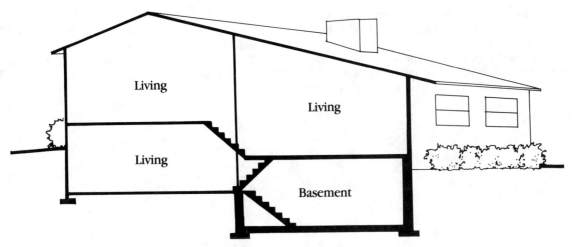

Fig. 13-21. *A multilevel split-level.*

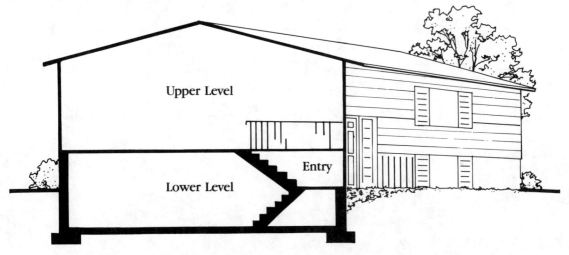

Fig. 13-22. *A split foyer.*

greater the modifications, the greater the costs.

It still comes back to the same thing: know the land and have exact measurements. Use these to design the home. It's much less expensive to modify the design than the land.

Again there are stairs or "half-stairs." One of the differences is that they are open. There isn't room for a door to close them, which means that the levels are also open to each other. While this tends to save as far as wasted space is concerned, it can cause problems in heating and cooling.

Warm air rises, cold air drops. With most standard two- or three-level homes, the floors are separated from each other by longer stairways if not by doors. The ducting brings the warmed or cooled air to where it is needed.

This isn't so with a split-level. While the split-level tends to improve overall movement of air throughout the house, this can be a disadvantage. Unless the ducting is properly designed, and unless the heating and cooling unit is powerful enough to move the air as needed, the upper floors are going to be overly warm during the summer, while the lower floors will tend to be too cool in the winter.

When designing a split-level, great care must be taken. Although the overall design can be one of the most attractive, it brings with it the possibility of flaws inside and out.

The key is to know the land, and design the house to fit it without causing the house to break in so many directions that it looks odd. Be sure the interior has a logical placement of rooms and stairs.

14

Garages, carports & patios

In America, those homes without at least one motor vehicle are a minority. That vehicle (or those vehicles) has to be parked somewhere.

Even if you're one of that minority, don't just dismiss the idea of having a garage or carport out of hand. *You* might walk or take the bus, but if the home is to be resold, you'll be limiting the market to those who are in the same situation, or who are willing to park on the street—if that is allowed.

Even if it *is* allowed, parking in the street, or even in the driveway, is a poor solution. For most people, a vehicle is the second largest investment made. Quite often your livelihood depends on it, even if only to the extent of getting you to and from work. It's an investment worth protecting.

Parked in the open exposes the vehicle to the weather. It can suffer from damage by the sun, rain, snow, ice, heat, cold, dust, and so forth. (This isn't limited to just the paint and upholstery, either.)

Parking on the street adds an additional danger, that of careless or drunk drivers moving along that street. Sooner or later, you might find yourself awakened by a loud crash, and then find out that your vehicle served as a stopping point for some other driver. Then there are other kinds of damage. Kids playing ball in the street, for example.

In some parts of the country, regular maintenance of the street is necessary. If the street needs to be torn up for repairs, all of a sudden you have

no place at all to put your car. During the winter there might be days when the street might need to be snowplowed, and again you have no place to park until the job is done.

In short, if at *all* possible, build at least a covered carport. The extra you'll pay is small for the return.

Garage or Carport?

Despite appearances, a garage and carport are almost the same. A garage is just an enclosed carport; a carport is just a garage that is missing one or more walls and a garage door. The differences are utility, cost, and appearance.

The two great advantages of a garage as opposed to a carport are protection from the weather and increased security. The enclosed nature of a garage makes it possible to shield whatever is inside from rain, snow, excessive cold, and so on, while keeping it locked and out of sight. This generally makes it more functional for its purpose.

Of course, you pay for the advantages. The simplest carport consists of little more than some beams to hold a roof, and the roof doesn't need any insulation. There is a cost, but it's considerably less than that of a garage.

The trade-off is protection. Anything put in a carport is still in the open. It can be damaged by

167

the weather or stolen. (More, a car parked is a sure sign that you're home, and an empty carport is an indication that no one is there.)

If you wish, your garage can even be heated and cooled. (In this case, be *sure* to specify that the walls and ceiling be insulated. For that matter, the cost of insulation is relatively low. Consider having it done anyway, even if you don't intend to heat or cool the garage. You *might* change your mind. While adding insulation to the ceiling is fairly simple, putting it inside the walls after they're closed isn't as easy.) Of course, this isn't possible with a carport. However, with just a minimum of planning, you can design the carport in such a way that it can later be closed in as a garage.

A step between is a carport that is already essentially closed in (FIG. 14-1). The savings is primarily on the garage doors, which is relatively minor, but you end up with something with the advantages (and disadvantages) of both the garage and carport. Also, it will be fairly easy to convert it to a full garage later.

Whatever you decide should also take appearance into account. The garage or carport can make quite a difference in the overall appearance of the home. It can be used to add to the appearance. Likewise, careless planning can cause the parking area to ruin the concept.

Will the garage be attached to the home and a part of it? Or will you have a separate garage? If separate, will it be standing by itself or semiconnected to the home by a roofline extending over a covered breezeway?

Keep these things in mind. They'll be covered in more depth later in this chapter. First some general considerations.

Size

When I was sixteen I helped my father on a construction job for a family friend. The home they owned was older and had a garage in the back. Like so many garages built in its day, it was made to fit a particular-sized car and nothing more. The car would squeeze in, and the door would close up against the rear bumper.

They bought an Eldorado. Most of it fit into the garage, but the door came down on the trunk, leaving the last two feet hanging out. Worse, once the car was parked inside, everyone had to exit the car from the passenger side. The driver's door hit the wall before opening far enough to allow anyone to get in or out.

The only valid solution was to tear down the existing garage and build a new one of the appropriate size. They didn't want to undertake such a

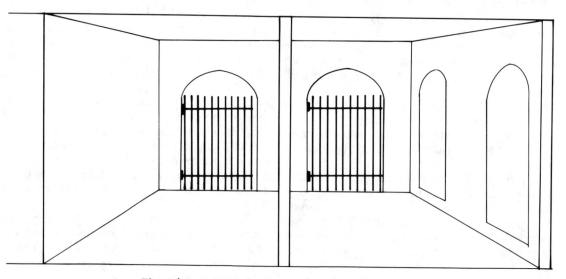

Fig. 14-1. *Halfway between a carport and a garage.*

project. So, to make the car fit, we had to remove a section of the front wall to allow the nose of the car to fit in. They still had to use the passenger door to get in and out, but at least the car was somewhat protected from the weather.

The mistake the builders made was to assume that no one would ever get anything larger than the scaled-down (by present standards) automobiles of the 1920s.

You might own a subcompact. By designing a garage that will hold *only* a subcompact, you limit use of the garage to that size. Nothing larger will fit. If you design the garage so that the clearance is for a vehicle no taller than 5 feet, nothing larger will go through the door no matter how wide the garage or how tall the ceiling.

Additionally, most people use the garage for storage of other items. Lawnmowers, snowblowers, rakes, shovels and other tools are stored inside. That further reduces room for movement.

The opening should be set to fit standard doors. The smallest standard door is 8 feet in width. Although you can fit a car through, some very careful steering is needed, and a large car with side mirrors may not fit at all. Much better is a standard garage door 10 feet wide. Both close a 7-foot-tall opening. (See also "Doors" below.)

The standard 10 by 7 opening will be sufficient for most single stalls (FIG. 14-2). It provides roughly 2 feet of clearance all around for the average car.

Allowing just 1 foot on each side to hold the door, the minimum garage becomes 12 feet wide. This allows for the mounting of the door, and gives you about 3 feet on each side for getting in and out. That's squeezing it a bit, which is why this is a minimum. The garage won't do much but hold the car.

Better is to allow more space. A 1-foot-deep shelving unit on a side wall is going to require that the garage be 13 feet wide as a minimum. And because of the way lumber comes, it's just as economical to go to 14 feet. This is the standard single stall for many builders. (Some will go to 16 feet in width as a standard.)

The exact width—and the size of the door—depends on your own needs. When we designed our home, our vehicle was a very large 4 × 4. From ground to the top of the roof was just slightly over 7 feet. Obviously it wouldn't fit through a 7-foot-high door. We needed an 8-foot-tall opening. (The 10-foot width was fine.)

The depth of the garage can be calculated in much the same way. The vehicle has to be able to pull all the way in so that the door can close. In addition, there should be a minimum of 3 feet of clear space for walking (usually in the front) and at least 2 feet of clearance behind. It can be smaller,

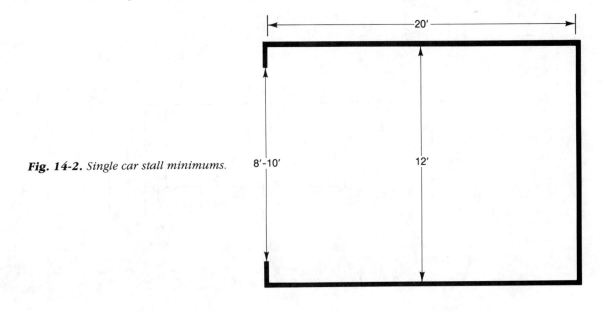

Fig. 14-2. Single car stall minimums.

but you get back into a squeeze again.

A 14 by 20 garage (or carport) is fairly common for a single stall. It's still a little tight inside, but functional. Better is to give the garage extra length. A garage that is 14 by 24 isn't too large.

Sizing is also determined by the number of vehicles and other things you wish to put into the area (FIG. 14-3). If you have two cars but only a one-car garage, the other vehicle is going to be out in the weather.

Think of the average car being 6 feet wide, then allow 1 more foot for side mirrors. The minimum for each vehicle is then 7 feet or 14 feet for two vehicles. Now allow 3 feet on the outside of each car for opening the doors and 3 feet between the two cars. That comes to 23 feet total as a rough approximation.

As always, you want to try to make the dimensions come out to even numbers. Thus the overall width of a highly functional two-stall garage or carport can be 22 or 24 feet wide, depending on how generous you wish to be with space. (My suggestion is to go for the larger dimension.) The 22-foot width allows for a single 20-foot-wide (or smaller) door or opening. The 24-foot width easily allows two 10-foot doors or openings.

Once again, you *can* squeeze a car into a 10-by-14 space through an 8-foot opening, but why?

The savings aren't that great; the inconvenience and lack of utility *is*. Keep in mind that a garage is less expensive than the house itself, even if the walls are insulated. A carport is cheaper yet. Considering this and the value of the area for storage and work, it's generally wise to design larger than the bare minimums.

Location

Locating the garage or carport isn't difficult. For efficiency, it should be near the kitchen, and hopefully with the front entrance easily visible from the drive (where guests might park).

Having it near or even directly connected to the kitchen makes it easier to unload groceries and such. Most people will be carrying in groceries at least once a week. Having the garage on one end of the house and the kitchen on the other means a *lot* of extra walking through the house.

If a part of the garage is to be used for storage of garden tools, for example, it should also be accessible from the yard, or yards, as the case may be (FIG. 14-4). This can be done with doors or with gates in the fence, depending on how you have things set up.

The garage or carport can also be situated to shield the house. In colder areas, by placing the garage to the north, it serves as a windbreak for

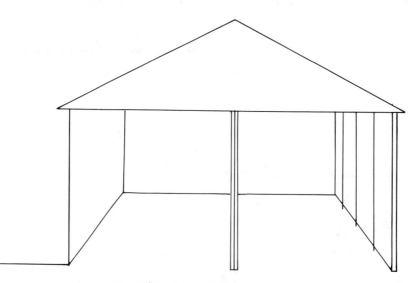

Fig. 14-3. *A two-stall carport.*

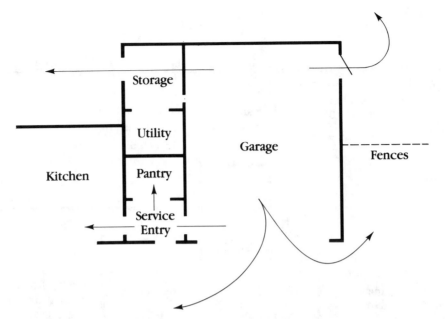

Fig. 14-4. *This garage is located to be accessible to the kitchen area and to the yards.*

the cold wind. In warmer areas, it can be placed to help block the sun: on the east side to block the morning sun, on the west to block the afternoon sun (which is generally the preferred side). Either plan, used in conjunction with trees and other plants, can be an effective way to reduce utilities.

This kind of positioning isn't always possible. It depends largely on the direction the lot faces. You *can* choose a lot that allows you to do what you want, however.

A garage or carport can also be used to block noise. Usually this isn't crucial, but it's possible that your lot has one side where there is more noise than on the other. Perhaps there is a freeway or other busy road on one side.

Don't forget appearance. Quite often the garage roof will break from the one over the house. It might be on a different level, or perhaps the garage is placed at an angle to the home. Try to envision how that is going to look.

Attached or Separate?

Most commonly, the garage or carport is physically attached to the home. It's more convenient and efficient while being less expensive (FIG. 14-5).

Imagine a separate garage, and a rainstorm or a few feet of snow on the ground. To unload the car, you'll be walking back and forth until the job is done. By then you—and the groceries—might be soaked or cold. By having the parking area as a part of the home, bringing in groceries and such is easier and more comfortable. Also, less dirt is being tracked into the house, which doesn't just mean that there is less cleanup. It also means that the floor coverings in the home will tend to last longer.

Another advantage of an attached parking area is that it makes the home look larger and brings with it the opportunity to do some things with the overall design that would otherwise be difficult (FIG. 14-6). Although the garage roof might break away from the main roofline, it's still a part of the whole. Most people find this to be more attractive, especially since a separate garage tends to look too much like a box.

On the other hand, a separate garage isolates the house from the fumes and noise (FIG. 14-7). This can be very important if the garage is to be used for noisy activities, and especially so if those things will be going on while others sleep. The same applies to anything that will create fumes.

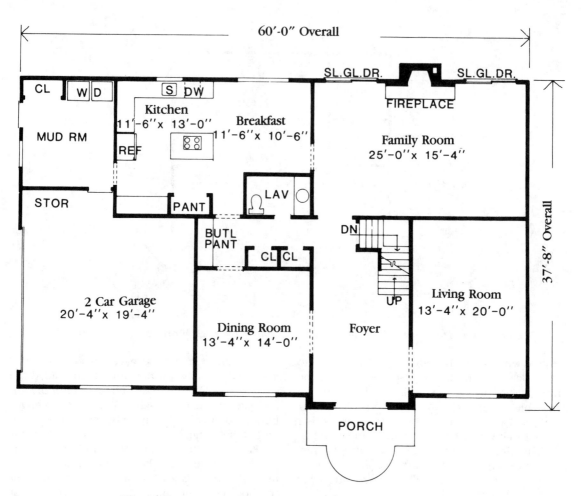

Fig. 14-5. An attached garage is more convenient and efficient.

This can be simply letting the engine warm up or using various solvents.

A separate structure is safer. Flammable materials are often stored in the garage, making it a potential fire hazard. If it catches on fire, there's less chance that the fire will spread to the home. The fire is also a little easier to contain.

There is a way to get the best of both. The garage can be separate from the house while still attached to it. Between is a covered walkway (FIGS. 14-8 and 14-9).

Depending on your needs and preferences, the walk between the garage and home can be totally open or partially enclosed. The second is often preferred, but it costs more because of the additional construction needed to make the enclosure. You can reduce this by specifying half-walls, or by using some other material, such as a trellis, as a wall.

Inside

The inside of the garage or carport is also important if the area is to serve its purpose. Some years ago it was common for a garage or carport to have a dirt floor. While this is still found, most have concrete floors. To begin with, it's cleaner and easier to keep clean. This in turn translates into a

Fig. 14-6. *When the garage is a part of the house, the house looks larger.*

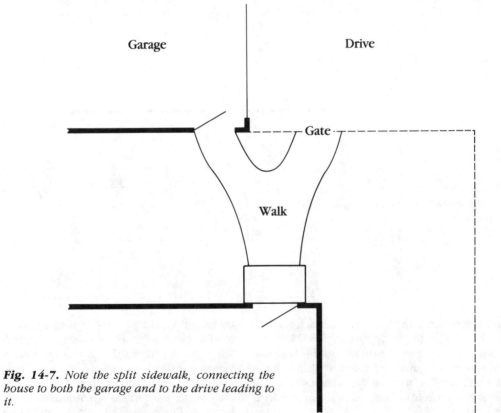

Garage

Drive

Gate

Walk

Fig. 14-7. *Note the split sidewalk, connecting the house to both the garage and to the drive leading to it.*

Fig. 14-8. *The breezeway can be as simple as a covered walk between the garage and home . . .*

Fig. 14-9. *. . . or it can be partially enclosed.*

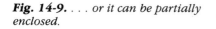

financial gain, since the less dirt you track into the home, the longer the floor coverings will last.

Since a vehicle will be driven on this concrete surface, some care must be taken. It should be at least 4 inches thick, with a solid base beneath, and preferably with reinforcing wire (a 6-inch grid is sufficient).

Vehicles have the tendency to drip oil and other messy fluids, or the tires might bring in hard-to-clean substances. Since concrete is somewhat porous, these things can be absorbed and become difficult to remove. You can reduce this problem by making sure that 2 or 3 coats of concrete sealer are applied when the concrete floor is installed. (This is a fairly simple job, and one you can do yourself.)

Floor drains are nice to have in a garage, but unnecessary in a carport. Either way, try to get the floor to slope toward the main opening. Not much is needed, just enough to be sure that water will flow out of the area instead of into it. One inch in 10 feet is generally enough.

To further help drainage, be sure that there is a sloped lip at the opening. It shouldn't be so steep that getting in and out is troublesome. It can be a gradual slope onto the drive, or it can be a 6-inch slope across about 3 feet or more.

A 4-inch-high step at the back wall of the garage is now the standard (FIG. 14-10). It serves several functions. The step serves as a pad to prevent you from hitting the back wall of the garage. By having the pad about 6 feet wide, the tires will touch the step before the front bumper touches the wall, and you'll still be able to get around the car. (It can be narrower, if you wish.) If the garage is attached to a home, this step also provides a curb to help prevent carbon monoxide from seeping into the home. (Carbon monoxide is heavier than air and will tend to drop to the floor.)

In many areas, a step is mandated by local building codes. This is one time when you don't have to worry about seeing if the code exists or not. *Do it*! That step has too many advantages in a garage for the slight extra cost.

The possibility of fumes building up inside a garage also dictates a need for good ventilation. Many people simply open the doors. That's sufficient in many cases, but doesn't do much good if you intend to be working inside with the doors closed. (This obviously doesn't apply to a carport, which is already open.)

If you intend to be working often in the garage, consider having it heated and cooled. That means that the walls and ceiling will have to be insulated. It also means that at least some of the ventilation will be provided. (More might still be needed, depending on what is being done in the garage.)

Some books recommend that every garage or carport have a minimum of two outlets. In my opinion, that's not nearly enough. The minimum should be the same here as in any other part of the home: that is, one for every 12 running feet and at least one on each wall. Even that may not be enough. If you intend to be putting a shop in the garage, it definitely won't be.

My suggestion is to have five electrical outlets in a single-stall structure (two on each side wall and one on the back wall), and at least six in a double-stall. In addition, there should be electrical wiring in the ceiling for future installation of automatic door openers. If you intend to have the openers installed during construction, the wiring will be there. If the contractor is not going to be installing the openers, those wires will be missing unless you specify otherwise.

Lighting in the garage or carport is very important. The usual choice is ceiling-mounted fluorescents, preferably two double fixtures per stall. This provides plenty of diffused light for the

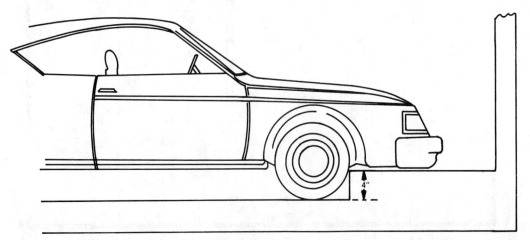

Fig. 14-10. *A 4-inch-high pad at the front of the garage can reduce the carbon monoxide that gets into the house and helps to protect the front wall from accidents.*

general area, but don't forget that there might be a need for task lighting in specific areas. That usually means using one of the outlets (FIG. 14-11).

Every home should have access panels to the attic space. One is usually located in a closet inside the home. A common error is to place another in an open area, such as a carport or patio. Don't make that mistake! It's too easy for a burglar to go into the attic through the access panel, and then come down through the ceiling inside the home.

The exposed access panels should be protected. One way is to have them made of sturdy material and locked. Easier is to place them in a protected area, such as a locked garage. By doing this, and then locking the access, you'll be protecting the rest of the house. This plan also gives you an easy option for getting into the attic, namely that of installing pull-down steps (FIG. 14-12). The other choice is to have a ladder at hand. The steps are safer and more convenient.

Pull-down steps won't work for a carport unless you have a way of locking the steps. You'll probably need a ladder to get at the lock, but don't do without that lock.

Garage and Carport Storage

If you're going to be using the attic space for storage, consider having plywood decking laid down. This is much easier to do during construction, and usually, if you don't specify the decking you won't get it.

Storage inside the garage is also important, especially so if you'll be doing any building or shop work. As mentioned in Chapters 7 and 12, and earlier in this chapter, the garage is often used as storage for various tools and other pieces of equipment used in and around the home.

Proper, efficient design can make the difference between a cluttered area and one that functions well (FIG. 14-13). It helps to keep one trick in mind: Try to keep as much off the floor as possible. Not only will this make cleaning the area easier, it forces you to make use of the walls rather than the floors.

Perforated hardboard is an excellent way to hang tools on the walls. Special hooks go into the holes of the board to hold the various tools. Some people will paint the outline of the tool on the board to help keep things organized.

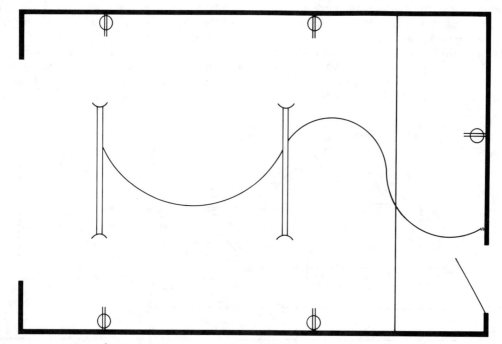

Fig. 14-11. *Electrical and lighting minimums for a garage or carport.*

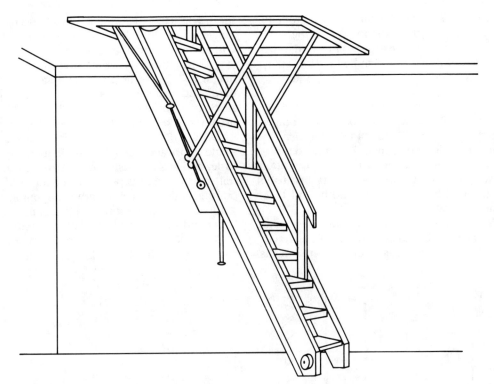

Fig. 14-12. *Pull-down steps to the attic space.*

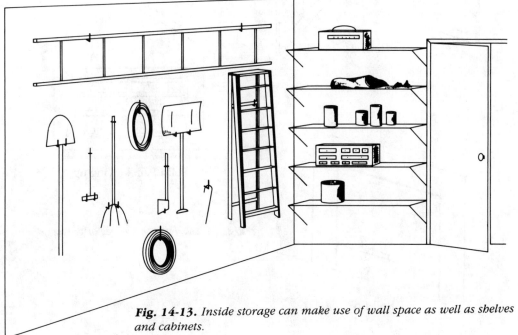

Fig. 14-13. *Inside storage can make use of wall space as well as shelves and cabinets.*

Heavier items can be hung down from the walls with larger hooks anchored into the studs. (Be sure that the hooks *are* into solid wood, otherwise pieces of the drywall can be torn loose.)

Doors

There are three basic types of doors: hinged, swing-up, and roll-up (FIG. 14-14). The first and second are single, solid panels. The hinged type—much like a standard door—isn't used very often. The swing-up has also lost popularity because it tends to be difficult to handle. Both tend to be large and heavy.

The roll-up door is made up of smaller, hinged panels. It bends as it rolls up along tracks. Although it's still heavy, as it rolls onto the tracks, the tracks take the weight. The bending at the hinges makes this kind of door perfect for use with an automatic door opener.

As mentioned earlier, the most common height is 7 feet. A height of 6½ feet is also standard, and many manufacturers will also have a stock of 8-foot-tall doors. Single stall doors are usually stocked in 8-, 9-, and 10-foot widths.

Quite often when a garage is two-stall, two single doors are used (FIG. 14-15). Such a garage is easier and less expensive to construct since a central support pillar is provided for the roof. Without this, if the garage (or carport) opening is to be without a central support, the beams must be larger and stronger to hold the weight above.

The central pillar makes construction easier and less expensive, but it also means that you have

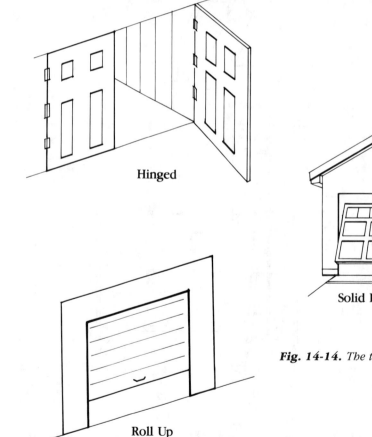

Hinged

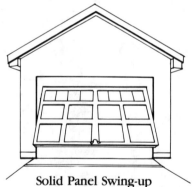

Solid Panel Swing-up

Roll Up

Fig. 14-14. *The three types of garage doors.*

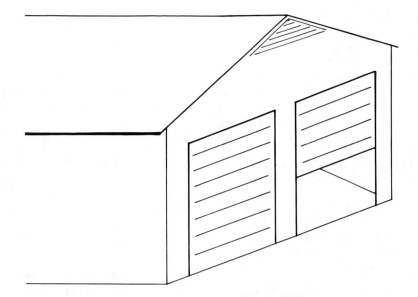

Fig. 14-15. *A two-stall garage with dual single doors and a central pillar.*

to maneuver around it. While that's rarely a problem with the average automobile, it can be with a trailer, boat, or even a large truck.

The option is to have just one larger door. The most common width is 16 feet. Also available are 15 feet and 18 feet, with some suppliers also carrying 20-foot widths in stock.

You need to make a few phone calls to local suppliers to find out what is readily available, and how much extra it will cost for nonstandard sizes.

Pads and Driveways

As already mentioned, it's wise to provide the garage or carport with a concrete floor, to have that floor sloped toward the opening, and to have a sharper slope at the opening. You know the importance of specifying 6-inch grid reinforcing wire in the concrete to be sure that it can hold the weight of a vehicle without cracking.

All of this is true of driveways as well. More so since there is the possibility of larger, heavier delivery trucks using the driveway.

As with the floor of the garage, it sometimes helps to give the driveway a bit of a slope, with the center just a little higher than the edges. This lets water run off to the sides.

A very common mistake is to not allow enough room to back out of the parking area and to turn around. This isn't always possible because of room limitations, but try to figure a way to do it. The alternative is to always back out into the street.

You have three basic choices in making the driveway: concrete, asphalt, or "something else." Which you choose is determined partially by where you live, partially by what you can afford, and partially by the overall effect you want.

Concrete is durable. If laid properly, it can last 30 years or more—much more in areas where climate is mild. It's also one of the more expensive materials to use for a drive. And some people find all that gray unattractive, even when it is given a texture (such as by exposing the aggregate).

There are two options for making the concrete look better. One is to add a dye to color the concrete. It's best to have this dye mixed into the concrete before it is poured so that the color is mixed all the way through instead of just on the surface.

The other option is to have the concrete "stamped" with a pattern. For example, the concrete can be made to look like paving stones, or tile, or brick. This in combination with a color can make a very attractive drive or sidewalk with a fairly small extra cost over concrete alone.

Asphalt is generally much less expensive. Some people also prefer the appearance. It's darker than plain concrete (it doesn't have to be dark black). It tends to be more flexible than concrete, which can reduce cracking. One disadvantage is that asphalt has to be resealed and otherwise treated on a regular basis if it is to last and look good.

The "something else" is a broad category, beginning with dirt and ending with inlaid brick or other stone. The first is virtually free. The only cost will be any grading that must be done. A step up is to have rock put down. This reduces the amount of mud and also helps to prevent depressions caused by erosion. Neither is a good solution in snowy areas. The same is true of any irregular surface.

Brick roadways and drives were once fairly common. The cost of the bricks and the installation has skyrocketed, making such drives very expensive. The other disadvantage is that these drives tend to require a large amount of maintenance if they are to remain smooth.

Patios

There are dozens of books just on patios. It's not the purpose of this book to cover all of that material in a few paragraphs. The variety possible is endless. A few options are listed below:

- It can be concrete or wood or inlaid brick or . . .
- It can be covered or open.
- It can be in the back, in the front, to the side, internal and private, or external and exposed.
- It can be at ground level, below ground level, above ground level, even up in the air. It can be stepped or flat.

The only real limitations are cost and imagination.

A good place to begin is to look through a few books about patios and decks. Get some ideas of

Fig. 14-16. *A very simple wood patio deck.*

what you might like. Then determine what will look best with the home and with the lay of the land.

Once again, keep the purpose and function in mind. Is it to be a glorified covered entrance for the kitchen door? Or will it be used for gatherings and parties, or perhaps as a place for the family to sit on nice days?

Like the home itself, the patio is a reflection of your personal needs and tastes. It doesn't have to be large or expensive to be functional. Something as basic as in FIG. 14-16 isn't too costly, yet this plan gives the family and friends a place to sit outside on nice days (or nice evenings).

Some patios can be added after the construction is complete. Modifications can also be done. However, if the patio is to have a roof that is to be attached to the house, the best time to do at least that part is while the home is being built (FIG. 14-17). The roofline is then consistent.

Although you might be able to build the patio yourself, consider having it done at the time of construction. Materials are almost certainly going to be less expensive. For example, if the patio is to have a concrete floor, the best time to pour it is when other concrete work is being done.

It might also be possible to arrange with the contractor to order and have delivered the other materials you'll need. Most contractors will be more than willing to do this—sometimes at cost or close to it. In any case, chances are very good that even if he marks it up to allow a profit, it will still be less expensive than buying the materials yourself—and delivery will be free.

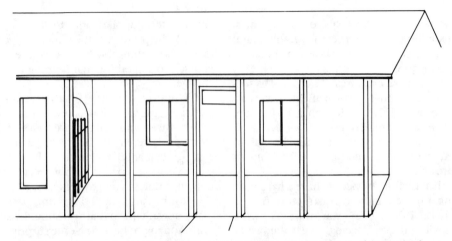

Fig. 14-17. *This standard patio is connected to the kitchen and is covered.*

Elevations

"Elevation" sounds like it refers to how tall something is. However, in architectural drawings an *elevation* drawing shows the house as it will appear (more or less) once complete.

People are visual creatures. We're used to seeing real, concrete things and are affected by that. Imagine two architects bidding on a major job. One brings in an extremely good floor plan, the other a scale model of the structure he has in mind. That second is much more visual and much more impressive.

More than that, many people have a hard time envisioning a three-dimensional structure from a two-dimensional floor plan. You can look at the floor plan without ever "seeing" what the resulting home will be like.

Unless your imagination is very good, you'll want an elevation before making the final decisions on your home (FIG. 15-1). It's also possible that those in charge of local restrictions—particularly when this concerns neighborhood committees—will want to see an elevation. The builder will also need it if he is to carry out your design the way you want it.

The term "elevation" is generally used only to define a drawing that represents a straight-on view of the outside of the home. It can also be used to describe interior views, also straight-on.

Somewhat similar are *presentation* drawings. These are drawn in perspective so that the object, room or structure looks more like a picture. (Usu-

ally, the term applies only to the outside of the home.) The purpose is the same: to give you a way to see how things will look before committing yourself to something that is going to be costly to change.

Whoever does the final drawings will automatically provide four elevations. (Most areas require these, and you certainly should.) The front elevation is generally the most detailed. The left, right, and rear views are usually much simpler. (See "Views" on p. 183) You won't get perspective drawings unless you pay extra.

Just because you'll be getting elevations eventually doesn't mean that you should wait until that time. You might be in for some surprises if you do.

You're designing the inside of the home to be just as you want it. Don't stop there. The outside is what people will see first—and all that most will see.

But I'm Not Artistic!

If you've been looking through books and magazines of home designs, you'll have seen drawings of homes. What you're usually seeing are *presentations*: the home as seen at an angle rather than straight on. To create one of these, it helps to have at least a little artistic talent. (See "Perspective" on p. 189).

It helps to have that talent in any case, but it's not absolutely essential for developing a suitable

Fig. 15-1. *A simple elevation will be an accurate representation of the home's features.*

elevation. Accurate drafting will do a respectable job in most cases. The home has certain dimensions. Put them on paper, just as you would a scaled drawing of the floor plan.

If the home is to be 60 feet long, and you've chosen 1/8 inch to represent one foot, your drawing will be 7 1/2 inches long. If the first window is 10 feet from the west wall, that's 1 1/4 inches in from that west edge. And if the window is supposed to be 4 foot by 4 foot, 3 feet off the ground, you'd draw in a 1/2 inch by 1/2 inch square, 3/8 inch from the base. Thus, by simply making accurate measurements, the end result will be at least dimensionally correct. You can repeat the process for each view desired. (Use the same scale for each.)

You'll need patience and a degree of imagination. The more complex the design, the more you'll need. A square chimney is still going to be square from the other views, a rectangular one is going to change in appearance. And the appearance will also change in other ways. (See FIGS. 15-2 and 15-3.)

Keep these changes of view in mind. If you do, the same drafting techniques will carry you through and each view will be dimensionally accurate.

Views

There are four basic views of concern, one from each direction. Knowing how the home will look from the front is generally considered to be the most important since this is what people see first, friends and strangers alike. It's also the side of the home that tends to get the most attention as far as general appearance is concerned. For example, the front might get a veneer of brick while the sides and back will be covered with less expensive materials.

Therefore, the front elevation will be given more detail than the others (FIG. 15-4). The professional will usually spend extra time in the rendering, and often some concept of landscaping will be added to make it look like a "real home."

If a perspective drawing is to be done, it is almost invariably done from the front (FIG. 15-5). This, again, is a *presentation* drawing, often done in color. Suitable for framing, so to speak.

Either way, when that point comes, provide some photographs of the land on which the home will be built. These, and an accurate site map, are the only way (other than visiting the site) that the person can make a meaningful rendering. Otherwise your home won't be drawn as being on your land. The photographs can also help you, if you care to add detail to your elevations.

The other three views—back and sides—may not seem to be as important to you, but should. They are to the builder. These show the home from the other directions: how the roof breaks and where, placement of windows, special features that might be present, and so on. (Refer to FIGS. 15-6 through 15-8.)

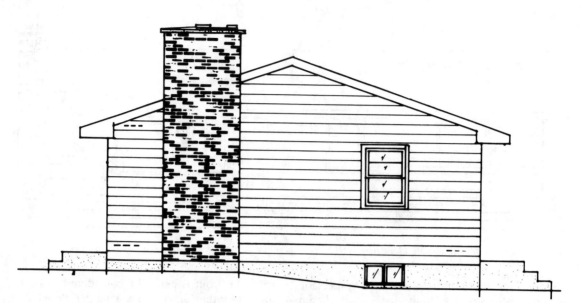

Fig. 15-2. *This view from the east side of the home shows the external chimney stack.*

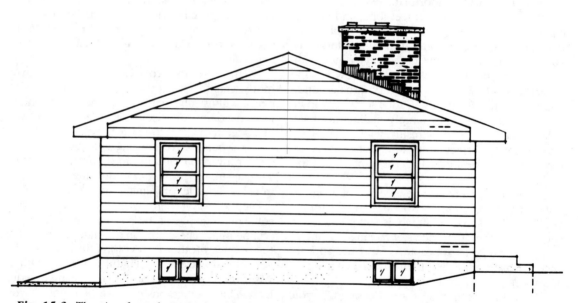

Fig. 15-3. *The view from the opposite side shows only the top of the stack, and a difference in the roof.*

If the home is to be nothing more than a basic rectangle, there won't be much difference between the two side views. On the other hand, there are bound to be some differences, and if the home is more than a box, those differences can be important, even if the views are not detailed.

Facings and Veneers

One of the advantages of elevations is to show how the home will look. It's not easy to picture this. "We're thinking of building a ranch home with a brick veneer," doesn't mean a lot to most people.

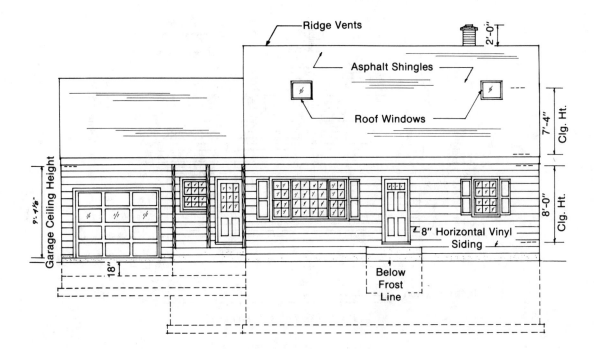

Fig. 15-4. *A front elevation.*

Fig. 15-5. *A front-view perspective.*

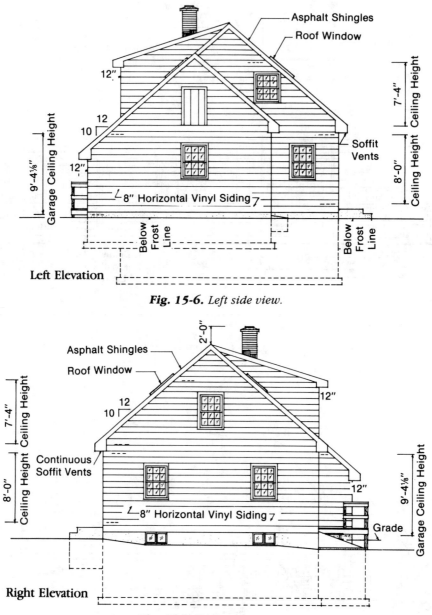

Fig. 15-6. *Left side view.*

Fig. 15-7. *Right side view.*

A detailed elevation can show just what the home will look like with a particular facing or combination of facings (FIG. 15-9). (And also how it will look with different window styles, with or without shutters, and so forth.) It does make a difference.

The variety possible is endless. You can have an all-brick exterior. Your tastes might be more towards a brick or block for the first few feet and stucco or siding the rest of the way to the eaves. You and a dozen neighbors can all have the same basic house, but if each of you can exercise your tastes, each of the houses will look different.

Your goal is to match the facing to the design,

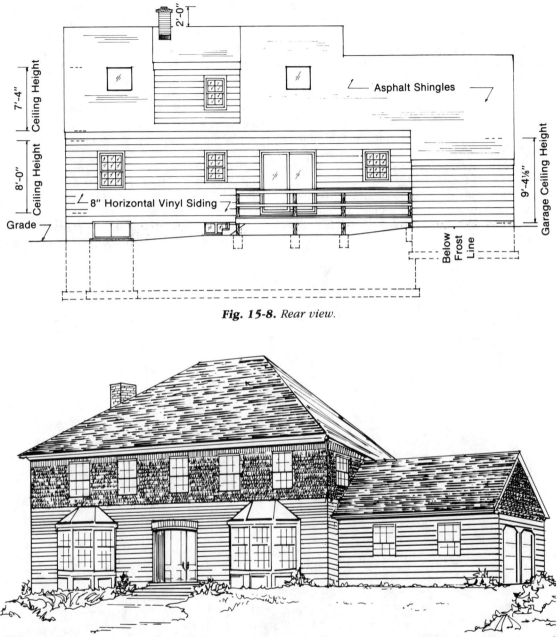

Fig. 15-8. *Rear view.*

Fig. 15-9. *Using two facings on a home—shown here are wood shakes and clapboard—add texture and visual interest.*

to your tastes, and to the surroundings. Typically, the house will blend in with the landscaping and with the nature of the land. At very least, the one side should enhance the other rather than take away from it.

An easy way to explore some possibilities is to make photocopies of at least the front elevation before detail has been added. The dimensions will be correct, the locations for the windows and doors will be set. You can then play with the copies as much as you want. For instance, one can be given a brick veneer, another wood siding, another a combination. You can also use different colors to get approximations of how that factor will affect the appearance of the home.

Chimneys

Years ago there was no such thing as central heating. If the home was to be warm, there was a fireplace, or fireplaces. Most homes had a stack coming out of the roof.

Then came the "modern" era, with more efficient means of heating the home. A small vent pipe was the only thing needed. Fireplaces all but disappeared.

A short period came about during which false chimneys became popular. There was no fireplace in the home, just a sealed and useless chimney stack for the sake of appearance. (A similar concept is used with false fireplaces inside the home. Some of these are decorative "boxes" with no real function but decoration. Others are electric fireplaces, with electric logs, and lights used to simulate flame.)

With the energy consciousness we have today, fireplaces and other wood-burning devices are back in vogue, especially in those areas where wood is abundant. Even with all the rationale aside, there's something pleasant, and even romantic, about having a fire.

In any case, if you have a fireplace or other wood-burning device in the home, an external

Fig. 15-10. *Some chimney shapes.*

venting stack is required. You can't get away without it. To be safe, the stack that vents a fire has to be of certain dimensions, which includes a height above the existing roof (usually set by code to be a minimum of 2 feet above the peak of the roof).

At this point, you still have a wide variety of choices. Will it come out of the roof or go up the side of the house? Will it be brick, block, stucco, or covered with the same siding as the home? (And, if your siding is wood, will local codes allow a wood-covered stack?) Will it be straight, rounded, or otherwise sculpted?

You might prefer the chimney to be a straight column of brick, but you aren't limited to just that. By changing the design of the stack, you also change the overall appearance of the home (FIG. 15-10 and FIG. 15-11).

Perspective

As with the front view, the rear view might have significant landscaping and other features that can't be effectively shown without using perspective. For example, if the home has an inset patio, it won't be seen from any direction except the rear. Even then, a straight-on view doesn't clearly define the feature (FIG. 15-12).

Although perspective views aren't necessary for construction and almost never are a part of the plan set, they can be important for an accurate visualization of many things, inside and outside. Quite often, even an amateurish perspective drawing is what makes the difference. Since such perspective views are almost never a part of the set, if they are needed, you'll either have to pay for them or do them yourself.

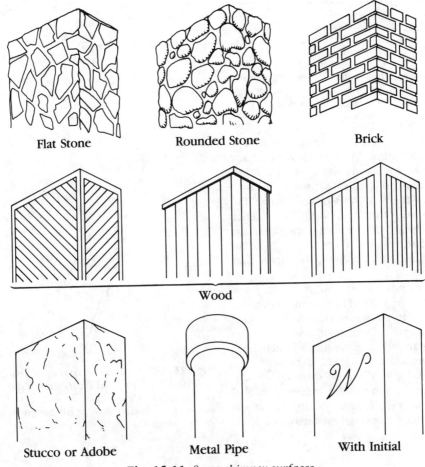

Fig. 15-11. *Some chimney surfaces.*

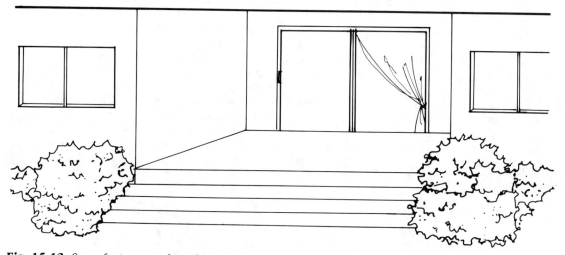

Fig. 15-12. *Some features, such as this indented patio with steps, don't show except on the floor plan and from the back. Even when shown from a standard rear elevation view, it isn't clearly defined. At such times, a perspective view might be needed.*

This book is not intended to be a course in art, nor in the uses of perspective. However, a few pointers can take you a long way with little effort and without the need for great artistic abilities.

Perspective refers to your point of view and how things are seen from that point. The essence of it is that things farther away appear to be smaller. The farther away they are, the smaller they appear; the closer they are, the larger they appear.

This applies not just to objects but to lines. The effect is to make parallel lines seem unparallel, which is just what is done in FIG. 15-13 to create the illusion of depth. (See also FIG. 15-14.)

It's important to keep in mind which lines should be parallel and which angled to one another. For example, if you're showing a room with a window, the top of the window is parallel to the ceiling, and the bottom of the window is parallel to the floor. Although they may not do so

Fig. 15-13. *A classic example of perspective is a railroad track or road vanishing in the distance. In reality, what appears to your eye as a receding track is just two angled lines with progressively smaller cross pieces.*

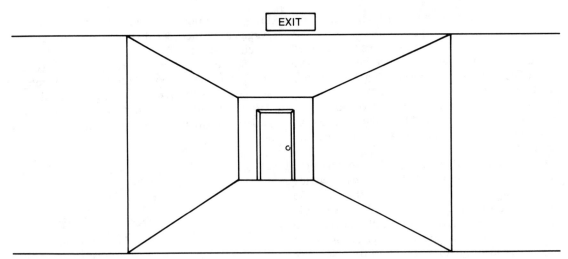

Fig. 15-14. *A wall receding from your point of view does the same thing.*

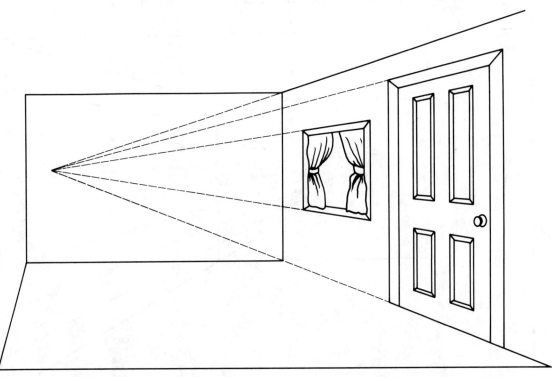

Fig. 15-15. *Note how the windows and door are drawn in this perspective. The dashed line shows the theoretical vanishing point, which would be off the paper.*

Elevations **191**

on the paper, the lines converge. They meet at a vanishing point (FIG. 15-15).

The combination of angled lines and decreasing size makes the drawing seem to be in 3 dimensions. Once again, you're not going to become a great artist and certainly not an expert in perspective with just this overly simplified version, but it can help you to make passable drawings. The only problem remaining will be in determining distances.

A perspective drawing can't be measured the same way that a purely 2-dimensional drawing can. One way to illustrate this is by thinking of a drawing of a ruler sitting on a table. (Or simply hold one up at an angle and see the effect with your eye.) The measurements will seem closer together at the more distant parts of the ruler (FIG. 15-16).

The same is true of anything drawn in perspective, both horizontally and vertically. The lines, real or not, will either be at an angle (to converge at the theoretical vanishing point) or closer together (FIG. 15-17).

To get it all down properly takes years of study, but the purpose here is to keep things as simple as possible (FIG. 15-18). Your job, unless you care to take art courses and learn how to handle a variety of situations, is to estimate that which

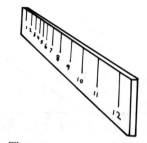

Fig. 15-16. *The measurements seem to be closer together at the more distant parts.*

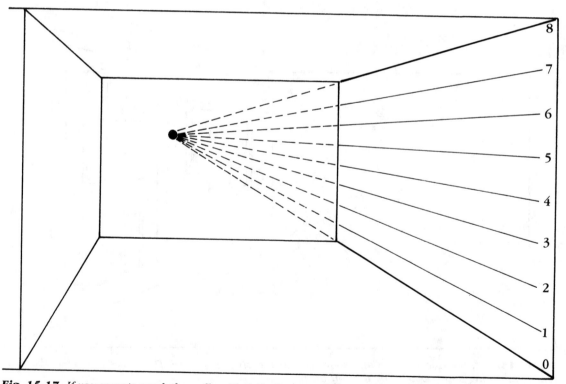

Fig. 15-17. *If you were to mark the walls with their dimensions, paint those lines along the walls and photograph the room, those parallel lines will appear to be angled along the side wall and closer together on the back wall.*

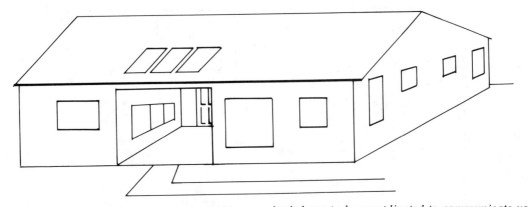

Fig. 15-18. *Perspective drawings, such as this one, don't have to be complicated to communicate your idea.*

can't be measured—to keep a "mental ruler" in your mind, and to keep things as simple as possible while still getting your idea across.

Uses of Perspective

This will sound oversimplified, too (and it is). Perspective views are used whenever a straight-on, flat view will not do. There may be times when you'll need to get certain information or details across that aren't completely clear in flat views. Other times it will be used simply to make envisioning the final result easier (see FIGS. 15-19 and 15-20).

You'll find the same techniques valuable for other kinds of detail, now and in the future. Although more complicated, you can use the technique above to help you design the landscaping. If you've already created a perspective drawing of the home (also complicated, but a good idea), once again you can have as many photocopies made as you wish. (You're going to be reading a lot about making photocopies in the next few chapters!) The copies can then be used to draw and redraw any number of schemes and ideas—easier now because the house and basic land forms are already on the paper.

More immediately, you can make interior drawings of the various rooms, complete with furniture, so you can get an idea of how they'll look. Once more (in this chapter, anyway), don't forget the value of copies. Once you've made the drawing, have it photocopied and put the original safely away. Photocopies are inexpensive and

nearly instant. Redrawing is more difficult and time-consuming. More, once you have the drawing done, you can make as many copies of it as you wish and experiment to your heart's content on details. For a room interior, you can color the walls, or draw in a wainscotting to see how that will look, or you can "try" different drapes and other window covers of different styles and colors.

A Special Kind of "Elevation"

The *scale model* has been mentioned in passing at the beginning of the chapter. With a little effort, you can create a scale model of your home. This can be as simple as using pieces of cardboard cut to size and glued or taped to an appropriate board. Or you can go to the trouble of making removeable ceilings and walls complete with studs and supporting beams inside, and sometimes with lights as well.

Professional architects will sometimes build models to illustrate major projects. Other than this, models are fairly rare, due primarily to the amount of time needed to build them. (It can take as long to build a good model as to build the structure itself.) A simplified model isn't too difficult to build and makes an interesting display for your new home.

The two most common materials used are cardboard and balsa wood. Both are easy to work with, but still require care. Usually thin stock is used for the same reason. Also 1/4-inch stock would represent 1 foot on most drawings, and

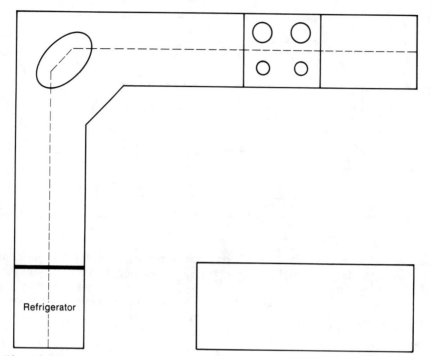

Fig. 15-19. *A standard cabinet detail tells the contractor what he needs to know.*

Refrigerator

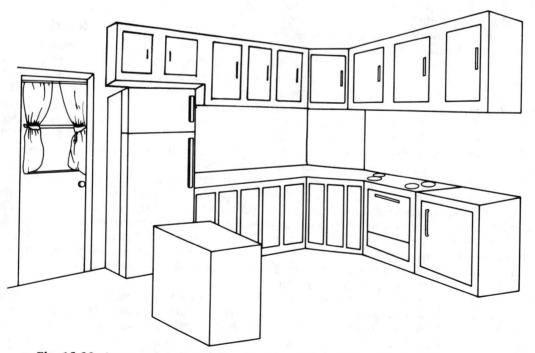

Fig. 15-20. *A perspective view of the same thing gives a different kind of information.*

even more on smaller scaled models.)

Making the three-dimensional model is very much like making the floor plan. The key is accurate measurements. In fact, it helps to have a floor plan as a base, both as a guide and as a means of seeing the various inside features (lights, plumbing fixtures, doors). Even if you don't care to have it as a permanent "floor" for your model, it will still serve as an excellent guide for making accurate cuts.

If you're enthusiastic, the walls can be joined together with keys and notches. (Carve a notch into one wall, and a flap in the one to be joined to it.) This makes a much sturdier structure than one that is simply glued or taped at the edges.

A few companies make kits from which you can build a scale model. (Unfortunately, none of these responded to my requests for samples for testing, so I can't personally recommend any particular one.) Another solution is to visit a well-stocked hobby shop and ask for their advice. Even if they haven't built that specific kind of model before, chances are very good that they'll know enough about other kinds to guide you.

One caution: Building a scale model can take a lot of time. For most people, that's time better spent in other ways, such as making sure that the design is what you really want, or later, that the details of finishing the home are picked. In short, unless you're in no hurry, the value of a scale model doesn't usually justify the time it takes to build it.

16

The rough drawings

Expect to make a lot of false starts. What first seems to be an ideal plan in your mind may not work out in reality. That's okay. "Tearing down a wall" on paper is as easy as erasing the line. And the end result will be a home in which you'll live for years to come. The time to make changes is while it's easy to do so, namely while the moving of a wall means erasing one line and drawing in a new one. Don't be afraid to make mistakes. *This* is the time to make them, not later.

At this point, you should have read all of the previous chapters and have at least some idea of which rooms will go where, why, and how big you'd like them to be. Closets and other storage areas will also be a part of it.

Your first job will be to juggle these concepts into some semblance of a whole, and then to refine this with a series of sketches until you end up with exactly what you want. This can be time-consuming and often frustrating, but it's critical that you take all the time and care needed.

Before You Start

Armed with the information in this book, look at floor plans of other homes. By now you should have a solid idea of what makes a good design and what makes a bad design. Studying floor plans with all this in mind can be a great help in bringing your own ideas together.

As has been mentioned several times, there are plenty of books and magazines filled with floor plans. Some have a broad spectrum of design types. Others concentrate on a particular type or size of home.

I would again recommend Ernie Bryant's *The Building Plan Book* (TAB, #2714) to remind you that a home is more than just a floor plan. This, along with visits to building sites, can be a great help in designing an effective, efficient home. You don't need to learn how to build a home or even how to calculate and draw all the details, but you should have at least an idea of how a home goes together.

Another good idea is to have the builders you're visiting select a floor plan for the job. You'll be accomplishing several things at once. Obviously, you'll be looking at floor plans and at the model homes made from them. You'll then have a much easier time envisioning your own floor plans as a completed home. Simultaneously, you can pick up some ideas on how to modify your design.

Sooner or later you'll be choosing someone to build your home. (See Chapter 20.) As you're touring the model homes, you'll be looking for quality or lack of quality. Just as important, you'll be getting an idea of the kind of homes that contractor is building. He might be a fine builder for standard ranch homes, but can he handle your particular design?

Floor plans are giveaways for most contractors showing model homes. It's not dishonest to bring them home, even if you have no intention of using them, as long as it's a part of selecting the right contractor.

As a side note, many of those floor plans are copyrighted. With rare exception, you do *not* have the option of copying them, and usually it's not financially feasible to do so anyway.

You should consider making lists of general specifications as you go. Having a separate sheet for each part of the home is an inexpensive way to organize your plans. These notes can help to guide you both in shape and in size.

It can help to measure your own furniture that will go in the various rooms. Some standard sizes apply, as covered in the appropriate chapters. In other cases, there is no such thing as "standard" except as a crude approximation. (How big is a recliner? Call a furniture store with that question! There's no answer to it other than the recliner will require anywhere from 4 to 7 feet of space in one direction and 2 to 4 feet in the other.)

The First Sketches

Your first drawings can be as crude as you wish (FIG. 16-1). In fact, the best way to start is to make the roughest line drawings, without much consideration to proportion or scale other than what comes naturally to you. The goal at this stage is to come up with a relative room arrangement and traffic flow.

For cost purposes, most people prefer to use the cheapest 8½ by 11 typing paper, or whatever else is either handy or inexpensive. That's fine, but I would suggest that you also get some quad-ruled graph paper (as described in Chapter 1).

These preliminary drawings will involve nothing more than scribbling some of your ideas onto a piece of paper. The goal of those first sketches is to simply get a basic layout that *might* work. It should be accurate enough to make some sense, but the main idea is to not waste a lot of time putting in detail for a sketch that is likely to be thrown out.

For these very first sketches, don't worry about details. At this point it matters more where the rooms will go than where you'll be locating the light switches. All those details can come later.

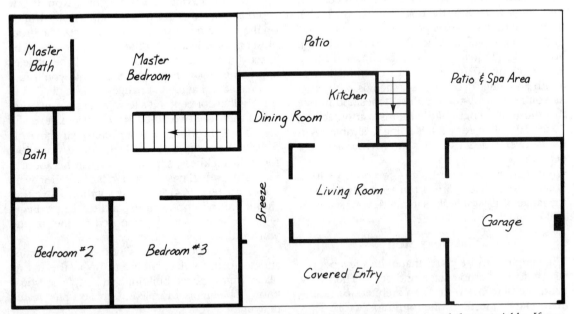

Fig. 16-1. *The first sketches are nothing more than crude ideas meant to be jotted down quickly. If you make only 30 or 40 such sketches to consolidate your ideas, you're doing very well.*

One person ignored this advice. He was determined to make each and every drawing perfect, accurate, and detailed. Consequently, he would spend the better part of a day getting the bedrooms and bathrooms in with 100 percent accuracy, only to find that the kitchen wouldn't fit and he'd have to start over again.

If one room is 10 by 10 and the one next to it is 10 by 20, try to make that second room roughly twice as long as the first. That's accurate enough for now. It's not necessary (at this point) to get out the ruler and make everything absolutely accurate right down to wall thicknesses.

You should have some idea of how large the final home will be. This is based primarily on lot size and how much you intend to spend. Will it be a 1200-square-foot home or a 2000-square-foot home? Another example: if you know that the maximum you can afford is 1500 square feet, and the minimum you can tolerate (or are allowed by deed restrictions) is 1200-square feet, then 1200 to 1500 is your range.

From there, it helps to have an idea of how that range translates into reality. As a simple rectangle, 1200 square feet is 30 by 40 (or 20 by 60, 25 by 48, and so on.) It doesn't matter so much that this will or will not be the final shape of the home. All you're trying to do is provide a guideline.

For example, assume that your maximum home is 1500 square feet. That becomes a rectangle of 30 by 50 (or any other combination of width and length you choose, such as 25 by 60). As you're drawing the rough sketches and notice that the added length of the rooms is approaching 70 feet, the allowed width is going to shrink down to just over 21 feet (which is too narrow for most people).

It's so easy to overdesign—to end up with a home design that is *much* too large. By keeping the range of allowable sizes in mind, your sketches will be much easier to make.

The Next Step

What might surprise you is that quite a few people take it to that crude stage and stop. Then they hand the drawings over to an architect or draftsman. The end result is often not satisfactory.

A client came to the architect with just such a sketch. It lacked so much detail that he hadn't even allowed for closets. It showed the rooms and the dimensions he wanted for them and nothing else. He *had* worked very hard to make the measurement specifications so that the home comes out to be exactly 73 feet long (for some reason), but the specifications didn't take into account any of the interior or exterior wall widths.

The architect's preliminary drawing came as a shock to the client. There was a choice. Either the rooms would maintain their dimensions and the house would be considerably larger, or the exterior dimensions could be maintained at the cost of shrinking the rooms inside.

Crude sketches *are* fine. They are the best way to start, in fact, the *only* way to start. However, they're *not* the place to stop.

The next step is to begin to turn those most rough drawings into something that makes some sense (FIG. 16-2). You will still not be adding a lot of detail. Your goal, once you have a couple of decent crude designs, is to bring in some accuracy.

The purpose of the crude sketches with just lines is to develop a basic concept without wasting time. The purpose of this step is to find out if the concept will actually work.

Choose a scale and use a ruler. Now if one room is twice the size of another, it really will be on the paper, not just approximately so. If a 5-foot closet is to be in a 10-foot room, the closet will be exactly half the length. More, you'll be at least approximating wall thicknesses. What you'll find as a result is that some changes will be needed to the original concept if it's to work at all. For example, if there are two 10-by-10 rooms next to a single 10-by-20 room, the first sketch will show the walls as lining up (FIG. 16-3). But once you allow for wall thickness, the one wall will be about 5 inches (the thickness of a standard interior wall) out of line (FIG. 16-4). The easy solution is to either shrink the two rooms or expand the larger. Begin with the walls that are supposed to line up and you won't have any difficulty.

Just as important are windows, doors, stairs, and so forth, which often end up in the wrong places on the actual building. The only way you'll know for sure is by making an accurate scaled drawing.

An accurate drawing becomes even more crucial if there is more than one floor in your plan. At

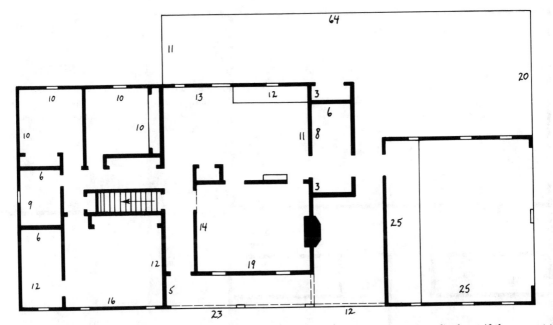

Fig. 16-2. *The next step is to add more detail and some accuracy. The purpose is to find out if the concept developed in the rough sketch will work.*

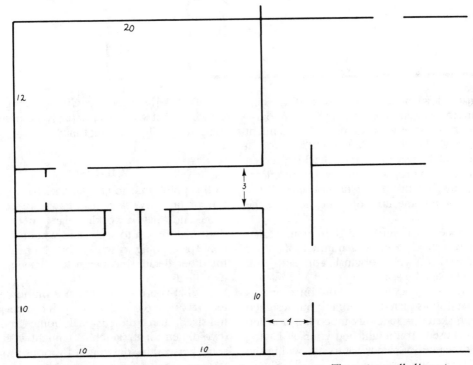

Fig. 16-3. *This rough first sketch simply shows the rooms. The outer walls line up.*

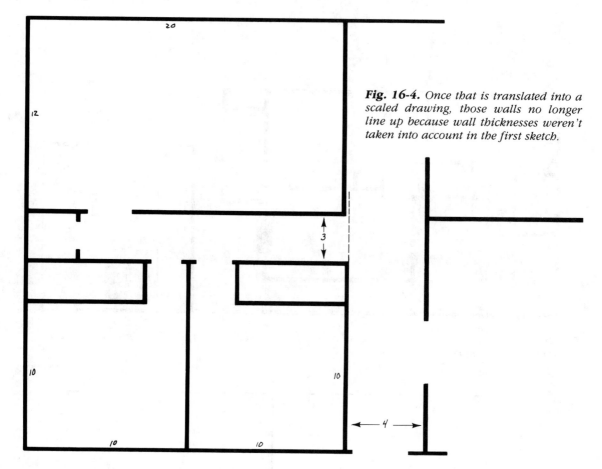

Fig. 16-4. *Once that is translated into a scaled drawing, those walls no longer line up because wall thicknesses weren't taken into account in the first sketch.*

times just a few inches can make a difference. There are things that "connect" the two floors—stairs are the most obvious example. There might also be weight-bearing walls that extend from a lower floor all the way to the roof. Stacking certain kinds of plumbing can save money and problems in the future, but this plan will be useless if the stacking doesn't line up from one floor to the next.

Don't be at all surprised if in your scaled drawing you have to make a number of minor modifications to your original concept. And expect to make false starts.

What can be even more disconcerting is when that 1500-square-foot home you designed as a rough sketch is suddenly much larger when accuracy is used. You might find yourself having to shrink the interior somewhat to stay within the range of sizes you've selected.

This is the reason you're spending time on drawings that will never actually be used. In the long run you'll be saving time.

What Next?

At this point your rough sketches have led you to the preliminary sketches drawn to scale. You should now have a working plan. Once you have a floor plan drawn to scale, and you know that the concept is going to work, you can begin to plan for other details and begin the drawing of your own finals.

What you do next depends on how you prefer to work and on how well you can envision the full-sized, three-dimensional home from a flat (two-dimensional) sketch. You might wish to make some perspective drawings of various rooms or of the entire home from the outside. Some help on how to do this is in the last chapter. You don't have to be a great artist to come up with sketches that help you picture how something will look.

Elevations were also covered in the last chapter. Now is the time for you to make some of the first ones. Your goal isn't quite the same as for the person who will make the final elevation drawings. At this point, you're merely helping yourself envison what the home is going to look like (FIG. 16-5).

One easy way to do this is by putting the floor plan and elevation on the same sheet of paper. In a sense, you're getting two views at the same time—one from above, and one straight on from the front.

If you have more than one floor, you have two choices. One is to make it easy on yourself and, for this drawing, use the main floor only. Another way is to use a larger sheet of paper so that the other floor or floors can be shown (FIG. 16-6). This second requires more work, but allows you to have the entire house on a single sheet of paper.

This is *not* how the person making the final drawings will do it. (See Chapter 17.) This kind of

drawing is for your own benefit—to help you envision the home. It's possible that a floor plan you just love will create a house that doesn't look right to you from the outside.

Your Final Drawings

Once you have an accurate scale drawing, you *can* stop. However, you'd be wise to take it one more step and make a final set of drawings similar to what the draftsman or architect will be making. Your main goal this time is to be sure that your ideas are communicated exactly, and that the details you need are clear. (There's not much sense in designing your own home if the end result is only an approximation of your ideas because everyone had to guess.)

It's a good idea to review the appropriate chapters in this book as you're finalizing your plans. And be sure you keep any lists or notes you've made on hand.

Because of the additional details, this drawing should be larger. How large depends on the size of the home. "Full-size scale" is usually 1/4 inch to the foot. Using this scale, a home 70 feet long will

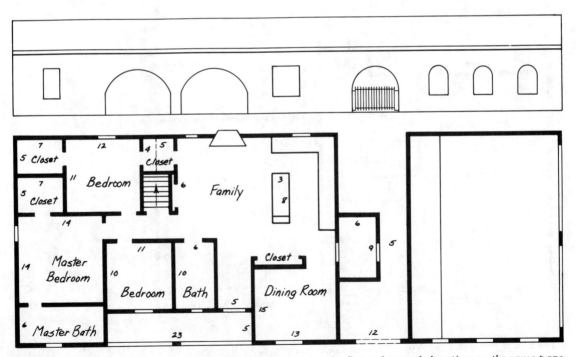

Fig. 16-5. *One way to help you envision the home is to have the floor plan and elevation on the same page.*

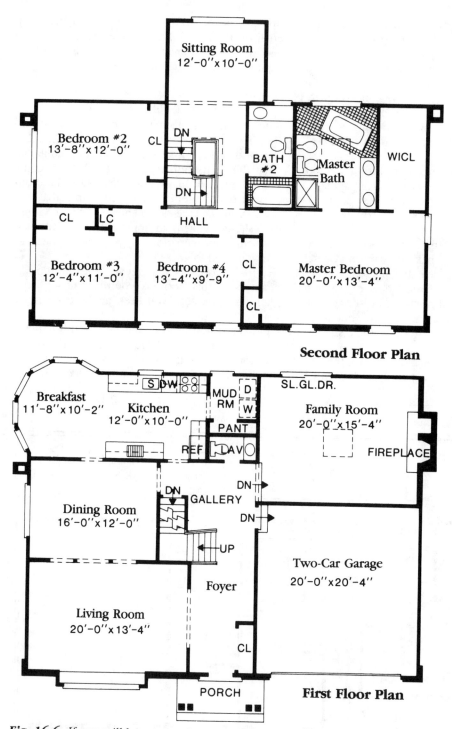

Second Floor Plan

First Floor Plan

Fig. 16-6. *If you will have more than one floor, you can show the others on the same sheet of paper.*

need 17½ inches for the actual home, plus a few more inches for dimensioning and margins.

Normally, you'll have one sheet for each of the floors, one sheet for the elevation or elevations, and however many other sheets needed for separate details.

What Details Are Needed?

Whoever makes the final drawings will automatically put in the proper number of outlets, as per code (FIG. 16-7). This may or may not suit your needs. In certain areas you may want additional or special outlets. Don't forget to show plenty of outlets on the outside of the home.

Lighting is even more important. The location, type, number, and more needs to be specified, both inside and outside the home. Also needed will be location of the switches—especially for lights that will be operated from more than one location.

Once again, don't ignore the outside of the home. That's a common error. It will often be given too few outlets, too few lights, and too few hose bibs (faucets). As you're making your final drawings, be thinking of the future as well as the present. And don't forget the past. How many times in your present home have you wished that there was just one more place—or a different place—to attach a hose, for example?

Various other details will also go on this drawing such as placement and size of the tubs, sinks, cabinetry, counters, and other items. You should also include any other details you feel are important (and some that you might not think are as critical). Don't assume anything. It's your job to tell the person who will be making the final drawings everything possible. Whatever you don't specify will either mean a guess on his part or that the item will be left out.

Some of these things can be taken care of later. Adding another outside light isn't too difficult, but if you're careful now, that won't be needed. There's no such thing as having too much

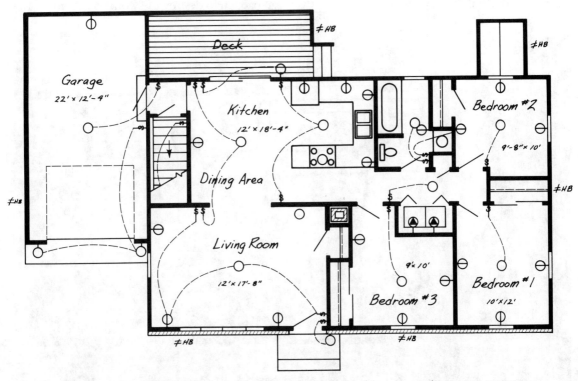

Fig. 16-7. *Your own final drawing will show detail needed to communicate your concepts.*

information for the person who will be making the finals.

Scale Furniture

You can draw in scaled furniture on the preliminary sketches if you wish, but they will only be confusing on your final drawings. There is a solution, however—one that gives you an additional way to be certain that the home is going to work for you: making scale-sized furniture. This is a nice technique even after you move in. (You can rearrange a room with your fingers, instead of your back.) Once you have a drawing that is to scale and accurate, you can make some scale furniture, appliances, and other items from paper and move them around on the drawing to see how things fit.

Many people have a very hard time visualizing what the room will actually look like. If you're one of those, don't worry about it. Cutting out scale furniture will still tell you if things will physically fit in the room and how much space will be left over (FIG. 16-8).

You can increase the visibility of the scaled items by coloring them or otherwise marking them to make them distinct from the background paper. For the same reason, it's also good to give each at least a dark outline and to write the name of the object on the piece.

If picking them up is a problem (it will be), a sharp point can be used to "stick" and lift the piece. This can be either a needle or a thin-bladed hobby knife, such as an X-acto knife (FIG. 16-9).

Copies

Once you have what you consider to be your working plan, have a few copies made. Copying machines that handle the larger paper won't be found at the corner convenience market, and making the copies will be more expensive than copies of the standard-sized (8½ by 11) paper, but the investment is well worth it.

There is always the chance that the person hired to make the final drawings will accidentally ruin yours. Or you might. Any number of things can happen to destroy the work you've done. The

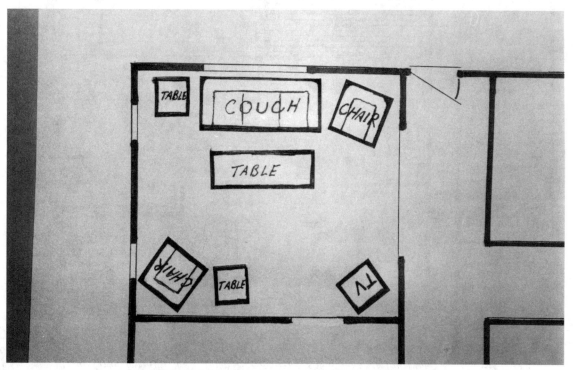

Fig. 16-8. *Making your own scale furniture and appliances.*

Fig. 16-9. *A thin-bladed hobby knife with a sharp point or a standard sewing needle can be used to "move the furniture."*

few dollars to make copies might save you hours of work.

Those copies can be used for other things. With them you can begin to plan other details and specifications while you're waiting for the true final drawings to be made. Which rooms will have carpet, and which will have sheet vinyl? How about paint colors? You might want to have some special wiring and cabling, such as for stereo equipment and intercoms. Those can be marked onto a copy (never on your original!) and later transferred, if need be, to a copy of the final renderings.

Be sure to keep one clean copy and preferably the original as well, with no peripheral markings or notes. (The time might come that you'll need more copies.)

17

The final drawings

You're almost finished with the planning stage. You have your rough drawings and are ready to have them turned into the final form that will be used by the builder. Hopefully you'll have been in touch with a few draftsmen or architects or both and have several in mind from which to choose. (If not, read Chapter 19 for some hints on how to go about this.)

It's going to take a few weeks for the final drawings to be done. Maybe shorter. Maybe longer. But that's fairly standard, depending on whom you select, how busy this person (or company) is, how large and how complex your design is.

This can be a hectic time. It'll seem to be taking forever, and all of a sudden you'll have a million new decisions to make—and quickly! That's often followed by another waiting period and then another batch of decisions.

The more prepared you are for all this, the better. If you've spent the time coming up with the design that you should—including research into what the constructional procedures will be like with your particular design—and especially if you've gone one step farther and already have a very good idea of all the specifications (see Chapter 18), you shouldn't have too much difficulty getting through this stage.

One Last Time

Before you bring your rough drawings to the draftsman or architect, go over them one more time—carefully. So far you've spent very little but time and personal effort, with the goal of coming up with the perfect home for you. From here on the costs go way up.

This is the last "best time" to make changes you want and to spot errors. Do you know where the home will be placed on the lot? If not, you'd better find out right away or all your efforts might be wasted. The house has to fit the lot, in size and in design. Does your plan take into account all the ordinary things, like plumbing and electricity? These items are so often given very little attention by the novice designer, much to their regret later. You can take care of *some* of the small details later, but the larger ones needed to be covered before you turn your ideas into final drawings.

Look at the layout as a whole. Do the rooms blend with each other in the way you want? Or do you have to walk through a bedroom to reach the only bathroom, or perhaps walk across the entire house to bring a bag of groceries from the car to the kitchen? Imagine yourself once more moving around inside and outside the home you have designed. Does it work? Or are there too many inconveniences?

Go through the plan room by room, section by section. Are the rooms large enough? Maybe they're too large, or perhaps you've given so much space to one area that others suffer. Do you have sufficient storage throughout? Or have you forgotten that people have things that need to be tucked away in every room of the house—and outside as well?

In short, is your design sound and workable, or will it be a growing headache?

What to Expect

The first step is to meet with the draftsman or architect and discuss your ideas. *You* know what you want. That professional knows what can and cannot be done. What is going to be standard, and what in your design is going to cost a small fortune (while a simple modification will make it work).

You may or may not have to redraw your roughs. If you do, chances are pretty fair that you haven't done your homework. Little changes are normal. Larger changes, or having to start over again, generally means that you have gone to a professional too soon.

If things are going as they should, you'll get the professional's version of "rough draft." Then you'll sit down again and go over those drawings, done to scale, to find out where you have gone wrong (and where you have gone right!). Once again, if your own sketches have been accurate, and if you've communicated your desires effectively, these preliminaries should be nearly identical to your own concepts. A room might be a few inches in another direction; there should be no large differences. (On the other hand, if your "roughs" have been made up of lines only, without the effort to take walls into account, the architectural renderings could come as a shock.)

If you can, bring these drawings (or copies of them) home with you. That way you can take your time to make sure that everything is just right. Make arrangements for this ahead of time. Some professionals will not be willing to let you take the preliminaries with you. All of them will need the time to have copies made. (It's not a good idea to take the originals.)

Once you've made the corrections and have

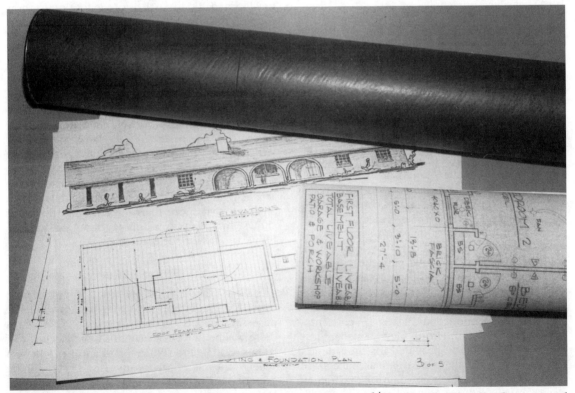

Fig. 17-1. *The originals are in the container. Full-sized copies and 8¹/2 by 11 reductions are the ones used for normal handling.*

approved the preliminaries, the final drawings will be made, followed by yet another meeting. Hopefully everything will be perfect by this point.

Bring a container with you to protect the drawing. (You should already know the size. If not, call and ask.)

Your next job, if it hasn't been done for you, is to take the originals—in the container—to a blueprint shop and have copies made. (Some print shops may also have the equipment needed to copy such a large size.) I *urge* you to have two full-sized copies made right away. It's also an excellent idea to have reductions made, so that the drawings are also on standard $8^{1}/_{2}$ by 11 paper (FIG. 17-1).

The originals should be tucked back into the protective container and left there. The only time they should come out is for last-minute changes (by the draftsman, not you—unless you made the drawings) or to have additional copies made.

Do not use the originals for the detailed examination, and certainly don't make notes on them. The idea is to touch the originals as little as possible. That's what the copies are for.

The Basic Set of Plans

How the pages are arranged depends somewhat on who does the drawings. Sometimes the first page will be the elevations. Other times it will be the detailed plan of the main floor (FIG. 17-2). We'll deal with the latter, since this is a little more common. The reason for this is that the contractor will be referring most often to this page.

After the main floor plan will come the page, or pages, for the other floors (FIG. 17-3). In addition to the usual floor plan details, these pages may contain other details, such as those for stairs, structural details for the floors, and so on.

With the major sections out of the way, the next page will probably cover the footings and foundations (FIG. 17-4). This tells the contractor where and how the supports and concrete are to go.

A sheet of elevations will also be included (FIG. 17-5). As mentioned in Chapter 15, concentration will be on the front view. Smaller, less-detailed views will be provided for the side and rear views. Some draftsmen and architects will also use this page to show some of the framing details. Others will put it elsewhere, perhaps even on its own sheet.

Just how much of the framing is shown in the drawing depends on what is required by local codes. Some areas want every wall drawn to show placement of each joist, stud, hanger, and frame. Others go on the assumption that any competent builder already knows how to build a wall and how to frame in a door or window, and are satisfied with ceiling, floor, and roof framing details (FIG. 17-6).

At least one sheet will give sectional drawings (FIG. 17-7). This might show just a portion of the home or it might show the entire thing. The purpose is to give vertical details, such as placement of insulation, how the floor is to be built up, and how the roof will be.

The final page—sometimes kept separate from the others—is the plot plan (or site plan). This tells the contractor where the home is to go on the lot, where the boundaries are, and other necessary information about the lot (FIG. 17-8).

Quite often other sheets might be made. Local code might require that a sheet of specific details be included, such as of the footings or how the wall is to be anchored to the foundation. Specific details might be needed for certain features, especially if those features are unusual. On many plans you'll find notes to refer the builder to a detail on another sheet.

You can also have other details drawn. You might want a professional rendering of the cabinetry, for example; however, such drawings are not part of the "basic set."

As mentioned in Chapter 15, the person making the drawings may also provide you with a *presentation drawing* (FIG. 17-9). This is a more artistic rendering of the home, usually drawn at an angle so that more than one side of the home shows. In a way it's a "photograph" of how the home will look once complete.

Floor Plans

The floor plans can be presented in one of two ways. Most common are those that give all the necessary details on one drawing. Other times there will be one floor plan to show placement of rooms, doors, and fixtures, and another that will specify the electrical layout (FIG. 17-10). Which presentation will be determined partially by local codes, or perhaps by the personal preference of the person who is making the drawings or even of

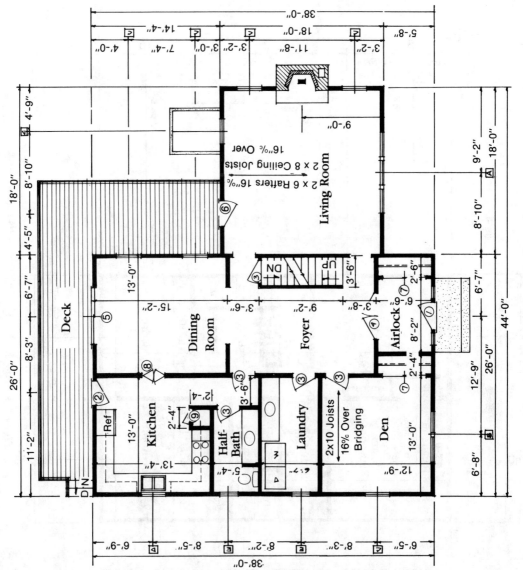

Fig. 17-2. Page 1—The main floor plan.

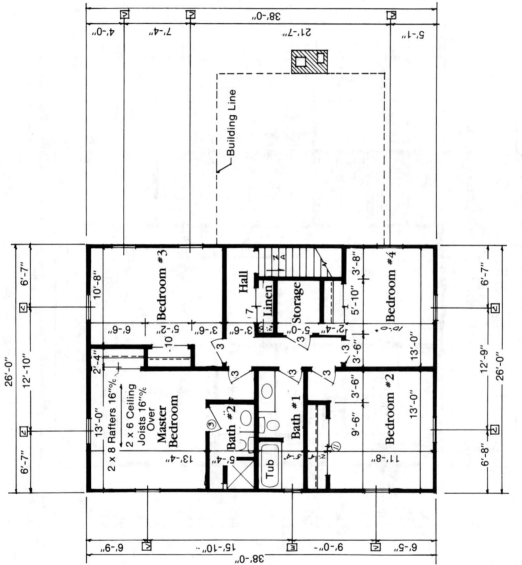

Fig. 17-3. *Page 2—Floor plan for the other level.*

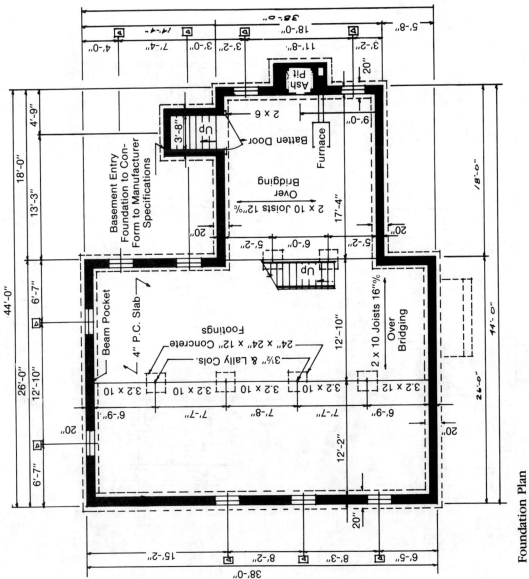

Fig. 17-4. *Page 3—Foundation details.*

Foundation Plan

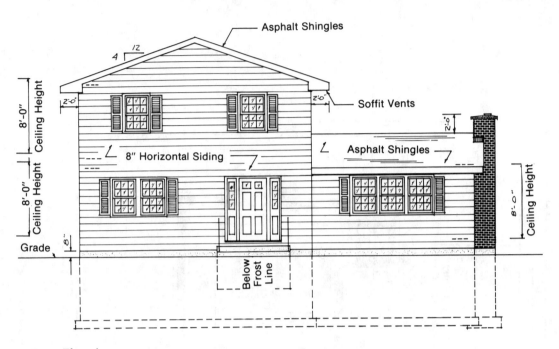

Front Elevation

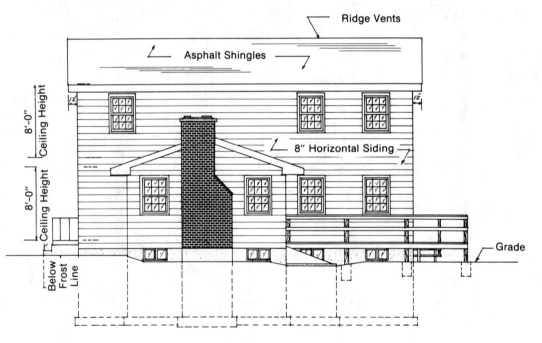

Right Elevation

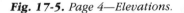

Fig. 17-5. *Page 4—Elevations.*

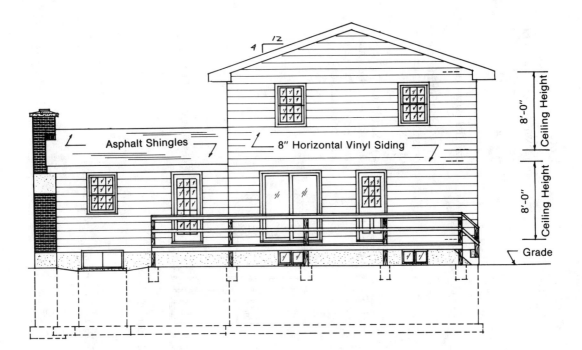

Rear Elevation

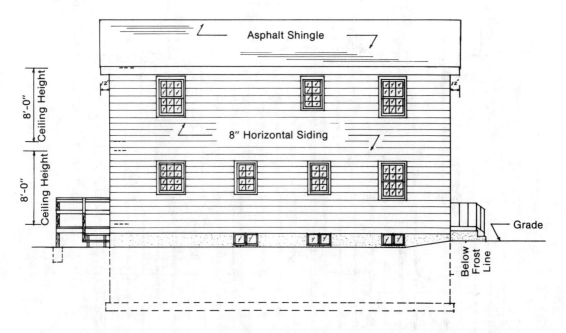

Left Elevation

Fig. 17-5. Continued.

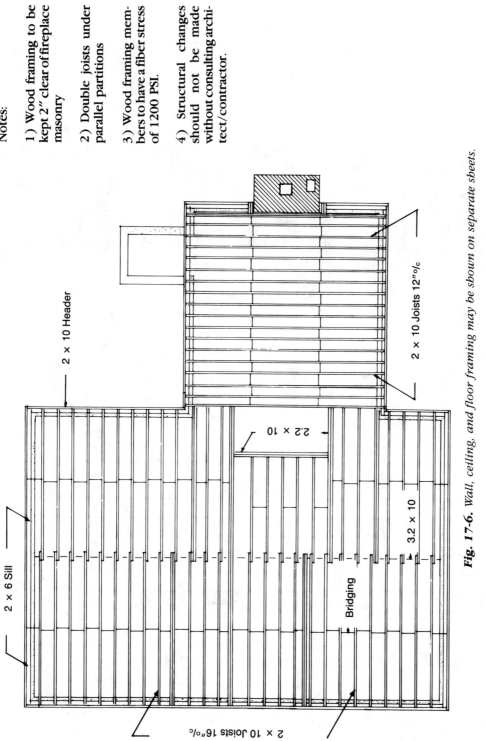

Notes:

1) Wood framing to be kept 2″ clear of fireplace masonry

2) Double joists under parallel partitions

3) Wood framing members to have a fiber stress of 1200 PSI.

4) Structural changes should not be made without consulting archi-tect/contractor.

2 × 10 Header

2 × 10 Joists 12″o/c

2 × 6 Sill

2.2 × 10

3.2 × 10

Bridging

2 × 10 Joists 16″o/c

Fig. 17-6. *Wall, ceiling, and floor framing may be shown on separate sheets.*

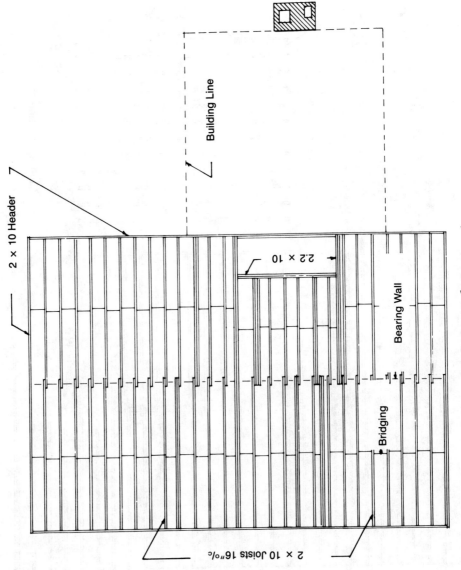

2 × 10 Header

Building Line

2-2 × 10

Bearing Wall

Bridging

2 × 10 Joists 16"o/c

Fig. 17-6. *Continued.*

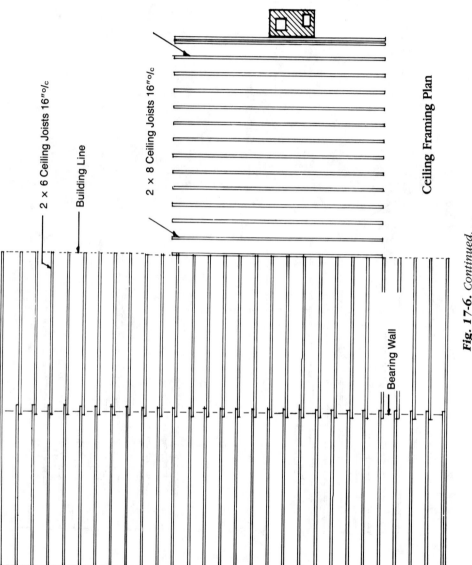

2 × 6 Ceiling Joists 16"o/c

Building Line

2 × 8 Ceiling Joists 16"o/c

Bearing Wall

Ceiling Framing Plan

Fig. 17-6. *Continued.*

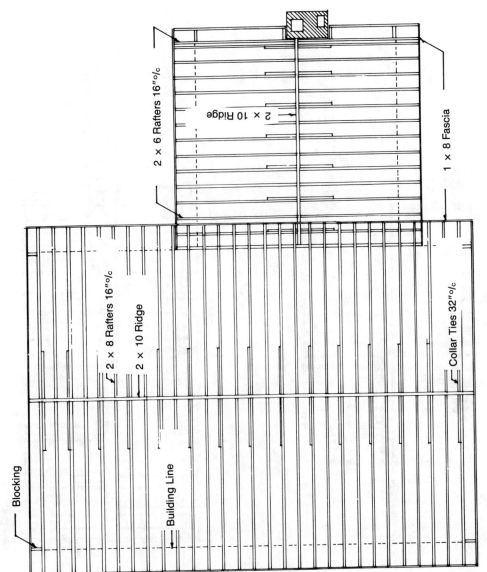

Blocking

2 × 8 Rafters 16"o/c

2 × 10 Ridge

Building Line

2 × 6 Rafters 16"o/c

2 × 10 Ridge

1 × 8 Fascia

Collar Ties 32"o/c

Fig. 17-6. *Continued.*

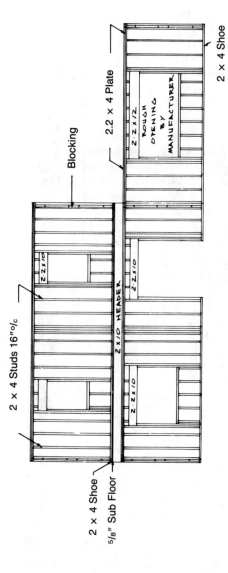

Front Framing Plan

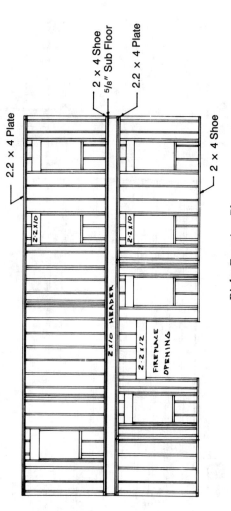

Right Framing Plan

Fig. 17-6. Continued.

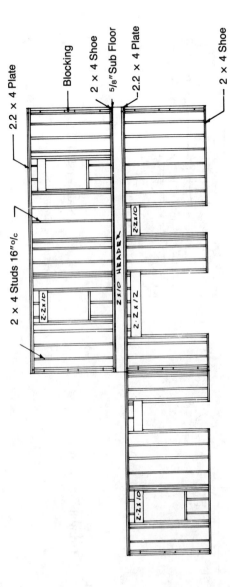

Rear Framing Plan

Labels on rear framing plan: 2.2 × 4 Plate, Blocking, 2 × 4 Shoe, ⁵/₈" Sub Floor, 2.2 × 4 Plate, 2 × 4 Shoe, 2 × 4 Studs 16" o/c

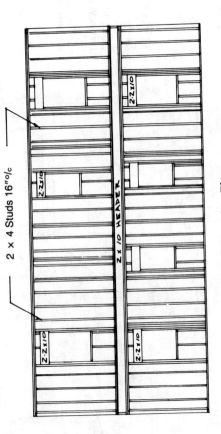

Left Framing Plan

2 × 4 Studs 16" o/c

Fig. 17-6. *Continued.*

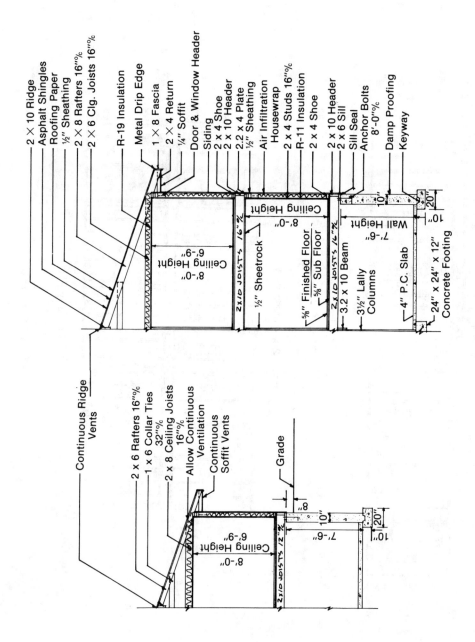

Staff Section

Living Room Section

Fig. 17-7. *Page 5—Sectional drawings.*

The following labels appear in the drawing:

2 × 10 Ridge
Asphalt Shingles
Roofing Paper
½" Sheathing
2 × 8 Rafters 16"%
2 × 6 Clg. Joists 16"%
R-19 Insulation
Metal Drip Edge
1 × 8 Fascia
2 × 4 Return
¼" Soffit
Door & Window Header
Siding
2 × 4 Shoe
2 × 10 Header
2.2 × 4 Plate
½" Sheathing
Air Infiltration
Housewrap
2 × 4 Studs 16"%
R-11 Insulation
2 × 4 Shoe
2 × 10 Header
2 × 6 Sill
Sill Seal
Anchor Bolts 8'-0"%
Damp Proofing
Keyway

Ceiling Height 6'-9"
8'-0"
2x10 Joists 16"%
½" Sheetrock
Ceiling Height
8'-0"
⅝" Finished Floor
⅝" Sub Floor
2x10 Joists 16"%
3.2 × 10 Beam
3½" Lally Columns
Wall Height 7'-6"
4" P.C. Slab
24" × 24" × 12" Concrete Footing
10"
20"
0"

Continuous Ridge Vents
2 × 6 Rafters 16"%
1 × 6 Collar Ties 32"%
2 × 8 Ceiling Joists 16"%
Allow Continuous Ventilation
Continuous Soffit Vents
Grade

Ceiling Height 6'-9"
8'-0"
2x10 Joists 16"%
7'-6"
8"
10"
20"
10"

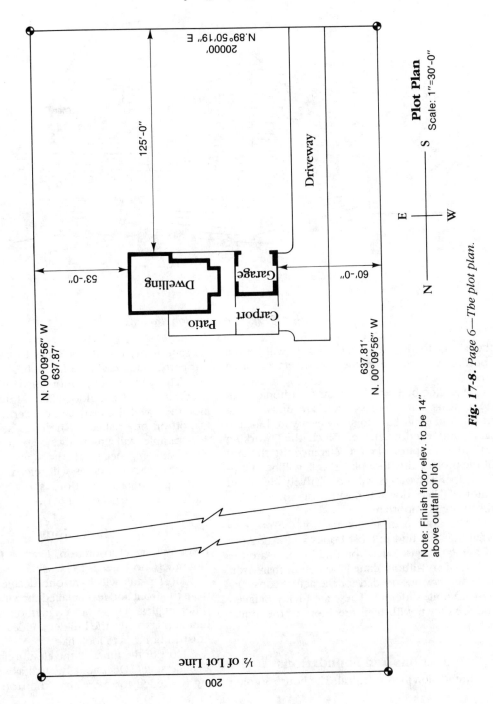

Fig. 17-8. *Page 6—The plot plan.*

Fig. 17-9. *A presentation drawing.*

the contractor. In any case, each crew will get the appropriate sheets (although the sheets are often shared).

A skilled builder can construct a home from floor plans alone (unless there are unusual features). You don't have to show every stud, beam, door, and window frame. Watch the "working set" that is kept on site for reference. By the end of the project, the floor plan sheets will be in pitiful shape. The others will be relatively clean and untorn. (That doesn't mean that those other sheets are unimportant.)

The floor plan sheets are not the same as what you will find in most books and magazines of home designs. What you find in those are the basics, often without dimensions other than overall. The drawings needed for the actual construction are quite different. These are highly detailed and are drawn with high precision, as they must be!

Sections and Foundations

The foundation plan is critical. The house is going

to sit on that foundation. If it isn't constructed properly, neither will the house be.

The general foundation plan will be a top view (like the basic floor plan). More often than not, there will also be details concerning the foundation on other sheets. The cross section sheet, for example, will almost always go from footing to roof, showing details all the way. If needed, or required by code, notes will refer the builder to drawings on other sections showing important parts in more detail (FIG. 17-11).

Elevations

Elevations were covered in detail in Chapter 15. Not much more needs to be said.

Most plans will have one detailed elevation from the front and less detailed drawings from the other angles. These are straight-on views. The function is to give the builder an idea of what the finished home is to look like.

Most of the time, all the elevations will be on a single sheet. Occasionally, such as when detailing is needed for more than the front view, the

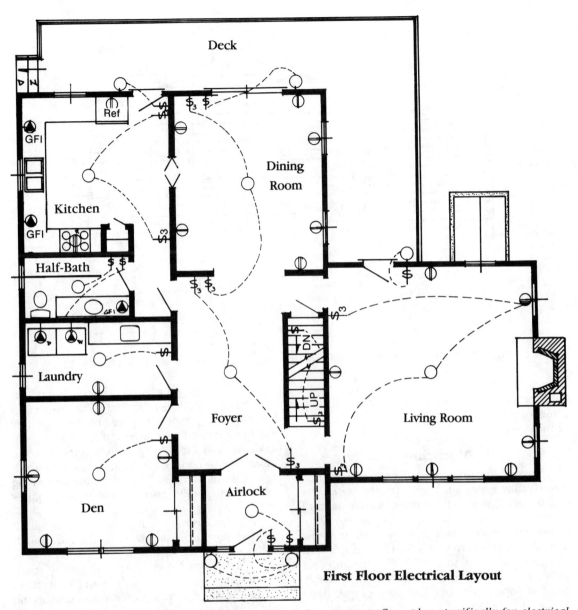

Deck

Ref

GFI

Kitchen

GFI

Dining Room

Half-Bath

Laundry

Foyer

Living Room

Den

Airlock

First Floor Electrical Layout

Fig. 17-10. *Sometimes the set of drawings will include a separate floor plan specifically for electrical details.*

four elevations will take up more than one sheet. A separate structure, such as an unattached garage, will almost certainly be on a separate sheet. In fact, such a structure is likely to have its own complete set of plans. (Most areas require a set of plans for every structure.)

The detail of the elevations is dictated by need and by the working habits of the person making the drawing. That person might be highly skilled as a draftsman. Each measurement will be precise, but he or she might lack the artistic talent to do a more artistic rendering. Generally, it's not

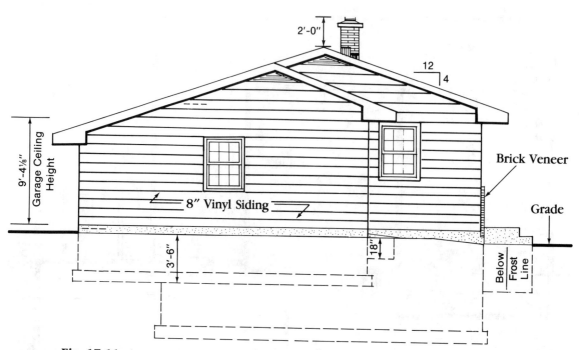

2'-0"

12
4

Garage Ceiling Height
9'-4⅛"

Brick Veneer

8" Vinyl Siding

Grade

3'-6"

18"

Below Frost Line

Fig. 17-11. An even more detailed drawing than the one shown might be called for.

needed anyway—at least not for the builder. The main purpose of an artistic elevation is to give someone unfamiliar with construction a "picture" of the home.

Blueprints

The name "blueprint" comes from a process that has basically gone out of use. Treated paper was put through a process that turned the dark lines of the drawing white and the white paper blue. Photocopying machines and new processes are now used almost exclusively. You'll rarely see an actual blueprint except in someone's files for an older building. Even so, the term is still used. It simply means a copy of any building plan, even if there isn't a hint of blue.

As mentioned in the last chapter and earlier in this chapter, have plenty of copies made. This is one of the least expensive parts of the job and one of the most important. Eventually you'll need at least between 5 and 7 complete sets, not including those you'll want for yourself. One is needed on the building site. One is needed in the contractor's

office. Others are kept by various subcontractors.

The county or other building inspection department might only require one copy; or they might require two or three complete sets. It could be that you'll be dealing with several different departments—county and local—with each wanting to have its own sets. You might also be dealing with a homeowner's association that also requires a set.

You can save some money by waiting until the plans have been approved by the local building inspection office, but in my opinion, this is not a wise way of saving. Already you've spent 100 hours coming up with your ideal plan, another $1000 to have a professional make up the final drawings, and you're about to spend many thousands to have the home built. Trying to save an extra $10 by skimping on copies of the plans is foolish.

As stated earlier, go directly from the office of the person who made the drawings to the place where the blueprints will be copied and have at least two sets made. You now have something on which you can make remarks and comments without having to touch the originals.

Once you're absolutely certain that everything is just as it should be, you can make all the needed copies. Don't forget to have at least two sets for yourself and at least one without *any* markings on it.

The moment you have copies, store the original in a protective container and put it away. The original or at least a copy or both should be stored somewhere other than in your home.

Once again, having a reduction made is a very good idea. Most blueprint shops that have the machinery to make large copies also have what is needed to reduce large drawings to smaller sizes. Once you have a set of plans reduced to standard 8½ by 11, you can make as many other copies of the same size at will—and cheaply. These smaller drawings are very handy in a number of ways, not the least of which is that they are easier to carry around and mail to family and friends (to show off your new home). You *will* need to carry drawings around—at least of the floor plans. Imagine visiting the company that is to supply all the floor coverings. You can lug along the rolled blueprints and struggle with them, or you can have a smaller, easier to handle 8½ by 11 sheet.

The difference between making notes on a separate sheet of paper and making notes on a copy of the floor plan is one of obvious convenience. You can easily jot down carpet, linoleum, lighting fixture, and other specifications for each room. If you wish to transfer these notes later to the larger set, fine. Meanwhile you won't be fighting those large sheets that like to roll back up the second you lift up your hand to jot down a note.

Mistakes, Mistakes, Mistakes

Even at this stage, mistakes can come into play. We're all just human, after all. You are, the draftsman is, the contractor is—so is the building inspector.

No matter how carefully you design the home or how carefully you make your drawings, no matter how carefully and accurately everything is done each step of the way, including your own inspections, there is a great possibility for mistakes. There shouldn't be any major problems. Not if you've been diligent. And little mistakes are generally fairly simple to correct, even late in the game.

If the draftsman hasn't faithfully put your concepts down on paper, chances are pretty good that a part of the fault is your own: for not communicating, for not doing your homework, or for not noticing the mistakes in the preliminary drawings.

Then comes submission of the plans to the agency responsible for approval. Call it red tape, or a "flexing of muscles," or just some official doing his or her job. In any case, it's fairly common for the submitted plans to come back from the inspector with comments and requirements for changes.

The best way to handle such problems and mistakes is to just handle them: one at a time, calmly and efficiently. Expect them to happen. You'll have sufficient time to find and handle them if you and the contractor are diligent.

Yes, some of the difficulties might not appear until construction is underway. Be *sure* that your contract clearly specifies that you will be notified in good time about such things.

Part
THREE

18

Other specifications

An entire book could—and perhaps should—be written about making the hundreds of final decisions concerning the home. Just when you thought you had everything done, along come more decisions to make in a few days than any person should face in a lifetime.

Where do you want carpet and where do you want vinyl and where do you want tile and where do you want . . . on and on. Of the 18,394 styles, colors, qualities, and other options, which do you want? If for some reason those aren't available, what are your second choices? Third choices?

Which paint colors do you want in each of the rooms? Walls and ceilings the same or different? Two coats or three? What kind of windows do you want? And doors? And hardware for both?

What about lighting fixtures? Which of the dozen-plus manufacturers' brands and which of their lines do you want where in the home, place by place?

That's just the beginning. There are literally hundreds of choices to make and thousands of ways to decide each. Details, details, and more details. The array of choices and decisions can come as a shock to many.

Hopefully, you'll have some ideas in mind even before the first line is put on paper. You'll have seen a number of homes and will know what you like and don't like. You'll have lists, and maybe a box full of samples and swatches.

As a piece of advice, take it seriously. Spend some time looking at homes, at magazines with pictures of homes, at catalogs, at samples, at everything possible.

Usually, you'll have what *seems* to be plenty of time for all these decisions. The home will be designed. The designs will be made into blueprints. The blueprints will go through the approval stages. You'll find a contractor and draw up the arrangements, including financial. Then construction will begin. That will be a few months to about a year, depending.

But if you wait until the point when the deadline is nearing, you'll not only be squeezing for time, you might find yourself forced into choices you don't want, while making those choices early would have allowed you some alternatives. In addition to this, the more you know about the project before even talking to the contractor, the more accurate the bids will be—and the fewer "surprises" there will be at the end for unexpected extra costs.

A stone tile roof is much more expensive than bottom-of-the-line asphalt shingles. If the contractor has bid your home to have those shingles, and you then see them and decide that they're just not good enough, you *will* pay extra for the change.

With many—even most—contractors, you will be given "allowances" in certain areas as part of the overall bid. (See Chapter 20.) The choices will be your own. For example, the bid might allow you $3000 for floor covering. It's up to you to look at samples of carpet, vinyl, and other coverings.

As a part of your specifications prior to getting the bid, it's your job to let the contractor know the quality you expect of the materials used. "Base grade" can be the least expensive available, and therefore, the lowest quality. If you have a 500-square-yard area to cover and specify that $10/yard flooring is sufficient, the allowance on the bid will be $5000. If you then find out that only the $17/yard material will do, you'll be facing an extra $3500 in costs.

To avoid these pitfalls, plan ahead. Find out what things cost. Visit a flooring company, for example, and find out how much the kind of carpet and vinyl you have in mind is going to cost. The same applies to everything else in the home.

Windows

By this time you'll have some idea of where you'll locate the windows and what size they'll be. You'll also have to figure out what the windows are going to look like.

A common misconception is that a window is a window—that glass is glass. Not true. There are a variety of styles, types, and qualities (See FIG. 18-1). For example, will the framing be wood or metal? If wood, will it be pine? Oak? Paint-grade or stain-grade (or perhaps you'll paint it outside and stain it inside)? If metal, will it be steel or aluminum? Painted? Anodized?

Each has advantages and disadvantages. There's nothing quite as beautiful as wood, but it often costs more and is subject to warping. Metal windows are often less expensive than comparable-quality wood-framed windows, but too often the metal used is thin and has the tendency to bend or warp under stress. (This is particularly true of window screens).

How thick will the glass be? This is determined somewhat by the size of the window. Smaller windows can be $1/8$ inch. Large windows might have to be made of $1/4$-inch or thicker glass.

For increased strength, safety, and insulation value, you might prefer to use glass that is thicker than normal for all windows. This is a good idea for the glass in doors. Going from $1/8$ inch to $3/16$

inch might not seem like much, but it can make a difference. (It also might not fit.)

There are other decisions to make. Will the glass be single pane or dual pane? Will it be thermalized? Will it be smoked, etched, textured, coated with a film, or plain? Will it be a single sheet or divided into smaller panes? For that matter, will it be glass or plexiglass (FIG. 18-2)?

Inside, the contractor may or may not be taking care of the blinds, drapes, shutters, or whatever you decide to use to cover the windows. A part of this decision is up to you. Usually, you can save a lot of money doing it yourself. If the contractor supplies the materials and labor—especially if he does so through a subcontractor—his own profit will be tacked on to the total. It's a great convenience to have everything done and ready for you to move in, but you *will* pay a charge.

Doors

As with windows, doors come in a wide variety of types, styles, sizes, materials, and functions. There are hollow-core interior doors with simple locks (or no locks); steel-clad, insulated exterior doors; ornate, carved wood doors with glass inlays; passageway doors; swinging doors; garage doors; screen doors; storm doors; café doors; and so on. (See FIG. 18-3.)

Of prime concern are the doors to the outside. These must be secure and solid, preferably with both a handle lock and a dead bolt. (See "Locks" on p. 232). Your concerns with exterior doors are appearance and security, not necessarily in that order. It's fine to have a beautiful, hand-carved entrance door with stained-glass inserts, but those glass panels can be easily popped or broken out.

Sliding glass doors, often called *arcadia doors,* are like large picture windows that move aside so you can walk through. They bring their own special problems, especially concerning security. Also, because they tend to be utilitarian rather than attractive, they are usually located in the back of the house.

On less-expensive homes, hollow-core doors are often used even as exterior doors. In my opinion, this is a foolish way to save money, unless that door has been specially constructed to be secure.

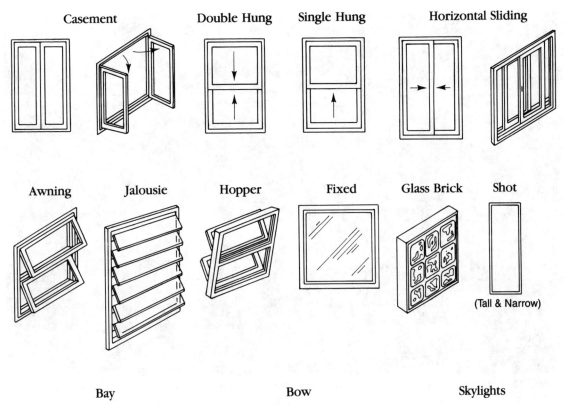

Casement Double Hung Single Hung Horizontal Sliding

Awning Jalousie Hopper Fixed Glass Brick Shot

(Tall & Narrow)

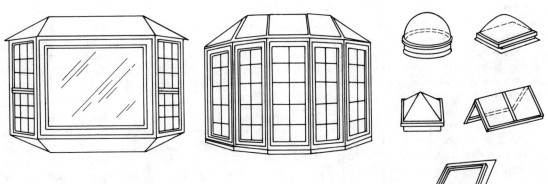

Bay Bow Skylights

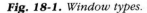

Fig. 18-1. *Window types.*

(A metal entrance door, for example, is by its nature hollow.)

Interior doors are meant to give privacy rather than security. They are usually hollow-core rather than solid wood. The locks can be simpler. All this saves money and does not lessen the overall security of the home.

As with exterior doors, the interior doors can be flat panels ("flush"), colonial, or have another pattern (FIG. 18-4). It's rare to have interior doors that are ornate, but there are other possibilities not available for exterior doors. For example, a louvered door provides a degree of privacy while also still providing ventilation. For an even more

Fig. 18-2. *These garage windows are plastic, not glass. The texture is to make it impossible to see in.*

open feeling, you can use café doors, either with panels or with louvers. French doors, with all that glass, close out sound while allowing visual openness. (For other door types, refer back to FIG. 7-2).

You don't have to limit yourself to standard hinged doors. As is so common with closet doors, other doors inside can be bifold, folding (accordion), sliding, or pocket. Each has its uses and its place. Choose carefully and sensibly. Think of how the door will be used and the space where it will be installed, and plan accordingly. Listed below are types of doors and their uses.

Hinged Door—Tends to be the most sturdy, least expensive, and requires the least maintenance. Easiest to seal (such as against weather) and make secure. Popular for entrance and passage. Requires floor space for swing.

Bifold—Relatively inexpensive. Takes up little space, since it does not swing but folds on itself. Popular for closets. Requires more maintenance than hinged door.

Sliding—Takes up no floor space. Popular for closets and for arcadia doors. Provides good accessibility since the door slides completely out of the way, but blocks an equal amount of space in doing so. Prone to functional problems and requires a fair amount of maintenance.

Pocket—Like a sliding door, except it slides into a pocket in the wall. Prone to the same problems as any other sliding door, but with the added disadvantage that access to the track is much more difficult. Requires space inside a wall without studs of a depth equal to the door width.

Folding—Also called an "accordion" door, since it folds. Takes up very little floor space. Provides least amount of security and durability.

Locks

Never try to cut costs where locks are concerned. You need the very best available for the exterior

Flush

Six-Panel Colonial

Four-Panel

French

Divided Light

W/Screen

1 Light, Divided

Tempered Glass

2-Panel Below W/Divided Light

Spanish

Colonial W/3 Light

W/"Wheel" Light

Fig. 18-3. *Some standard exterior door styles.*

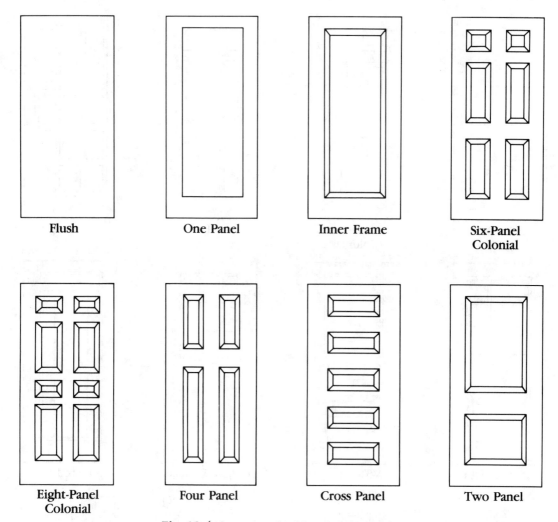

Fig. 18-4. *Some standard interior door styles.*

doors. (The interior doors normally don't need high security. The locks are more for privacy.)

Burglars fear three things: being in sight, making noise, and taking too long. Your job is to make things as difficult, and as dangerous, as possible for the burglar. Cheap locks aren't much of a deterrent. They can be picked, jimmied, or snapped too easily. Even if the door with this lock is in plain sight of the neighbors, the amount of time needed to get past the lock and into the home isn't a significant threat to the burglar.

Better locks can still be defeated, but it takes longer and generally causes more noise. A door with a standard beveled latch bolt *and* a sturdy dead bolt lock should be standard on all exterior doors in your home, and certainly where the entrance is secluded from sight (FIG. 18-5). Be sure to specify this in the building contract, and don't forget to be sure that the work has been done properly.

Windows and arcadia doors have several things in common; for openers, they are made largely of glass. Also, they are often made so that the sliding part can be lifted out. Finally, the standard locks provided tend to be rather pitiful.

Specifying dual-pane glass will help a little.

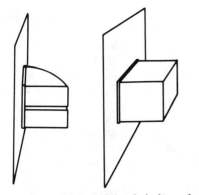

Fig. 18-5. *Standard beveled latch bolt and dead bolt.*

Such windows not only help to insulate, they also tend to be of heavier construction and give two layers of glass that must be cut or broken to gain entry. Beyond this, you can also specify that the windows and sliding glass doors be fitted with decent locks. Unfortunately, that will narrow your choices while increasing the cost.

You can take steps on your own. A simple stick placed in the track will prevent the window from sliding and can be easily lifted out from the inside. To prevent someone outside from prying the sliding panel up and out, you can drill a hole (or can specify this in the building contract) so that a pin can be placed through to prevent movement of the panel. (Be sure that this pin can be easily removed from the inside.)

Appliances

Most contractors "throw in" certain appliances. The cost is built into the bid. You'll get a water heater and some kind of heating, ventilation, and cooling system. In many areas, these are required by the building codes.

Generally, unless you specify otherwise, you'll also get a stove and often a dishwasher. In a few cases the contractor will also offer a refrigerator and perhaps even a washer and dryer.

Keep two things in mind: First, *nothing* is free. That the home will "come with" various appliances doesn't mean that they don't cost. You pay for those things. They're just an easy part of the overall charge. Second, it's entirely possible that the contractor has special contacts through which you can get appliances at a discount,

whether they are offered as a part of the deal or not.

For example, when we built our home, the range/oven and dishwasher were a part of it. We *could* have specified that all the other appliances were to be installed as well, but that would have meant that the cost for the washer and dryer would have been a part of the mortgage to be paid off with interest over 30 years. While it would add very little to the house payment, it would more than double the *real* cost of the appliances and fix them to a loan that would go on long after the two had died.

We opted instead to make use of the contractor's supplier and pay cash for those things we wanted. (We could have also taken out a separate loan.) As a consequence, we got all new appliances, including a microwave oven, for 30 percent and more below what we would have paid elsewhere. (Since we were buying so many other things, the supplier offered us the microwave at his own cost.)

The real key is to balance your needs and your wants, while keeping in mind that what you can't afford at the moment will become a part of the mortgage and will cost you dearly over time. In short, keep the number of mortgaged appliances to a minimum.

As to your choices: The three major appliances in the kitchen are the stove, the refrigerator, and the dishwasher. As mentioned above, the first and last are often a part of the package. Normally that means a basic appliance. If you want something different, you'll usually have to pay extra and call out for it in your specifications.

The standard stove has the oven inside and four burners on top. It's roughly 30 inches by 30 inches. Mounted overhead will be a rangehood with a fan and a light. You may prefer a different arrangement. Island-mounted range tops are popular, for example, often with the oven located separately along the wall cabinetry, sometimes with a microwave mounted above it. You can even have an indoor barbeque, either gas or electric (but keep in mind the need for extra ventilation).

When choosing color, keep overall coordination of color in mind. White will go with almost anything, but tends to be a little stark—almost sterile. Black will also go with most color schemes, but if not handled properly can seem dreary. Other colors, such as harvest gold and avo-cado, might blend in better with your present ideas, but keep in mind that you might repaint or repaper the kitchen in the future.

Cabinets and Counters

Cabinetry and countertops were discussed in some detail in Chapter 7. At this point you will have made use of that information and will know the sizes of the various cabinets. In the final speci-fications you'll also have to decide style and color (FIG. 18-6).

Most people live with the same cabinets for as long as they own the house—or nearly that long. Replacing the cabinetry is an expensive job. Con-sequently, it's advisable to make your choices carefully. You don't have to go with the most expensive handmade cabinets you can find, but neither should you make the bad "investment" of going with the bottom line.

The least expensive, usually, are those with plain, flat doors and fronts. With these you'll also find that there is often fewer color choices. Gener-ally, the more "carving" there is, the more the unit will cost. This cost can be reduced by going with one of the stock patterns.

Stain tone usually comes light, medium, and dark. There are a variety of colors, from a mild yel-low to an almost black. In addition to these are painted cabinets, which open the color choices almost to infinity.

Cabinets that are meant to be stained gener-ally have at least a veneer of higher quality wood.

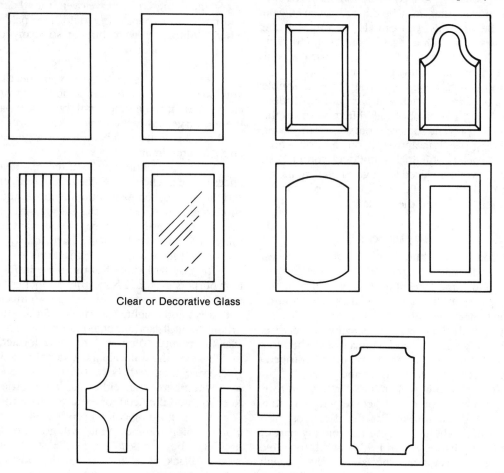

Clear or Decorative Glass

Fig. 18-6. *Some standard cabinet styles.*

"Paint grade" cabinetry doesn't have to be so fussy since little flaws in the grain will be hidden by the paint. Thus, paint-grade cabinets tend to be a little less expensive, although they can come out about even if you also have to pay a special labor charge for the painting.

With stained cabinets you have the natural beauty of the wood. With paint the grain is hidden but the variety of colors available opens up.

The type of countertop and material used depends both on your personal preferences and on the location of the counter (FIG. 18-7). Plastic laminates are the most popular throughout the home. The material is tough, attractive, and relatively inexpensive compared to anything else with those qualities. This material comes in literally hundreds of patterns and colors—from wood-look, to rock-look, to patterns and colors not otherwise available. Other choices are ceramic tile, special plastics such as Corian, synthetic marble (more of a poured and formed plaster-like sub-

stance), real wood, and even (if you can afford it) real stone.

The cabinets and counters in any single area should usually match. They do not have to match throughout the house.

Trim and Molding

Your choices concerning the trim are somewhat similar to the choices in cabinetry. It can be wood, plastic, or some other material. It can be stain-grade wood, or paint-grade. It can be smooth or have a "carved" look.

Trim is used to finish off the job. Cabinets mounted to the wall will have small gaps between the cabinet and wall. There will be gaps where the wall meets the floor and gaps around every door and window. All of this has to be hidden. In addition, there will usually be trim whenever two different materials come up against each other (FIG. 18-8).

Fig. 18-7. *Note that the countertop in this laundry room is at "desk height," allowing a person to sit on a standard chair and work comfortably.*

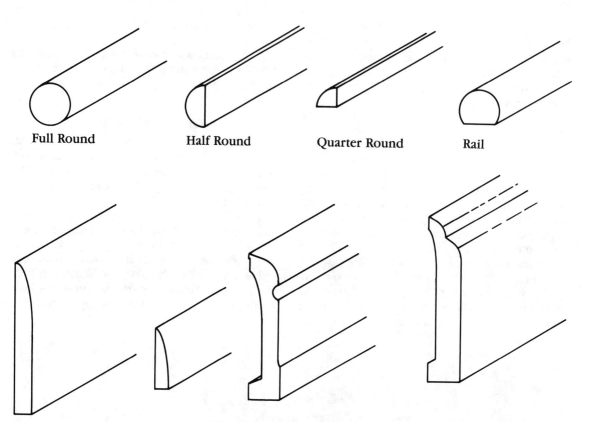

Full Round **Half Round** **Quarter Round** **Rail**

Fig. 18-8. *Trim and molding.*

Normally the trim job around the cabinets is a part of the cost of the cabinets. Unless you specify otherwise, it will probably match the cabinets.

Other trim will be provided along the wall bases, around doors and windows, and sometimes (but not always) inside closets. You can also specify other kinds of trim. For example, you may wish to have a chair rail behind the table. This was originally meant to prevent damage to the wall when someone slides a chair back too hard, but today it is often used simply for appearance (FIG. 18-9).

Painted wood is the least expensive. The wood can be of lower quality, with flaws and joints. If the wood is to be stained, any flaw or joint is going to show, so the wood must be of higher, and more expensive, quality.

Floor Coverings

The two most common ways to cover a floor are

with carpet and vinyl (either sheet or tiles, and often called *linoleum*). Other choices include wood, stone tile, and various kinds of concrete finishes. Each comes in a variety of types, styles, colors, finishes, and qualities.

A general rule of thumb is to get the best you can afford. The floor gets a lot of wear. Cheap floor coverings are going to have to be replaced much sooner, which means another cost both for material and installation.

Carpet and vinyl are relatively inexpensive (when compared to other coverings) both in material cost and installation cost. Carpet comes in 12-foot widths and occasionally as 1-foot squares. Vinyl comes in sheets of 6-foot and 12-foot widths and as tiles usually 1 foot square.

The life and comfort of the carpet can be increased by using a higher quality pad beneath. The cost is minimal compared to the benefits, so it's generally advisable to call out for a 1/2-inch or 5/8-inch pad of very good quality. It might cost

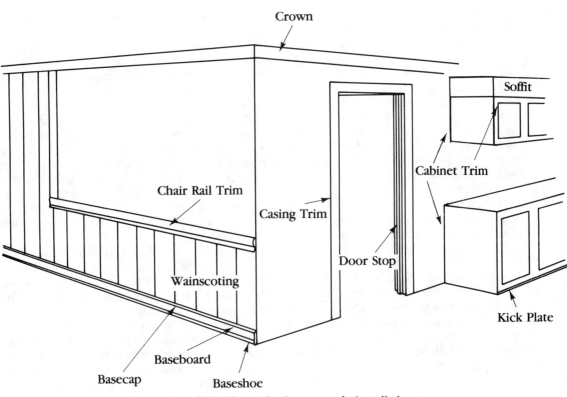

Fig. 18-9. *Where trim is commonly installed.*

you another $1 per square yard extra, but it can greatly increase the lifespan of the carpet while also making it feel more luxurious.

Carpet comes with a variety of different piles, from long-stranded shag to extremely dense and short tufted "indoor-outdoor" carpets. The usual warranties range from one year to 20 years, increasing in time as the cost of the carpet increases. If you have carpet, be sure that the contract specifies that the installer will come back once during the first year to restretch as needed.

Vinyl floor covering is the most common in any area that might get wet, where spills might occur, and where frequent cleaning is necessary. For this reason, it is almost always used in bathrooms and kitchens.

As with carpet, vinyl floor covering comes in a variety of styles, colors, qualities and an even greater variety of patterns. You can get types that require no waxing, others that have the pattern through extra thickness so that scratches don't show, still others with a cushioned backing to

make the flooring feel a little softer.

Wood floors are usually installed as squares or as strips of wood. Either way, it's one of the more expensive kinds of floors. Only high-quality hardwood material will do, and it must also be free from visible defects. In addition, it's a high-maintenance floor. Even light use of the floor will require that it be resurfaced every few years.

Stone tile floors are also expensive, due mostly to the cost of installation, which is invariably a time-consuming job. (Even basic, rough stone that costs $1 per square foot of tile can cost you $45/yard with installation. Do keep in mind that the cost of installation is fairly constant, regardless of material. Just as it costs the same to lay down a yard of $60/yard carpet as $8/yard carpet, with the difference in cost being material only, the same applies, more or less, to the laying of tile.)

Stone tile is durable, but not indestructible. With proper care, the tile will probably never have to be replaced in your lifetime. If something heavy is dropped on it, repairs might be needed. This emphasizes the need to collect any leftover material—something you should do with all floor coverings. It's standard for the builder to leave the carpet and vinyl scraps, but often you'll have to specifically ask for—and be sure you get—the extra tile. (All of this applies to any ceramic tile in the house.) Those doing the job will probably estimate the materials fairly closely, but at least a few pieces will be leftover. This demand on your part will also prevent any chance of the subcontractor ordering too much material, at your expense, and then storing it for the next job.

Another kind of stone is man-made. Although most people think of concrete as suitable only for things like foundations, garages, and driveways, it can also be used as a finished interior floor. A dye can be mixed in with the concrete to add color. The surface can be polished to smoothness if you wish, giving it the appearance of compacted clay.

Another option is the use of pebbles or rock flakes. The first will give a rough floor, generally suitable only for the outside; the second can be floated to a smooth surface that has somewhat the appearance of granite.

Wall Coverings and Painting

The three basic choices are paint, wallpaper, and paneling—or any sensible combination of these. Ceramic tiles are also popular, especially in kitchens and bathrooms. Walls of mirrors are sometimes used for beauty and to make a room seem larger and more open than it really is.

The possibilities are so endless that an entire encyclopedia could be filled and still not exhaust every scheme. Not only do you have an almost infinite choice of material and color, you can blend and mix to suit yourself. Your choice will be a matter of personal preference, and this goes on from room to room—inside and outside. The choices are all yours to make.

Planning wall covering schemes can begin very early. What kind of look do you want for the house? What kind of color scheme? Will the colors blend or contrast? Will they be subtle or bold? Look at other homes, at magazines, and at books on interior decorating. Get some ideas that have worked for others and then come up with your own.

No matter how you do it or what materials you use, be *sure* that the contract specifies that you get all the leftovers. It might mean just a few extra squares of tile, maybe a quart or so of each paint color, some trimmed strips of wallpaper, but insist on them. It will make minor repairs much easier. Even though a can of paint in the store has the exact same name and code number and is made by the same company, one batch of paint is going to be slightly different from the next. Consequently, the best paint for touching up is the same as what was used in the first place. The same is true of other materials, made worse because sometimes a particular style or pattern will disappear. A simple repair then becomes a difficult or impossible task.

A fair number of homeowners choose to do the painting themselves. The advantage is the savings. If you have the time, you can do the job skillfully enough and with enough care so as to not cause damage, go ahead.

The greatest disadvantage is that if you make a mistake—if you spill paint or cause other damage—the cost of repair is yours. If a professional painting crew does the job and ruins something, they're responsible for the repairs. (Be *sure* that this is clearly specified, that the contractor is licensed, bonded, and insured, and that he takes responsibility for the subcontractors he hires.)

Lights

By this time you will already know where the permanently mounted fixtures will be placed and how many you'll need. This hopefully will have been determined by need, with care taken to be sure that the number, location, and wattage of the lights will be sufficient and that the switches are all properly located. Now your goal is to choose those lighting fixtures that will do the job needed while creating the appearance you want.

With most contractors, the lighting fixtures are on an allowance. You'll be "given" so much to spend, and it will be up to you to make the choices. Usually you will be given at least one source—generally one through which the contractor deals often and can get a discount. One of your first jobs in this regard will be to visit the showroom and to get catalogs and prices of what is available.

The two basic types of lighting are *incandescent* and *fluorescent*. Both have a variety of bulbs available, both in wattage and in style. Usually, the type of bulb used will determine what the lighting fixture will look like, and, in many cases, how it will be manufactured.

Lights can be made to mount to the wall, to the ceiling, or on a pole. The first two can be mounted to a surface or can be recessed. Finally, there are stand lights that sit on the floor or on a desk or table. These last are usually plugged into an outlet. The others are almost always "hard wired" through a switch. (Outlets may also go through a switch.)

You'll have quite an array of styles, from fancy crystal chandeliers to a very basic bulb holder (Refer to FIG. 18-10 on pp. 242 and 243.) Prices range from about $3 to several thousand, with most standard fixtures costing between $10 and $50 each.

Your first and primary consideration is where the light will be and how it will be used. This might mean that the fixture will have to have two bulbs instead of one, or perhaps even more. If you have your heart set on a particular fixture but it won't do the lighting job, you may have to talk to the contractor about a modification to the house plan. Perhaps two fixtures can be used. If the fixture you want, for appearance sake, is to be on the wall, you might be able to choose a ceiling fixture to augment the lighting. Or vice versa.

It's time for another reminder: Don't wait until the last minute. If a change is needed very early in the job, the added cost will be minimal or possibly nonexistent. Wait until the walls are up, finished and painted, and the charge is going to be considerably higher.

When planning your lights, don't forget the outside. The entrances *must* be well lighted. A peephole in the door isn't going to do much good at night if you're looking into darkness. On a more regular basis, if the entrance is dark, guests are going to have a hard time.

Outside spots to light the yard are inexpensive at the time of construction and a great investment (FIG. 18-11). The same applies to a lesser extent to lights out in the yard or along a walk.

Landscaping

Many people think of landscaping as having no

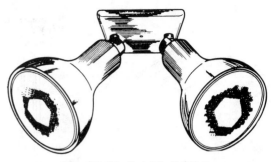

Fig. 18-11. *Outside lighting.*

purpose other than to beautify. It's also there to reduce erosion by wind and water and to protect the home from the elements. Trees can shade the home during the summer and (if evergreens are used) block a cold northerly wind in the winter. Slope of the land can help with drainage problems (FIG 18-12).

At the very least, be sure that the land immediately around the home is graded to a slope to keep rain away from the house. This usually means a drop of about 6 inches across the first 10 or 15 feet from the outer walls. More might be needed, depending on if you have a basement, where you live, on the soil conditions, and on the plants (FIG. 18-13).

Whenever possible, try to use the natural landforms. Every change you make is going to cost money. In addition, each change is likely to make some other change necessary elsewhere. If you've looked over the lot well ahead of time—before you began the home design—you'll have designed the home to best suit the land. Hopefully this will mean that major changes will be minimal.

One of the first places to start is with the ground cover. The most common is grass, which can be either seeded or put in place as sod. Seeding is initially less expensive, but will require a great deal of water before it comes up. Even so, it is almost always less expensive than sod. The two great advantages of sod are that you'll have, almost literally, an instant lawn—and one with its own topsoil.

Other ground covers are available. Which you choose will depend on where you live. Local nurseries can tell which plants are most suitable for your area, and usually what other options are available (such as crushed rock for landscaping in desert areas).

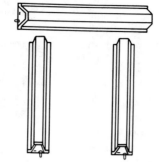

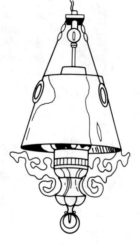

Fig. 18-10. *Some standard lighting fixtures.*

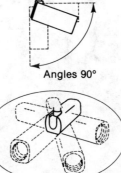

Angles 90°

Rotates 360°

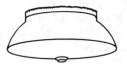

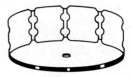

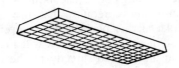

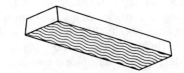

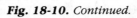

Fig. 18-10. *Continued.*

Fig. 18-12. *Landscaping.*

To oversimplify, there are two basic kinds of trees: *seasonal* and *evergreen*. The seasonal trees, such as deciduous, will have leaves for shade during the summer, but will be bare during the winter when you want the sun's warmth on the house. Of course, this means that each fall you'll be facing the job of raking up and disposing of the fallen leaves. Evergreens keep their leaves (needles) all the year. That can cause a problem with shade, but evergreens can be used to block the cold winter winds. The key is proper placement so that the plants and trees do what you want them to.

While much or all of the planting can be left for later, you might consider asking the contractor (at the beginning) about the cost of installing fences or walls. He may or may not be able to provide a better deal for you. If not, or if you put it off until later because of finances, at least plan your overall yard for such things. If you never intend to have any kind of fence or wall, fine. If you do, perhaps only in the distant future, your landscaping plans must take this into consideration (FIG. 18-14).

If the contractor is to handle the landscaping, be sure that the contract allows you to withhold that amount until the work is done. This is often one of the last jobs, and it's not uncommon for the work to be still going on after you've moved in. It's always easier to get satisfaction when there is money still due, but due *only* after the work is completed.

Other Needs

The building codes just about everywhere in our country now require that fire or (preferably) smoke alarms be installed in every new home. Most of the time the bid will include only the basic unit, wired directly to the house current. That's fine, and certainly better than nothing, but if a fire knocks out the power, or melts the wires to the alarm, it won't do anything to protect you. Much better, but more expensive (and still not

Fig. 18-13. *Placement of trees, bushes, fences, and walls can add to the overall beauty while also serving a purpose.*

completely secure) are those units that have battery backups.

Burglar alarm systems are rarely an automatic part of the bid, and surprisingly few new homeowners take them into consideration before the construction, which is when running the wires is the least expensive. The oft-cited reason for not installing the burglar alarm is that the money is needed elsewhere. Don't forget that a compromise is possible. If you figure where you want the main control unit and which sensing devices will be needed and where, you can run all of the wires while the walls are still open.

Putting wires of various kinds is relatively easy while the walls are open. You can run wires for intercoms, for stereos, for cable or satellite television, for extra telephones, and so on. You can have the contractor run all these lines if you wish, or you can do the work yourself. If you plan to do the work, there is only one time when it can

be done, and you can't expect everyone to stop all progress.

Within your list of specifications, require that the contractor tell you when the walls are up and the electrical wires are in, but *before* the walls are covered. This is the best possible time to run your extra wires.

Beyond all this are possibly hundreds of other little items, many of them dealing with your own personal preferences and needs. Some will have to be specified in writing with the contractor, others will not. When in doubt, ask.

I work at home, and the design and specifications reflect this special need. Dedicated electrical outlets were "called out" in the plan. Perhaps more appropriate here is the darkroom next to the library (which is next to my office). A darkroom is unusual as far as "standard home" is concerned and has special needs. In my own list of specifications, the room had to be equipped with light-

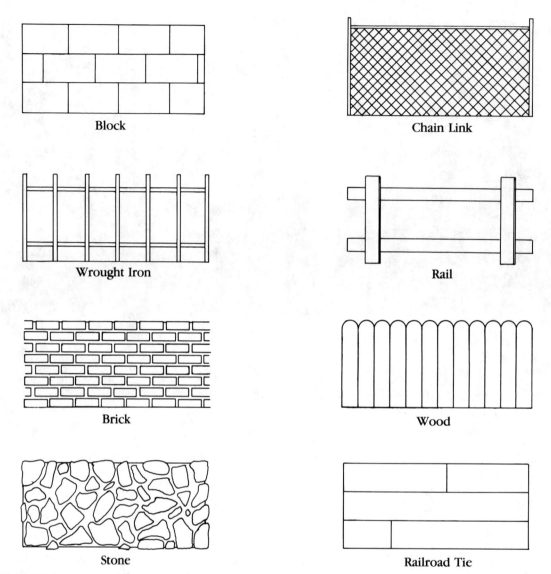

Fig. 18-14. *A variety of fencing and landscaping materials can be used to achieve a multitextured effect.*

proof doors, lightproof and efficient ventilation, switched outlets for the safelights, and special plumbing.

You may not have a darkroom in your home, but you will have other things unique and special to you. The easiest and best time to make the adaptations is in the design stage, with a second-best time being before the construction begins. In either case—or, for that matter, at any time—it's your job to clearly specify *exactly* what your needs and expectations are.

Keep a notepad close at hand. Jot down notes and questions and special needs as they occur to you. Then, put everything you've specified on paper, make copies, and have the contractor sign it so that there can be no question at all as to whether or not those points have been discussed and agreed upon.

An Easy Way to Keep Track

Keeping track of everything sounds complicated, and it is. There are so many things involved. However there is an easy way to do so. Once you have a completed drawing of the house, have a number of 8¹/₂ by 11 copies made up of the floor plan.

These are wonderful for jotting down which material goes where and where any special wires go. Colors, code and model numbers, and so forth can all be written down in the appropriate areas, and the sheets are small enough to be easily folded and carried in your pocket when you go shopping for the materials.

19

Draftsman vs. architect

Once the design is complete, you have three choices. One is to attempt to finish the drawings all on your own. At the other end of the spectrum is to hire an architect for the job. In the middle is to find a draftsman who specializes in architectural drawings. Each has advantages and disadvantages.

Finishing the drawings yourself brings with it the greatest investment of your time and the greatest risk that the local building inspection office won't approve the plans. There's more to passing approval than having a floor plan, however detailed.

Hiring an architect will increase the chance of having the plans approved without hassle, and also the chance of having the person you hire spot problems. It's also the most expensive.

The third option is a compromise of sorts. Although many architectural draftsmen are just as competent in home design as many architects, they don't have the degree and often don't have the education. In some areas, the law limits what they can and cannot do. What matters is that they are specialists in at least rendering ideas into workable blueprints. If you already know exactly what you want, maybe all you need is someone familiar with constructional basics and local codes.

Doing It Yourself

Usually finishing the drawings yourself is not a good idea. As stated above, there is a lot more to a home than just a floor plan. There are structural members that have to be calculated for size. This varies from home to home, even from room to room and floor to floor.

Learning and researching the basics of construction isn't difficult; it's almost a requirement if you're going to design a home. You should have some idea of how the home goes together. That's part of your job. The job of the draftsman or architect is to take care of the details.

If you don't know how much stress a white fir 2 by 10 of a particular length can bear, if you don't know what kind of supports a 20-foot-wide floor will need and how many and what kind of rebar is needed for the foundation that will support your particular house (and the individual parts of the house), you can look up the information in resource materials. There are certain national standards, which does not guarantee that the same figures will apply in your particular area in every instance. And the codes are also a matter of public record. All you need to do is spend the time to find out what they are—each and every one of them—and how they apply to what you have in mind.

You have to ask yourself if you have the time and patience to do the needed research. Can you spend the time needed to research structural, electrical, and plumbing codes? Are you prepared to redraw parts of your design to meet the requirements of the local board?

You also have to ask yourself if you have the artistic talent to do the job properly. The drafting skills alone take a while to learn. The lines have to be straight where needed, the measurements have to be extremely accurate. (See FIG.19-1.)

Usually, the money spent to have a professional make the final drawings is a wise investment. If you've done a good enough job on the design, the cost can be reasonable. (With my home, it cost roughly 1 percent of the total building costs.)

Hiring a Draftsman

These days, the generic term should be "draftsperson." There are a number of highly competent and skilled women working in the field. Gender has nothing to do with competency.

With that disclaimer out of the way, choose your draftsman carefully. Almost every area in the United States requires that an architectural draftsman have some kind of certification. There are often limits applied. For example, the draftsman might not be allowed to design any structure over 5000 square feet, or any commercial structure of any size. In other areas, the field is left wide open. The reason for size limits is that any very large structure requires special knowledge to design properly.

The basic difference between draftsman and architect is the amount of formal schooling required. It's possible that the draftsman will have more actual experience and knowledge of construction; there will also be times when the draftsman will get into the field because he or she takes "the easy way" by avoiding all of the college hours (or simply because they can't handle all the math involved).

You must use your own judgment to decide. At times, a particular draftsman will be better qualified to handle the job than a particular architect. At other times, you'll need that extra schooling.

The cost for making the drawings can be as low as about 55 cents per square foot and as high as nearly $1.70 per square foot. It depends on what you need done, how much work is involved, and how much that particular person or firm chooses to charge. This fee should include an initial consultation to explain your design and needs, to be sure that everything is as it should be on your own drawings, and to discuss any possible problems.

Next comes the draftsman's preliminary drawing done to full size. Some draftsmen will do this without fee or obligation, which gives you the chance to see if this person is the one you really want to hire. Normally it is followed by another consultation to be sure that it was as you wanted.

Last comes the final set of drawings ready to be submitted for approval.

The Architect

An architect earns a degree by spending years in college. While this doesn't guarantee that the person you hire is competent (the cost of a college education doesn't "buy" talent or competence), that degree *was* earned by a concerted effort of five to six years, and sometimes more.

That education, ideally, provides the person with the knowledge and skills needed to engineer almost any kind of structure. Some specialize in residential designs, others in office buildings and larger structures. All can come up with designs that are structurally sound, practical, and usually beautiful.

Architects learn how to calculate stresses and loads and how to choose materials that will handle them. They've had to learn something about soil conditions and how to make the land support the structure built on it.

If you have an unusual structure, or unusual land, your chances of success are better with an architect. They're generally more used to handling such problems than a draftsman.

Because of all of this, and other reasons, the average architect will cost more than the average draftsman, even if the only thing the architect is

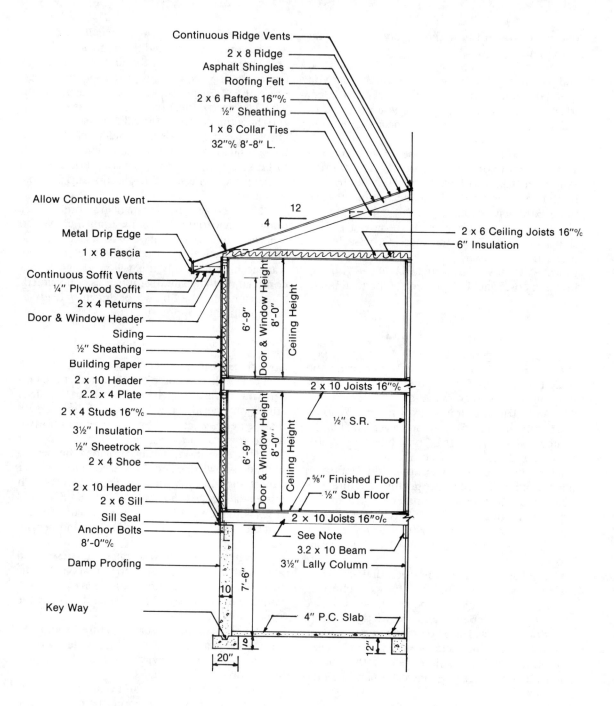

Continuous Ridge Vents
2 x 8 Ridge
Asphalt Shingles
Roofing Felt
2 x 6 Rafters 16"%
½" Sheathing
1 x 6 Collar Ties
32"% 8'-8" L.

Allow Continuous Vent

Metal Drip Edge
1 x 8 Fascia
Continuous Soffit Vents
¼" Plywood Soffit
2 x 4 Returns
Door & Window Header
Siding
½" Sheathing
Building Paper
2 x 10 Header
2.2 x 4 Plate
2 x 4 Studs 16"%
3½" Insulation
½" Sheetrock
2 x 4 Shoe
2 x 10 Header
2 x 6 Sill
Sill Seal
Anchor Bolts
8'-0"%
Damp Proofing

Key Way

12
4

2 x 6 Ceiling Joists 16"%
6" Insulation

Door & Window Height 8'-0"
6'-9"
Ceiling Height

2 x 10 Joists 16"%
½" S.R.

Door & Window Height 8'-0"
6'-9"
Ceiling Height

⅝" Finished Floor
½" Sub Floor

2 x 10 Joists 16"o/c
See Note
3.2 x 10 Beam
3½" Lally Column

7'-6"
10

4" P.C. Slab

20"
12"

Staff Section

Fig. 19-1. *Can you do this?*

doing for you is rendering your drawings into final form. It's fairly common to spend 5 to 6 percent of the total cost for just the drawings (while the draftsman may cost you as little as 1 to 2 percent). The major difference is that the licensed architect will bear more liability, even if the design is yours. (By putting his "seal of approval" on the plans, he is certifying that the structure will be sound—something few draftsmen do.) If you wish, the architect can do more.

With a draftsman, the drawings are made and the rest is up to you. The architect will often oversee the project, either with a contractor they pick or with one you choose. (The latter is usually better. At the very least you should have a say in the matter; if you don't, find another architect.) They'll go by the building site regularly to be sure that everything is being done properly.

You'll pay for this service—sometimes as much as 20 percent of the cost of the home (with 12 to 15 percent being more common). But if the architect is competent, it takes the worry out of having the home constructed and completed the way you want.

Of course, you can perform many of the tasks yourself. You can find a contractor on your own, for example. This is a pretty good idea anyway since it lets *you* pick who will build *your* home. You can also monitor the construction. Although the architect will be much more familiar with the proper way things should go together, you'll be able to recognize when something is obviously wrong, and the building inspector will catch most or all of anything else.

You can also handle all of the other details. Whether you communicate them to the architect or directly to the contractor, subcontractor, or supplier, it works out to be about the same. (It's also important that you *do* remain a part of it, even if you have hired someone to take care of the details.) This is not to say that hiring an architect isn't of value. It can be, and especially so if you just don't have the time to keep track of things during the construction.

Monitoring the job doesn't mean being on the site all day, every day. Stopping by once or twice a week is minimum but is usually sufficient (assuming that you've picked the contractor carefully). Whether or not you have hired a professional—an architect or other person—to keep track of things, you should be stopping by that often anyway. What you're paying for, if you choose this option, is to have a professional's skill and experience to catch things that you, as an amateur, might miss.

CAD

The abbreviation CAD stands for "computer aided design" (or "computer assisted design"). Special programs and equipment are used so that the computer handles the job of making the drawings.

The great advantage of CAD is that walls and other objects can be so easily moved and otherwise changed without having to redraw anything at all. The design is on the screen and can be changed at will. "Let's see how it will look if this wall is 6 inches in this direction" is an easy matter. "The house looks fine from the north, how will it look from the northeast?" is also easy because the display can be rotated.

With advanced programs, even the interior can be shifted and rotated. You cause the computer to "draw" the floor plan of a room. The computer can then generate a perspective of that room, and even the things that would go in it.

It might seem that all you really need to do is to get yourself a computer and a CAD program. You can do so for a cost of less than having drawings made for you (if you shop carefully); however, there is a very large problem.

CAD programs are amazing. Some aren't all that difficult to learn; others are very confusing, with the ones that do the most obviously requiring more time and effort to learn. To use any of them effectively you still have to have some knowledge of how things go together. More, you have to be willing to spend the time and effort to learn the program.

For example, when you move a wall, what stresses change and what structural elements do you need to take care of the changes? Will the local building codes allow it? Also, do you have the time and patience to learn how to use the program well enough to get it to do what you want and need?

Although you may not wish to spend the time and effort to learn CAD yourself, it can be an advantage if you hire a draftsman or architect who makes use of such a system. You'll pay a little more for it since it's one more skill you're "buying," but if done properly you'll be able to see your design in three dimensions and from different angles, before ever committing anything to paper.

The problem is one of cost. With rare exception, a service that can also provide CAD will charge more. If you intend to sit in the office and watch as each and every room is being turned and twisted and changed, expect to pay extra for the time.

Finding a Draftsman or Architect

The key to finding a reliable professional is always the same, whether you are looking for a doctor or a designer. Don't just open the Yellow Pages and pick the first one you see.

I, personally, would avoid any person who does not list an address in the phone book. Some have only a phone number. To find out where they are, you first have to call. This may mean nothing; however, it could mean that they don't want the location known for one reason or another.

Make some phone calls to explain what you have in mind and to get some rough prices. Get a "feel" for the person you might be hiring. Then set interviews with four or five (or more) who seem to be the best for you. Meet with them in person. The interviews don't have to be long. The idea is to have them look at your drawings (more to convince you why you should hire that particular person or company).

Never forget that you are the customer and the employer, and that the person you hire is a salesperson and employee. The reason for hiring them is because of their special expertise in the area, which means that you owe it to them, and yourself, to listen to their advice. But *you* are still the boss.

If you get the idea that the person you wish to hire *demands* to be in control, find someone else. Such a person probably won't let you be a real part of what will become your own home and almost certainly be difficult to get along with. Of course, this doesn't mean that you should walk in and become instantly dominant or shout, "If I hire you, *I* am the boss!" That will end the relationship right there (or, if the person gives in, it should end it).

It's important to keep an open mind. You should never be "bullied" into accepting something you don't want, but neither should you forget that you are an amateur and the person you've hired is a professional. It's possible that some suggestion the person makes will be the difference between a barely livable home and a remarkable one. He or she, from experience, might notice a potential problem you didn't.

Basically, you'll be hiring this person to do a job. A part of that job is to point out flaws in your design—not to dictate, but to at least point them out. (In other words, although it's your design and your home, don't be so sure of yourself that you can't accept the advice of a professional.)

The person in question should have some actual construction experience. That doesn't mean that he or she must have been hammering nails or soldering pipes in the past, just that they have practical experience on a job site and have seen homes being constructed.

Book learning is fine, but the practical experience can be as much, or more, valuable. Unfortunately, some draftsmen, and even architects, have designed hundreds of homes but have never taken any other part of the construction. How much experience of any kind has this person had? A draftsman who has spent the past 35 years in the business might be vastly superior to a degreed and licensed architect just out of college.

"How many homes have you designed?" and "Can I see any of them?" are good questions to ask. Even if you intend to use your own design, it's helpful to see a standing structure that the person has designed or has made the drawings for.

Don't forget to ask for references. Past customers are a fair guide. Even though the person is unlikely to give you the names of dissatisfied customers, a list of the satisfied ones can help.

Preferably, the person should be licensed. Although most areas don't require it, it shows that the person you're about to hire has taken the time and effort to learn enough about construction and codes to be able to pass certain tests.

Most architects are licensed. Those who are not are most often called "designers." The education required is the same, but the "designer" hasn't gone through the formal testing procedure to get the license—which may or may not mean anything.

If you decide to hire an architect, also look for membership in the AIA, or the American Institute of Architects. Although membership is not a requirement for architects, it shows one more step of certification on the part of the person.

A draftsman might be a member of AIBD, or the American Institute of Building Design. Within this organization is voluntary certification. The test is fairly rigid and shows that the person so certified knows enough that many states recognize the AIBD stamp as just a step beneath that of an architect.

Handling Problems

No matter how careful you are, there are almost certain to be some changes needed to your design. Some will be your own and some will be flaws pointed out by the person you hire.

A home is a major investment. If a change is needed, don't be so inflexible that it can't be made, unless you have a very good reason.

One person brought a design in to the draftsman in which the traffic flow in the basement was a looping hall. The draftsman pointed it out instantly. The only way to get to the basement game room from the main floor was to come down the stairs and make a nearly complete circle around the basement through two other rooms. The owners had already decided that their design was perfect and ignored the advice of the draftsman, and then of the contractor who saw the same problem.

The solution, as suggested by the draftsman in the first place, was to have a door instead of a wall at the bottom of the stairs. The "look" wasn't exactly what they wanted, but a disaster was made practical. The only problem was that the lesson cost them quite a bit. (The wall had to be broken open and the door installed.)

Be prepared to accept constructive criticism (literally!). You're hiring this person because of his or her special expertise in the field. If you don't feel comfortable accepting advice, you shouldn't have hired them in the first place.

20

The contractor

At last the time has come to turn the dream you have on paper into a real home. There is still a lot to be done, beginning with finding and dealing with a suitable contractor.

This isn't as simple as it might seem.

You're entrusting someone to build the home you'll be living in. Everything they do incorrectly may be something you'll have to repair or tolerate. More serious, some of those errors could present an actual danger to you and your family.

You're also entrusting the contractor with a great deal of money. Even if you divide the payments so that portions are paid as construction schedules are met, with a final payment after acceptance of the home, you're not protected. (It has happened that someone has put down 25 percent and more of the total cost, only to have the "contractor" disappear, without the ground even being broken.)

You're making the largest purchase that most people ever make. If you've done it before and are using equity to build the home, at least a part of the investment has already been made but it comes down to the same thing.

The lesson is simple: *Take the time and do it right.*

Finding the Right Contractor

It's nice to know that most contractors, like most people, at least *try* to be competent and honest. That doesn't mean that all are, or that all the honest contractors are right for you.

Building a home is an important step in your life, and a major expense that will be with you for many years to come. Take the time and choose wisely. Be sure to locate a minimum of four prospective contractors and then go through a process of elimination to pick the one best for you. This means going out to model homes to see the quality of construction offered. It means taking the time to interview the contractors, preferably in person. Eventually it means making up dozens of copies of the blueprints for the home so that the contractors can make accurate bids (in writing!).

References and Recommendations

A sadly typical way that many people find a contractor is to simply open the Yellow Pages, pick one with a nice-sounding name, and assume that the job is done. Although the Yellow Pages are indeed one source for finding contractors, it's always better to get recommendations.

It might be that the architect or draftsman can recommend some contractors. The reverse may also be true: if you've started looking for contractors first, they might be able to recommend a quality draftsman or architect. In both cases, you're dealing with people involved in construction. The draftsman or architect has surely had some of his designs turned into homes; the home builder has certainly used designers.

If you can find out who the local building materials suppliers are—usually prospective contractors will give you a list—make a few phone calls. Is the contractor good at paying on time? This will tell you at least something about a contractor's reputation. It will also forewarn you about the possibility of problems.

Materials are almost always purchased on credit. The contractor will order a certain amount of material and have a certain amount of labor done before you owe him for that portion. Once you pay the contractor, he pays his suppliers. If he doesn't, there won't be more credit forthcoming, and you could find yourself with a half-built home and a contractor on the edge of bankruptcy. The suppliers *might* give you a clue as to whether this is a reasonable worry.

The same is true of the subcontractors the contractor uses. Are they paid on time? How about the employees? (You can find out quickly about the quality and attitude of the employees of the contractor and the subs by simply visiting one of the other homes he has under construction.)

In all of this, beware if the contractor refuses to tell you who his suppliers are, who the subcontractors will be, or where he is building at the moment. As long as you are seriously looking for a contractor, those are all valid questions, and you have a right to know.

Real estate people also know homes, although not necessarily home construction. Even so, it's a fair bet that they will know which contractors are reliable, and which cause complaints.

Banks or other institutions will be more concerned with people paying back their loans than with how a home is built, but at times the two are linked. Mortgage holders who are not happy with their homes are more likely to be reluctant to pay on time. This will quite often give the bank or loan officer a good idea which contractors cause problems.

The local Better Business Bureau, any local builders group, such as the National Home Builders Association, and the building inspection office are all good places to check. Not finding anything doesn't mean much. Finding one or two complaints usually means just as little (unless the contractor has only built one or two homes). What you are looking for is a string of complaints, and particularly unresolved complaints.

Along with lists of suppliers, subcontractors, and homes under construction, try to get the names and addresses of some homes already built and of the people who live there. If you can, try to find homes that are about five or six years old, as well as newer homes. This will give you the chance to find out how well the contractor handled complaints and how well the home stands up over time.

Other Questions

Normally it's not a good idea to ask the contractor the questions discussed directly. That has a tendency to begin the relationship on the wrong foot, as though you're going in expecting him to be either a poor builder, dishonest, or both (in which case, why are you taking his time?). However, you can find out what you need to know without making accusations.

How long has he been in business? How many homes has he built? What kinds of homes? Is he licensed, bonded, and insured? These are essentials. All of them. If he isn't licensed, why not? If he isn't bonded, you could find yourself having to pay for theft of materials by his employees. If he isn't insured, the same applies, but more important is that you could find yourself facing a lawsuit by an employee injured on your job site. Also find out what warranties are offered. Standard is between one and two years.

Where are his model homes (if any)? If he doesn't have any models you can see, where are some homes under construction, and some completed? If he doesn't have either or is reluctant to tell you, thank him for his time and find another contractor.

Very close to an absolute rule is to never hire a contractor without seeing the kind of work they can do. There are several reasons for this. First, and most obvious, if that contractor doesn't have any homes you can see, you should immediately wonder why. All people have to start somewhere—for all contractors there is a first home—but do you want *your* home to be that first? You might save a little money that way (which is doubtful), but you increase your risks, both in the quality of the work and in the chance of having that contractor "go under" during the construction, or during the warranty period.

Things to Avoid

First impressions aren't always the best or most accurate. If the builder seems a bit grouchy the day you meet him for the first time, it could simply mean that he has had a hard time lately or maybe isn't feeling well. Still, a warning bell should ring in your head.

Keep in mind that you're going to be dealing with this person over the months to come. Unless that relationship is mutually satisfying, it's going to be rough going for all concerned. This is *not* the time to have a personality conflict. Even if the builder is the best in the world, if you can't get along with him, you're generally better off finding someone else.

A grouchy attitude might be just a chance happening, or it might mean the person's nature. Having to make an appointment to meet with the person is normal. Accept it. But once in the meeting, you deserve some attention.

You are the customer. The contractor is the "salesman." It's his job to convince you to "buy" and to convince you that his "product" is the one you want. If he refuses to do so, you may find yourself facing a haughty attitude later when it's too late.

Be very leery of any builder from out of your area. That's going to make communications much more difficult. The farther away his office, the more difficult it becomes. You need to be able to call his office on the phone, without so much as a toll for distance. Hopefully, that office should also be within fairly easy driving distance. Now you have one more reason for getting a list of suppliers. As with the contractor, the subs and suppliers should be within easy reach.

Never base your decision on price only! *Never*! This opens you up to one of the most common scams, and the most common downfalls. If you get three basic bids of around $90,000 for what you have in mind, and a fourth of $60,000, something is wrong.

Looking at it most positively, you're not getting a fair bid: the $60,000 contractor is bidding in the lowest grades throughout (which still wouldn't explain a difference of 33 percent). It's also possible that the low contractor is "low-balling," and you'll find yourself facing "extras" later on. Perhaps worst of all would be the indication that the contractor is so inexperienced that jobs (such as yours) are going to create losses, which in turn means he won't be around for long.

This doesn't mean that you should go with the most expensive. Something could be wrong there, too. If five bids come in $60,000, $87,000, $89,000, $91,000, and $115,000, you can usually toss out the highest and lowest without concern. There is probably something wrong with those extremes.

One help is to get everything in writing. If you've handed over complete plans and specifications, the contractor should be able to give you an exact price for the structure as detailed and to do so in writing. There *should* be no surprises at the end, unless you have changed things. Even then, each change and the resulting costs will be in writing.

If everything is in writing from the beginning, the contractor has no excuse. "Oh, we didn't see that" is not a valid excuse if it's on the plans, or in the written and signed list of specifications. Don't accept anything orally. Not in the beginning, and not during construction. Think of this as any other standard business deal. It doesn't matter how much you like someone. It doesn't even matter if you feel they can be trusted. *GET IT IN WRITING!*

Other Hints and Tips

The first and most important hint is to get a lawyer who specializes in building contracts. The cost will be fairly small for him to read through the contract and to advise you on it. Most such contracts are standard. If anything varies from that, he'll spot it pretty quickly. This minor cost keeps someone on hand if there are other problems during the construction or afterwards.

One of the things he might recommend is to get approximate completion dates from subs on the contract. Things can happen, which has to be taken into account and allowed. If the foundation is to be completed by June 7th, but it has been raining constantly and heavily since May 3rd, that step will obviously have to be delayed. It's no one's fault, and it has to be taken in stride. The key is that *you* shouldn't find yourself paying extra because two other crews have been kept waiting.

With "acts of of nature" aside, you, the buyer, should *never* be responsible for poor scheduling on the part of the contractor. If he has scheduled the electricians to come in on July 2nd, but the framing isn't complete yet due to poor planning on the part of the contractor, any added costs should be his, not yours. (On the other hand, if you make changes that delay the framing, the fault is yours and so should be the cost.)

How is the property to be kept up during and after the construction? Builders and the crews are famous for just tossing scraps aside for the moment while the job is being done. Wandering around on a construction site can be dangerous! There are board ends, loose nails, and other scraps everywhere. That much is fine, as long as it isn't allowed to continue day after day through the entire building.

Normally, some kind of cleanup should be provided every day, even if only minimal. At least once per week useless scraps should be hauled away. Certainly a complete and thorough cleanup should be provided at the end. You shouldn't be mowing the new lawn on your new home only to have the blade of your mower chipped by discarded boards and nails.

If you have additional wiring to be done, such as for a stereo, intercom, or burglar alarm system, specify this in your list. Make the builder responsible to let you know in good time that the framing is done and the walls are to go up. There will be a period of *at least* a week when you can get in and run the extra wiring without interfering with the construction. If the contractor is on top of things, he'll know at least another week ahead of time when this will be.

It's then up to you to do what you want, but it remains a part of the contract that he let you know. A call at 6 AM with "They're putting up the sheetrock today, so you'd better hurry" is *not* sufficient. Rather it should be: "If it doesn't rain they'll have the framing done next Wednesday. The electricians and plumbers are scheduled to come in Friday after the inspection, so you should have holes for your wires no later than Tuesday.

The inspection for the wires and pipes is set for the following Friday, and the next Monday the drywall hangers are set to come in to close up the walls."

That is a tight schedule; it allows for no correction to be made after the building inspector has gone through, but it still gives you plenty of time to get in, run your wires and get out. The contract should specify that if you aren't given ample notice (1 to 2 weeks), the contractor faces the expense of running those special wires, which means that they would also have to be clearly specified ahead of time.

You should be visiting the construction site once or more per week. Daily is best, but usually it isn't necessary. In any case, bring a camera with you each and every time. Take plenty of pictures, especially of those things normally hidden (in the walls or underground). Film and prints are relatively cheap. If the processing and printing charge is too much for you, mark and store the film in the freezer. It will keep there for a couple of years in most cases. Better yet, have the film processed (about $2 per roll in most areas) and store the negatives in case prints are needed.

A roll of film will cost somewhere around $4 or less. Processing will be about $2, bringing the total to around $6 per roll. Add prints and it comes in as high as twice that, but for ease of figuring, think of it for the moment at $10 per roll. You visit the site and take 30 rolls of film. That might be overdoing it, but too many is better than too few. At 24 exposures per roll, it would give you 720 exposures. Cost will be somewhere around $300—*very* cheap when compared to the possible value later on.

Don't forget the possibility of video tape. It's probably not worth it if you have to buy or rent the camcorder, but if you have one already, video tape is an excellent and extremely inexpensive method for recording the construction of your home. In addition, it will be something that can be entertaining in the future as well as valuable.

Ask the contractor if he is in association with any local building organization that offers extended warranties. In some areas these are offered for a nominal fee. Although the standard warranty period normally lasts no more than two years (with one year being more common) such an

Fig. 20-1. *If you didn't have a photo like this one, would you know how to handle future problems?*

extension can warranty the home for up to 10 years and also covers you if the builder fails in his obligations to make repairs. You'll foot the bill for this insurance, but if it's available, it's often well worth it.

Bids

To get an accurate bid you'll have to provide completed blueprints and specifications. Going in and asking, "How much will a 1700-square-foot house cost?" is as meaningless as asking a dealer, "How much does a car cost?"

Even blueprints aren't enough. If you have 1700 square feet, is it to be covered with $10 per yard linoleum or $150 per yard stone tile? That all by itself is a difference of more than $25,000. Will you have $175 oak doors throughout, or will hollow-core pine do for the inside? Are the walls to be 2-by-4 frame or 12 inches of composite frame

and brick? Will you have three fireplaces in three different places or none at all?

Figure out your needs and wants. Have blueprints of the home and a *complete* list of specifications. The bid is made on this basis, and those conditions *must* be in writing. Any changes you make are then your own responsibility.

Get at least four such bids. Making up five complete sets of blueprints for each bid can be somewhat costly *(Always keep the original and one set for yourself!).* If you have the time you can make up fewer sets, but then time becomes a factor, and a bid is good for just so long. Prices increase over time. Just keep in mind that you are about to make the biggest investment you may ever make. An extra $100 for additional prints is minor in comparison.

Be careful that the bids are on identical specifications. If your blueprints and specification sheets are accurate and complete, this won't be a problem. Anything that varies *requires* an explanation. If one contractor bids in the Jacuzzi tub you have specified, and the next contractor has bid it without the tub, off goes the warning bell again. If you've planned for $30/square yard carpet, and the contractor is calling for "base carpet" (at $10/yard or less), either he hasn't been paying attention or you've just been "low-balled." Either way, find someone else.

Above all, insist on quality materials whenever possible—certainly on those concerning construction. If you have to replace a $20 faucet in five years because the one installed has failed, that's one thing. If you have to replace a sagging floor or a leaking roof because of cheap materials, that's quite another.

Sweat Equity

One kind of "specification" that will affect the bid is when the homeowner will be doing some of the work. Most contractors allow you to do certain parts of the job yourself to save money, although many will have certain limitations on this (as may be the locality). Unless you're licensed, you won't be allowed to do your own electrical wiring, but painting doesn't have the same restrictions or inspection codes.

The contractor may require that you sign a waiver concerning those parts of the work you choose to handle yourself. The reason is obvious. If a subcontractor splatters paint on the floor and cabinets, that subcontractor is responsible to make the needed repairs or replacements. If the sub somehow gets out of it or refuses, the contractor is still liable. But if you're the one who has done the careless painting job, the only person liable is yourself.

There are many things you might be able to do. The most important thing to keep in mind is your own limitations. A close second is the trade-off between money saved, the work needed, and the risks taken.

The Contract

As mentioned several times, *everything* should be in writing. Much of this can be taken care of by yourself. Lists of specifications, change orders, and other smaller items are usually within the average person's abilities to handle. Other things are not, which once again brings in the importance of finding a lawyer to go through the contract.

The sample contract on pp. 260–261 may differ from the one you'll be signing with your own builder, but the essence should be much the same. The key is to be sure that you understand and agree with every word of the contract. If there is anything strange in the contract, the time to act on it is *before* you sign, not after.

If something looks suspicious, the lawyer can tell you if it is or not. Some things seem vague, such as the clauses that allow delays for various things, but there is no choice in the matter. If the home is struck by a tornado during construction and destroyed (which should remind you of the need for insurance on the structure), or if all of a sudden there are no toilets to be had in the entire state, the contractor can't be held liable for delays.

The Contractor's Job

Many contractors have few, if any, crews of their own. More often than not, part or all of the construction will be handled by subcontractors ("subs") who specialize in the various stages of construction. The crew that installs the plumbing probably does nothing else but plumbing and aren't licensed for anything else.

Whether the contractor has his own crews or does nothing but subcontract, the primary job of the contractor is to be sure that everything is coordinated and stays that way. In a very real sense, the contractor is your employee, while the crews who do the actual building are *his* employees. Both are temporary relationships (until the particular job is done and for a time afterwards). Although you *can* go to the electrical sub, it's often better to deal directly with the contractor you've hired. At the very least, he should be informed of any changes or special instructions.

The contractor coordinates the job, sees to it that everything gets done in the proper order, and often oversees the quality of the work—or at very least works hand-in-hand with the subcontractor's supervisors and inspectors. He also handles any problems that come up and basically serves as a liason of sorts between the homeowner (his employer) and the subcontractors (his employees).

CONTRACT AGREEMENT
By and Between

Mr.	Robert E. Smith		Build-It Construction Company
Mrs.	Jane L. Smith	AND	13 S. Market St.
Address	111 No Name Street		Anytown, Pennsylvania
	Anytown, Pennsylvania		

Building Site Lot #35, Oakland Hills

THIS AGREEMENT MADE THIS _____ day of _____,
19_____ by and between _____ of the City of_____,
County of Erie, and State of Pennsylvania, hereinafter called "Owners"

AND

Build-It Construction Company, a corporation with principle offices in the City of Anytown, County of Anyplace, and State of Pennsylvania, herinafter called "Contractor."

<u>WITNESSETH</u> The Owners and Contractor for and in consideration of the mutual covenants of each other, and for and in consideration of the work to be done by the Contractor and the money to be paid by the Owners, as hereinafter set forth, it is agreed between the parties as follows:

1. <u>SCOPE OF WORK</u> The Contractor covenants and agrees to furnish all the labor, perform all the work that shall be required for the erection of a 2 story frame dwelling which is more fully set forth in plans, attached hereto and marked Exhibit "A", and specifications attached hereto and marked Exhibit "B", both of which documents have been initialed by the parties. Said dwelling house to be built on the property of the Owners, Lot #35 Oakland Hills Subdivision.

The Contractor covenants and agrees to do and complete all the work set forth in said plans and specifications for the erection of said dwelling house, in a good and workmanlike manner, and within a reasonable time after the construction job has been started. The Contractor specifically covenants and agrees to pursue the work diligently without delay after the construction of said dwelling house has been started by them. All work shall be new and all workmanship done and performed under this Contract, by the Contractor, shall be of good quality and shall be performed in a good and workmanlike manner. The Contractor shall protect all the parts of the work from damage by cold or other elements. The Contractor shall also be responsible for temporary electrical service. All the work and materials furnished by the Contractor shall meet or exceed the minimum FHA requirements. The Contractor shall be responsible for the building permit, gas permit, and sewer permit and for the expense entailed in obtaining said permits. The Contractor further covenants and agrees to sign a Release of Mechanic's Lien before any work is started.

2. <u>TIME OF COMPLETION</u> The work shall be started as soon as possible, weather permitting, and shall be completed as soon as possible, Acts of God, strikes, material shortages, government regulations, or catastrophes excepted. The Contractor covenants and agrees to pursue the work of erecting said dwelling house in a diligent manner after the same has been started.

3. <u>DELAY OF COMPLETION</u> If after the dwelling house has been substantially completed and livable, full completion thereof is materially delayed through no fault of the Contractor, the Owners shall, and without terminating the Contract, make payment for the balance due the Contractor for that part of the work fully completed and accepted by the Owners.

4. <u>ASSIGNMENTS</u> The Contractor shall not assign this Contract to others. However, this shall not prohibit the sub-contracting of parts of the work to others by the Contractor.

5. <u>CONTRACT DOCUMENTS</u> The Contract documents shall consist of the Contract Agreement, the Specifications, and the Plans and they are all as fully a part of the Contract Agreement as if attached hereto and herein repeated. The Parties herewith covenant and agree that upon execution of this agreement they shall, each of them, initial the specifications and the plans.

6. INSURANCE The Contractor shall insure himself against all claims under Workman's Compensation Acts and all other claims for damage for personal injuries, including death, which may arise from operations under this Contract, whether such operations be by themselves, or by anyone directly or indirectly employed by him. The Contractor shall save the Owners of this protection. The Owners shall maintain fire insurance and vandalism insurance on the structure as soon as the sub-floor is completed, and the Contractor shall be reimbursed from said insurance from any and all loss due to fire.

7. EXTRA WORK OR ALTERATIONS The Owners shall have the right to make changes or alterations, but any order for change or alterations shall be in writing and signed by the Owners and the Contractor; said amount shall be stated in the written order, and to be paid to the Contractor (or Owner if it shall be a saving) before final payment is made. The extra charges, if any, shall be considered a part of the contract cost.

8. CLEANING UP The Contractor shall, at all times, keep the premises free from all unnecessary accumulation of waste material or rubbish caused by his employees or the work and at the completion of the work he shall remove all rubbish from and about the building, and all tools, scaffolding, surplus material, and shall leave the work "broom clean."

9. ORDINANCE AND STATUTES COMPLIANCE The Contractor shall conform in all respects to the provisions and regulations of any general or local building acts or ordinances, or any authority pertinent to the area. The Contractor covenants and agrees that he has examined the land, plans and specifications, and understands any and all difficulties that may arise in the execution of this Contract. The Contractor specifically covenants and agrees that in laying out the house, he shall observe the building line required in the sub-division. The Owners, however, shall be responsible for providing an exact survey of the building site.

10. ARBITRATION CLAUSE In the event any dispute arises between the parties hereto which cannot be amicably settled between the parties, it is hereby agreed that each party shall appoint an arbitrator within three days after receipt of written request from the other, that the two arbitrators so appointed shall select a third arbitrator within three days after notice of their appointment, and that the arbitrators shall hear the dispute and, by majority decision, make a decision or award. It is agreed that any compensation required by the arbitrators shall be shared equally by the parties thereto regardless of the decision or award made.

11. ACCEPTANCE BY OWNERS AND OCCUPANCY It is agreed that upon completion, said dwelling shall be inspected by the Owners and the Contractor, and that any repairs or adjustments which are necessary shall be made by the Contractor. It is further agreed that the Owners shall not be permitted to occupy said dwelling until the Contractor is paid the full amount of the Contract. Occupancy of said dwelling by the Owners in violation of the foregoing provisions shall constitute unconditional acceptance of the dwelling house and a waiver of any defects or uncompleted work.

12. TIME OF PAYMENTS
   1st Stage—Platform: 10%
   2nd Stage—Under roof: 35%
   3rd Stage—Plastered: 25%
   4th Stage—Trim completed: 20%
   5th Stage—Completion: 10%
   (Or according to bank regulations that closely resemble the above schedule.)

13. WARRANTY The final payment shall not relieve the Contractor of responsibility for faulty materials or workmanship; and he shall remedy any defects due thereto within a period of one year, material free with minimum service charge. This warranty is only valid when the Contractor is paid contract cost in full.

   This contract shall be binding upon parties, their heirs, executors and assigns. And by this agreement, the parties intend to be legally bound in witness whereof, the parties have hereunto set their hands and seals the day and year first written above.

When it comes down to it, he's responsible for everything done or not done. He becomes, in a way, an insurance policy for you. If a subcontractor makes a mistake, it's up to the contractor you've hired to make good on it, whether he can collect from the sub or not.

The Subcontractor's Job

Unless you're doing your own contracting, the subcontractor won't be of direct concern to you. If they make a mistake, it's the contractor who must fix it. (If *you* are the contractor, it's *your* job.)

The subcontractor is a specialist. The most common jobs left to the sub are electrical, plumbing and household heating, cooling and ventilation, and certain specialty jobs. With some larger contractors with their own crews, the only subs will be those who handle unusual items.

In any case, the subcontractor invariably handles a limited amount of the total work and usually just one particular job. In theory, this specialization provides the highest quality workmanship for the lowest cost. In practice it doesn't always mean this, since you're still relying on the human factors, but it generally means that the work will be at least competent.

Your Job

Your primary job, other than to pay the bills, is to stay on top of things. It's your home. Especially since you've designed it, you know your wants and needs better than anyone else. This doesn't mean that you should be so involved that you get in the way. You've hired these people (or caused them to be hired) for a reason, which is to build your home. They are the professionals and hopefully know what they are doing. (If not, or if mistakes are being made, it's a part of your job to say so as quickly as possible. See "Problems During Construction" below.)

Stay involved. Visit the site at least once a week, and more often if possible. But try to stay out of the way. In other words, take part, while also making yourself welcome instead of someone no one likes to see drive up.

Being Your Own Contractor

Being your own contractor is not a job to take on without thinking it out carefully. The simple fact is that most people can't carry it off successfully. To do so, you need more knowledge than most people have. More time and more energy.

Hiring a subcontractor to handle the framing of the house when you have no idea of how that framing is to be done puts you in a position of having to trust that sub. The same applies all the way through. If you're the contractor for the house, it's your responsibility to handle all of the details and coordination. If something goes wrong, it's your fault and your job to get it taken care of.

It *can* be done. Others have done it. But others have also tried to do it and have failed miserably or have found themselves so overwhelmed by the details that they end up in serious trouble and paying more rather than saving.

If you're willing to spend the time, both in research prior to beginning and all through the project, and if you're willing to accept the risks, you can save the contractor's fee.

Problems During Construction

No matter how good the design, the plans, the contractor, the subcontractors, and all workers, there *will* be problems to solve, both during the construction and afterwards. Accept that and expect it. There is no such thing as perfection when it comes to building something as complex as a home.

You can minimize problems by taking the time to make a proper design and have that design properly drawn. Then comes the so-important choice of contractor.

As mentioned earlier, once all of those choices are made, the best thing you can do is to stay involved. Visit the site no less than once per week. More often is better. If you have questions, ask (but don't become a pest). And if you spot an error or other problem, let the appropriate person know about it right away. If you notice, for example, that a wall or window is in the wrong place, don't wait until the home is finished to bring it up.

There's no trick to dealing with people. It comes back to the age-old Golden Rule. Treat people as you like to be treated. No one likes to be yelled at or insulted, and certainly not in front of others.

If you have a complaint, take it to the proper person, which is usually the supervisor for the job or the contractor. Even then, take this person aside and let them know quietly and calmly. That doesn't mean that you shouldn't be firm—just that you need to be tactful.

Next, be sure to follow up. If you've spotted something wrong and no one seems to be taking steps to correct it within a decent period of time, bring it up again, but perhaps more firmly. (And that *after* finding out if there isn't a good reason for the delay.)

Keep in mind that you have rights, including the one to stay in control of what is going to be your home. Yet the moment you allow things to degenerate into shouting matches, real communication begins to break down.

If there is a total breakdown and you find yourself having to resort to legal action, all the photographs or video tapes you've made to docu-ment the construction will come in very handy. That is why you must be sure to carry the camera with you at every visit.

One tendency that homeowners have that contractors probably hate most of all is the inability to make up their minds. The design is handed over and construction begins. Suddenly, a wall needs to be moved or the laundry room area is changed to also have a toilet in it.

If the builder is informed soon enough, making a change is relatively simple. You'll pay extra if there are extra costs involved, but you'll pay a lot more—and have more problems—if you wait too long. (For example, the time to decide to have a toilet in the laundry room is before the concrete floor is poured.)

All in all, treat the project as a business deal and the people as human beings. Expect problems to occur, but don't make them where they don't exist.

21

The home under construction

Just because all the decisions have been made doesn't mean that . . . well, it doesn't mean that all the decisions have been made. More are to come. And there will be more problems to solve even after you've moved in. Just because the plans have been approved and the home is being built, it's a serious mistake to assume that you can sit back and put up your feet. For many, the toughest time is yet to come.

You may have taken months to design the perfect home, and another couple of months getting the plans drawn up and approved. All through this you have time to reconsider problems. Once construction begins, decisions have to be made under pressure. Quite often, the building can't continue until you've decided when something has to be changed. That means you may have to make a snap decision on something *very* important.

It also means that the contractor may make that decision for you. If he does so all on his own, you have reason for regress. But it's also possible that there was no choice. The contractor may also have to make snap decisions, and if you're not available or have kept yourself out of the process, there is little choice left open.

The Basic Schedule

The exact schedule of how a home goes together is based on a number of variables. Even if you

have a basic schedule from the contractor, it may or may not go *exactly* as specified. Sometimes a step set for next Tuesday will be pushed up because the crew is ready for it. Sometimes a step set for this afternoon will be delayed due to weather. There are many reasons why a set schedule might have to be modified: weather, supplies, crew schedule conflicts, owner changes, and so on.

Before anything else can happen, the plans for the house have to be submitted to the appropriate government building inspection agency. An inspector will look through the plans to be sure that everything is according to local codes. If something isn't quite right, that fact will be noted and a change will be required. Sometimes the inspector will suggest a solution that will bring the problem to within standards. At times he will say, "If you'll do this, this, and this, the plans and building will be approved, and I don't need to see the plans again."

If the changes are more extensive, the plans will have to go back to whoever drew them (or to someone else). Also, if changes are made to the plans during the construction that would affect the structure, you'll probably be required to submit at least a redraw of that section, along with any other portions that might be affected.

All through the construction, the building

inspector will be stopping by to be sure that everything is being done correctly. Formal inspections of various stages will be made. (For example, once the plumbing is done, it has to be inspected and tagged as approved before the walls can be covered.)

Assuming you use a general contractor, he'll probably be contacting subcontractors to handle various parts of the whole. Some contractors don't have even one crew of their own; they "sub out" all the work. In such a case, the contractor's job is more to serve as a coordinator (see Chapter 20) and to be sure that everything is done correctly and in the correct order.

Work to the land always comes first. If there's a basement, it will be excavated before the main foundation is set. Any other leveling, building up, or cutting down in the immediate vicinity of the structure will be done. This doesn't mean that the ground will be perfect everywhere. There might be piles of dirt 10 feet from where the front door will be, which might remain there until the final leveling job is completed.

Trenching for any incoming underground

pipes or lines will often be done at this same stage. Some of this—maybe all of it—may wait until later. Any pipes or wiring that will be under the foundation will be installed. If you visit the site of a new construction, you'll see the pipes sticking up with colored tapes on them. These mark the pipes according to use so there is no guesswork (FIG. 21-1).

The forms for the foundation will be set and then the concrete will be poured. In some parts of the country, termite-proofing is required, which generally consists of the spraying of a liquid on the ground very shortly before the concrete is poured. (The chemicals will begin to break down rapidly after being mixed and exposed to the sun and air. It's critical to have the concrete poured as soon as possible after the spray is laid down.)

Once the foundation has been poured and set, the forms are taken down. There's a curing time needed before any appreciable weight can be put up. This time is used to get the rest ready to go. Base plates are bolted into place. Chalk lines are snapped and markings drawn for placement of the various structural parts. In essence, you might

Fig. 21-1. *Laying and tagging pipes that will be buried comes early in the job. Be sure to take photos so you'll know later where they are.*

find yourself looking at a full-sized "blueprint."

The frames for the walls go up and any floors over a basement or over excavation are roughed in. Roof members are then put up. Within a surprisingly short time, the "skeleton" of the home is in place (FIG. 21-2). Priority is now given to enclosing the structure, to protect the interior from the weather. The house is, literally, given a "skin."

A number of crews are going to be working simultaneously now. One crew might be finishing the exterior walls. Another will be installing doors and windows. Meanwhile, electricians and plumbers are running their lines. Duct work is installed for the heating and air conditioning. Depending on the location and circumstances, still another crew might be on top of the house putting on the roof. Outside, some preliminary backfill might be going on.

Exterior and interior walls and ceilings (usually in that order) will begin to be finished. Any remaining doors will be fitted. Hopefully all the main painting inside will be done before the cabinet crew comes in, and before the tubs, toilets, and so on are installed.

If possible, also have the vinyl sheet goods (linoleum) installed before the cabinets and the like go in. (See the previous chapters on this subject for advantages, disadvantages, and special precautions that are needed.)

Appliances, fixtures, counters, and so forth are installed, and the finishing woodwork is put in. Carpet and remaining vinyl is laid down. (*Hint:* Insist on having floor covering beneath the cabinets and appliances.) Last-minute touches are done inside. Any contracted landscaping outside is completed. Meanwhile, everything is made clean and ready for occupancy.

The last step before you move in is called the "walk through."

The Walk-Through

No matter how careful everyone has been during the construction, there are almost invariably at least a few things that need to be corrected. You, the owner, walk through the home with the contractor or his representative. Anything you find wrong, missing, or incomplete is noted and hopefully will be taken care of either before you move in or shortly after.

Be sure that you have a notepad of your own. Don't merely trust the contractor to keep an accurate and thorough list. In fact, it's a very good idea to have your spouse also keep notes as you go

Fig. 21-2. *The frame (skeleton) of the home.*

through the home. Better yet, think about having at least one person carry a tape recorder, or even a camcorder. It's easy to miss things, even when you're looking for them and at them.

The walk-through is meant to protect both you and the contractor. It gives all of you the chance to note problems. For you, this means that the home will be as perfect as it can be. For the contractor, it means that all the little things can be taken care of all at once. That's less trouble for both you and for him—and it's considerably less expensive. In addition, it protects you in that you have a formal opportunity to point out errors. It protects the contractor in that if you cause damage while moving in, the contractor won't be held liable for it.

All in all, the walk-through is for everyone's benefit. Be as complete and accurate as you can. That doesn't mean that you are expected to find *every* problem area in the walk-through. You'll generally have a year after you've moved in. But the idea is to catch everything possible and leave the warranty period for taking care of things that weren't obvious.

Change Orders

The walk-through is *not* the time to start changing your mind. If you've picked a certain color for a bedroom, and now that you see it decide that another color would be better, that's your own responsibility. (However, if you picked one color and the color used is different, the contractor is responsible to do something about it.)

If things *do* need to be changed, the best time is before the design has been completed, then before construction starts, then before that particular item has been started, then before that item has been completed. The way it is handled is with a *change order,* which will probably be a form designed specifically for this purpose. On it, the change will be described in detail, along with the difference in cost, if any.

Generally, both you and the contractor will sign the sheet, and each will have a copy of it. (Be *sure* you get a copy of each.) Check it over carefully. It should be very clear, and very specific. Your goal is to keep the number of change orders to a minimum—and to keep each change itself minor. If you've thought things out well enough in advance, this will be fairly easy.

At the same time, don't be afraid to make needed changes. You'll be living in that house for a while. Something easy to change now might be difficult, and expensive, later. The time to change a paint color is before the painting has been done—before the paint has even been ordered. The time to move a wall is actually before you've finished the design—certainly before that wall is already up, sheetrocked, and painted.

Most of the changes will be minor, like deciding you want blue instead of jade in the guest bedroom. For the larger things you discover, get them in as soon as possible. If you want a more major change, it might still be less expensive to do it now than later. Talk it over with the contractor. He just might have some suggestions on how to do what you want without great expense.

Problems?

Although how to deal with unforeseen problems was covered in the last chapter, this is important enough to bear repeating—especially since it also applies to problems encountered even after you move in.

All through the planning and construction there *will* be problems. It's important that you take an active part. Visit the site while your home is going up. Watch what is being done and how it is being done. Take pictures (especially of buried lines). If you have any questions, ask. Chances are that something that doesn't seem quite right is merely a procedure you don't understand, but how are you to know if you don't try to find out?

It doesn't matter how good and how honest the contractor, subcontractors, and workers are. They're human, which means that they can make mistakes. Not only *can* they make mistakes, they *will*, and probably more than once. The more complicated the home and instructions, the greater the number of errors made. It's important that you keep this in mind. It will help you in dealing with those mistakes.

A too-common approach is that of screaming at the contractor or whoever else you feel is at fault. Yelling, cussing, and tossing accusations is *not* a good way to get things done—especially not when the mistake is an honest and human one. How do *you* react when someone screams at you?

Being pleasant doesn't mean you have to accept the mistake, simply that you point it out in a firm, but pleasant, manner. It also doesn't mean that you have to accept excuses. A simple "That's fine, but just fix it, okay?" will go a long way. There *is* a difference between getting what is coming to you and being so unreasonable that the workers mess things up almost out of revenge.

Other Concerns

Coordinating power and telephone connections with the completion of the structure often falls to the homeowner. The same applies to other utilities and services such as water, garbage pickup, and so forth. All will be in your name, which means that most of the time *you* will have to be the one to formally request the connect.

Communication with the builder is critical in this stage. There's not much sense in having everything connected and ready to go if you won't be moving in for another month. There's even less sense in moving into a "dead" house.

At the beginning of the job, the contractor will give you a projected completion and move-in date. Weather and other conditions permitting, the actual date should be fairly close to this. If you've been visiting the site as you should, you'll already have some idea of how things are progressing. You'll have plenty of warning, and plenty of time to get everything lined up and ready to go.

Make some phone calls. Find out how much time is needed for each utility or other service and exactly what steps and procedures (called "red tape") are required. One service might take a week, another a month. One might require that you put in the paperwork a month ahead, while another doesn't even want to talk to you until a week before the work is to be scheduled.

Will deposits be necessary? Which utilities require them? How much? If you don't plan for this, you could find yourself in a financial bind just when things should be easiest for you.

Unless you've paid extra for them, the windows will probably have no drapes. You should already have a list of all window sizes on the plans. Don't trust it. Go around and measure each window, just to be sure. Having drapes or other window coverings made can take a while. It's not at all uncommon for it to take a month or more. If you plan ahead, you'll know how much it will be, and

how long it will be. (Thinking ahead also lets you look for sales.).

Moving

Experts know that there is a trick to moving. It's a simple one. Begin the move weeks—even months—in advance. This includes stockpiling boxes to hold your belongings, along with newspapers to wrap and protect the items for transit.

Start by making lists and planning the move. What goes? What stays? What is of primary importance and what can stay in the boxes for a month or so until you settle in?

In our case, we had one somewhat unusual "item" to move—a horse. By thinking well ahead, the new corral and tack building was completed *long* before work on the home was anywhere near ready. We then had our own, on-site storage building. Nonessentials were packed up many months ahead of the real move. Each time we went to the site, a few boxes were carried along. This required some forethought and a little temporary sacrifice. It meant that some things were in boxes and unavailable for up to 6 months. But, when it came time to move, there wasn't as much left.

It's a matter of setting priorities. Things you won't need until next year at this time *can* be boxed up while the foundation is being poured. Things you use daily will be the last to go and the first unpacked.

Priorities are often mixed up by those not used to moving. The end result is confusion and a haphazard, often irritating, move. Experienced movers will get the living room at least basically set up first. It doesn't have to be perfect, just a place to sit down and relax in some kind of comfort (and with some kind of throws on the furniture to protect the furniture). Other than this, don't try to arrange and rearrange the furniture. Not yet. You can do that later.

A close-second priority is keeping out just enough kitchen utensils and enough food to make something to eat. This drops in order of priority if you intend to have dinner out. In fact, dining out is a wonderful idea. No one has to cook or clean up, and everyone sits down for an organized relax. If nothing else, it's a good way to end the day.

Be sure that you have an ice chest and plenty of soda, cold water, or whatever those helping you move prefer. However, keep alcoholic beverages to a minimum. You're asking for trouble otherwise. Strenuous work and alcohol are a bad combination.

It's often a good idea to assign specific tasks to certain people (or certain teams). Someone should have the job of "foreman" to keep an eye on things and to be sure that everyone takes regular breaks—especially those lugging the heavier items.

If there are children, they can carry lighter items. If you want to make them feel like a real part of things, let them set up their own rooms. Even if they can't carry in the beds and dressers, they can unpack their clothes. You may have to go back in to rearrange a little, but the main job will be done and the kids will feel important, more a part of the new home, which in turn softens the loss of the old.

Above all, don't try to rush. If you feel that you have to complete the move-in on the first day, you're going about it all wrong. Tempers can flare if there is too much pressure. If you watch professional movers at work, they might seem to be moving in slow motion. They take their time, stop now and then—rarely will they keep working for more than an hour without pausing at least briefly. When they begin to rush (usually at pressure put on them by an anxious homeowner), mistakes happen and the job doesn't really get done much faster.

As the old proverb says, "Slow and steady wins the race." This is appropriate when it comes to moving a houseful of belongings from one place to another. It becomes all the more important to homeowners who aren't used to handling heavy and awkward items. Imagine rushing the first day so much that everyone is too sore the second day to do much of anything. Everyone is tired, muscles hurt, backs and joints are strained. Maybe there won't be as much left to do on the second day, but if it takes a week for everyone to recover enough to complete it, you haven't gained.

Labels

A common mistake is to mark a box "Kitchen" with no other indication as to what is inside. Be as clear as possible. Get yourself a supply of marking pens and self-stick labels. One part of your label should designate the area of the home where the box belongs, such as kitchen, laundry, bedroom, or linen. Another part should say what specifically is in the box. The first allows you to unload the boxes to the appropriate spots in the home. The second tells you which box is which.

Hiring a Mover?

Renting moving equipment is something to consider. Most people don't have a vehicle capable of carrying all the large items. Even if you have a pickup truck, it won't hold a houseful, which means that you have to make a number of trips. Depending on the distance (and on how much you have moved ahead of time), the extra gas for all the trips back and forth can add up to more than rental of a truck large enough to make it in one load (or two).

There are any number of rental companies ready to help you out. U-Haul and Ryder are the two best known, but there are others, some national and some local. Your first basic choice is to rent either a truck or a trailer. The trailer will be less expensive, but even the largest is smaller than most of the rental trucks, and a trailer has to be hauled.

As with trailers, rental trucks come in a variety of sizes. They're often ranked by the number of average rooms of furniture they can carry inside. The rental company can help you to decide. Make a list of what you'll be hauling. How many beds, and of what sizes? How many major appliances? How many couches, chairs, and tables? The idea is to get the right size truck. There's not much sense in getting a truck that is much too large for the job. It will cost you more, and the larger truck will also be more difficult to handle. (Speaking of handling, take your time getting out of the lot and home. Try the brakes several times, especially with a large truck. Get used to the way it handles before you get out into traffic.)

Rental rates are usually a factor in a combination of size, time, and mileage. With some, only the first two factors will matter as long as you don't exceed a set number of miles.

Above I suggested that you don't try to make the move in one day. That, of course, depends on how many belongings you have. If you have a lot, definitely consider renting the truck for more than one day. The extra cost can be worth it.

In renting a truck, you do all the work, but if you have the time and help, you can save a lot of money doing it yourself. The other option is to hire someone (or a crew) to drive a rented truck or hire a moving company with their own crews and trucks.

The cost of hiring a moving service varies across a wide range. How far is it from one home to the other and how much do you have to move? Will you be needing storage facilities? Call several and get quotes.

There are some other important questions to have answered. Are they insured, licensed, and bonded? If not, you may have no easy recourse in the event of damage or theft. What are the limits of their insurance and liability? Unfortunately, it's common for a moving company to provide pennies per pound should something be damaged or lost. That $1000 couch of yours might weigh 100 pounds. If the mover is only willing to carry liability of 35¢ per pound per item, all you're going to get is $35 if something happens to it. A lost VCR might have cost $800, but because it weighs 12 pounds, it's "worth" only $4.20.

Ideally, you're looking for replacement cost for lost or destroyed articles and true repair costs for damage. (And don't forget possible damage to the homes. *Both* homes!) It's important to find out about such policies before you sign a contract with anyone. Don't just take their word for it. Read the contract carefully.

Steps for the Future

One of the first things you should do after moving in—or even before—is to record the serial and model numbers of all the new appliances and other appropriate items in the home. That includes the numbers for style and color for carpet, vinyl, tile, and all paints and wallpapers.

All of this, and all instruction manuals, need to be filed. So do all other important papers concerning the house and its construction. Contracts, maps, photos and negatives, anything that has anything to do with the house needs to be placed where you can get at it if need be.

Make a list of all phone numbers that are of concern and keep them handy. You probably already have a sheet with the numbers of the contractor and suppliers. But do you know the number of the nearest medical facility? (Or even where it is and how to get there?) How about the police and fire? Even with the advent of 911, there are some areas where a separate number is the fastest way to reach certain kinds of help.

Thinking of your regular maintenance schedule might sound strange since you have a brand new house, but you should plan it as soon as you are settled. Filters for the air system (heating and cooling) usually have to be changed monthly. (Do you have some in the house and ready? Personally, I buy them by the case so there are always some around.) Do you even know where the filters are located, how to check them, and how to change them?

Quite often, a part of what you've paid covers a checkup on certain things 6 months or a year after you've moved in. For example, it's fairly common for the carpet layers to provide one free re-stretch within the first year. (Well, it's fairly common for the better companies.) Many heating and air conditioning subcontractors will also come back out once during the first year to check, service, and readjust the system.

Appendix

Architectural Symbols

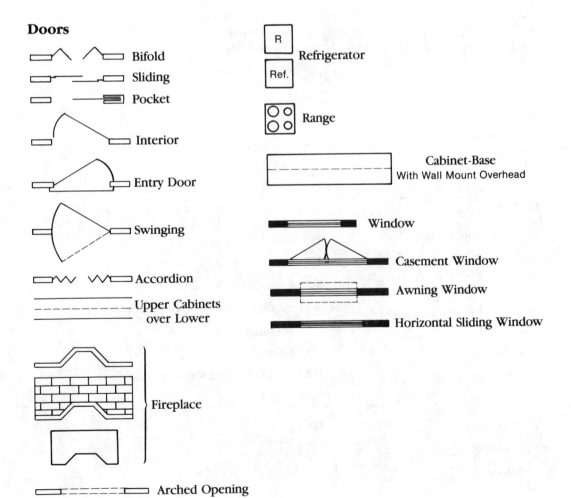

Doors

Bifold

Sliding

Pocket

Interior

Entry Door

Swinging

Accordion

Upper Cabinets over Lower

Fireplace

Arched Opening

R

Ref.

Refrigerator

Range

Cabinet-Base
With Wall Mount Overhead

Window

Casement Window

Awning Window

Horizontal Sliding Window

Plumbing

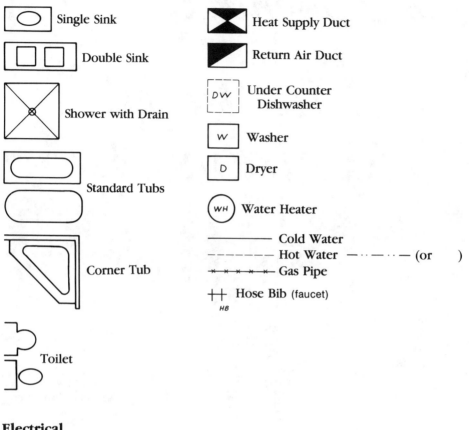

⬭	Single Sink
▢▢	Double Sink
⊠	Shower with Drain
▭▭	Standard Tubs
	Corner Tub
	Toilet

◨	Heat Supply Duct
◺	Return Air Duct
DW	Under Counter Dishwasher
W	Washer
D	Dryer
WH	Water Heater
———	Cold Water
– – – –	Hot Water —··—··— (or)
×–×–×–×–	Gas Pipe
┼┼	Hose Bib (faucet)
HB	

Electrical

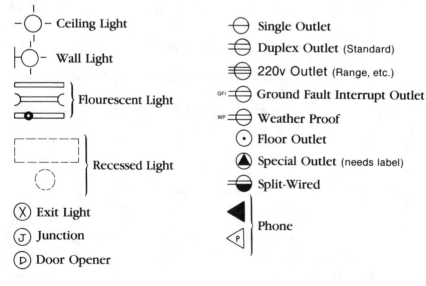

–◯–	Ceiling Light
⊢◯–	Wall Light
	Flourescent Light
	Recessed Light
Ⓧ	Exit Light
Ⓙ	Junction
Ⓓ	Door Opener

⊖	Single Outlet
⊜	Duplex Outlet (Standard)
⊜	220v Outlet (Range, etc.)
GFI ⊜	Ground Fault Interrupt Outlet
WP ⊜	Weather Proof
⊙	Floor Outlet
▲	Special Outlet (needs label)
⊜	Split-Wired
◀ ◁P	Phone

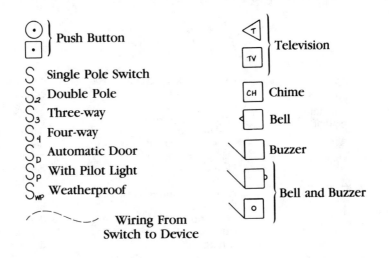

} Push Button

S Single Pole Switch

S_2 Double Pole

S_3 Three-way

S_4 Four-way

S_D Automatic Door

S_P With Pilot Light

S_{WP} Weatherproof

Wiring From
Switch to Device

} Television

CH Chime

Bell

Buzzer

} Bell and Buzzer

Materials

 Insulation

 Wood

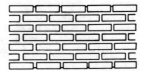 Brick or Block

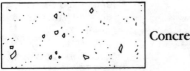 Concrete

 Post (Can also be Supply Duct)

Index

M

model homes, 84, 196
moving day, 268-270
mud rooms, 101, 141
multi-level homes, 150-166

O

office, home, 143, 144
oil heat, 35
open floor plan, living rooms, 126
outlets, electrical, 43-44
outside storage, 72-73, 75

P

paint, 240
pantries, 65-69, 97-98
paper, drafting, 5-6
parking areas, 179-180
patios, 180-181
pencils and erasers, drafting, 5
perspective views, 85, 189-194
photovoltaics, 36
plans (see elevation drawings; floor plans; perspective views)
plot plan, 221
plumbing, 46-50, 265, 272
  pipe size and type, 47
  septic tanks and systems, 49-50
  sewage, 49
  shut-off valves, 47
  water heaters, 47-49
pocket doors, 66
pool house, 75
pools, indoor, 129-132
presentation drawings, 182, 208, 222
problems during construction, 262-263, 267-268

R

R-values (see insulation)
risers, stairs, 61
roads, 14-16
roofs and roofing, 29-31, 159, 184, 229
ruler and straightedge, drafting, 6

S

scale models, 195
scale, drafting, 5-7, 183, 198
scheduling, contractors, 257
sectional drawings, 220, 222

septic tanks and systems, 49-50, 162
service entrances, electrical, 41, 43
setback restrictions, 14, 17
sewers, 49, 265
sewing center, laundry room and, 140
sheathing, 266
shelving, 72, 73, 143
shingles and shakes, 29-31
shop lights, 135
shops, 147-148
showers, 115
sitting rooms, 140
skylights, 135, 231
slate roofing, 30
sliding doors, 66
solar electricity, 36
solar heating, 35-36
special-use rooms, 133-149
  communications, 136
  electrical needs, 134
  lighting, 134
  location in house, 133
  ventilation, 136
split-level home, 163-166
stairways, 49-63, 152-156
  pull-down, attic, 177
  rise and run calculations, 152, 155
  split-level homes, 164
  traffic flow through house, 59-63
storage, 64-75
storied homes (see multi-level homes)
stucco, 24
studio, 142
subcontractors, 262, 265
sump pumps, 162
surveying, 12-13
sweat equity, 259
switches, 44
symbols, 9, 271-273
  appliances, 271
  cabinets, 271
  cooling, 272
  doors, 271
  ductwork, 272
  electrical systems, 44, 45, 272, 273
  fireplace, 271
  heating, 272
  insulation, 273
  lighting, 44
  openings, 271
  plumbing, 272

walls and wall finish materials, 273
windows, 271

T

T-square, drafting, 7
task lighting, 135
telephone, 9, 136-137
templates, drafting, 8, 9
tile, 30, 115-117, 238-240
title search, 13
traffic flow through house, 51-63
treads, stairs, 61
triangles, drafting, 8
trim and molding, 237-238
tubs, sizes and shapes, 114-115, 272

U

utilities, 14-16, 268

V

veneers, elevation drawings to "try on", 185, 187
ventilation
  basements, 161
  bathrooms, 114
  garages and carports, 175
  kitchens, 89
  special needs, 136
views, elevation drawings, 183

W

walk-through inspection, 266
walkways, 173
wallpaper, 240
walls
  coverings and paint, 240
  finishing, 266
  symbols for walls and wall finish materials, 273
water heaters, 47-49
waterproofing, 151, 160
windows, 83-84, 230, 231
  basement, 161
  garage, 232
  installation, 266
  insulation value of, 39-40
  kitchens, 90
  locks for, 232-235
  symbols for, 271
wood heat, 35
woodwork, trim and molding, 237-238

Z

zoning, 13-14